REDEEMING

Mama

PURPOSE-FILLED PRAYERS
FOR YOUR NEWBORN

KATHERINE HAGER

DEDICATIONS

To my beautiful daughter, Zoe Mae, who has impressed on me the necessity of prayer

To my wonderful husband, Jonathan, for his faithful prayers, constant support, and tireless enthusiasm in this work.

To my army of prayer warriors: Chris and Carol Arch, Stephen and Patricia Hager, Jim and Lori Davis, David and Barbara Hackmann, and Sara Hess; may your legacy of consistency in prayer be continued.

To the One who wrote my life story and redeemed me from myself; my eternal gratitude and praise.

TABLE OF CONTENTS

Introduction

CONFESSIONS FROM
A MAMA'S HEART

It's over.

I looked at my beautiful, sleeping daughter. Normally, her cherub-like sleeping state would have filled my heart with warm fuzzies. But that night a twinge of sadness overcame me as I watched her long lashes softly shut and her lips close into a dreamy stupor. I put down her empty bottle, tiptoed across the house, deposited her into her bed, and slipped her light purple blanket over her legs and belly.

My little daughter was weaned.

For the previous eleven months, I had fought through pain, embarrassment, and many tears (hers and mine) and had successfully nursed my first child. And now, she was done. It wasn't that I was unhappy to see my daughter growing and thriving on solid foods and the bottle, but there was something so special about being *needed* in such an intimate and tangible way. I had carried this little girl, felt her kicks, grown with her and helped her into the world. I had fed her from my own body, and now I was not necessary in this way anymore.

Over the months that I had spent nursing my child, I realized that I, like many other young mothers, had been given a very special gift. I had given several hours each day where I could sit quietly with my child, bond with her, and help her grow. In all my busyness, this opportunity helped me to slow down and enjoy the special, tender moments of the first few months of her life.

Suddenly, I regretted my wasted time. Not that I regretted nursing my child—I didn't. Nor did I regret giving my child formula when my supply seemed insufficient. What I did regret was the way that I wasted those precious hours given to me. Occasionally, I spent fleeting moments during those long hours praying or reading my Bible. More often, however, I fell asleep or found myself mindlessly involved in meaningless pastimes, scrolling social media or online shopping. As I saw this chapter of my daughter's life close, I mourned for my lost opportunity.

As I have considered the task of mothering, I have found that I get caught up in the *doing*. The chores are endless.

- Cleaning the house
- Doing the dishes
- Reading the books
- Making the doctor's appointments
- Going to story time

Somehow care for even one little person can get so exhausting!

I believe, however, that anyone can do the *tasks* required to raise a child. In fact, much of what I do daily could just as easily be completed by a maid or a nanny rather than myself. So, I began to ask, "what is my calling as a mother?" If I claim that I am called to raise my little ones, how do I differ from any other caregiver? Perhaps you've considered the same question: how is your role as a mother unique? As I have pondered these questions, I've added another to my list: what can I do that will impact my children eternally?

The answer to each of these questions can start on day one with the time we are each given to nurse our babies. Whether you choose to bottle or breastfeed, you are given the opportunity to sit quietly with your infant six to eight (perhaps more!) times each day and cease from doing. If these fleeting moments are redeemed for that which has value, this time can set the tone for the rest of our parenting journey.

How?

Prayer.

We will explore a selection of passages from the Psalms which gives a wealth of examples for praying for our children. We will consider who we pray to and the intrinsic value of praying for our children. If you commit to making this a priority in your life, your role as a mama will be invaluable.

So, don't lose this opportunity.

The prayers you offer for your child are priceless.

PRAYING PSALMS: MODEL PRAYERS

Have you ever been in a restaurant or at the grocery store when a loud, annoying song pours through the speakers? Although you may not like the song, it is catchy, and by the time you are paying your bill or loading your bags into your vehicle, you are humming right along with the refrain of the song.

I seem to have that tendency, and often I find myself singing along to lobby music without even thinking that the lyrics might not be something I want to fill my heart with.

The Psalms suggest the importance of "sticking" songs into our hearts and minds and, perhaps the most beautiful of all, hearing them repeated through the mouths of our little ones. In fact, Psalm 8:2 says:

From the mouths of infants and nursing babies you have ordained praise on account of your adversaries, so that you might put an end to the vindictive enemy.

What a thought—God receiving praise from the mouths of our precious children!

Perhaps such an idea seems completely far-fetched. Maybe your child seems capable only of screaming, and silence would be far more appreciated than speaking anything! If at this point in mothering, you are hoping just to make it through the day, allow the Psalms to be your place for refreshment, in addition to providing you with model prayers. Your children might not be making beautiful noises now, but as you learn to pray in tune with the heart of the Lord, perhaps your children will find your song catching.

For this prayer journey, we will be working through forty-two of the Psalms. One of the primary writers of the Psalms, King David of Israel, is often referred to as a "man after his (God's) own heart" (1 Samuel 13:14, NIV). If you study his life, however, you realize that he was far from sinless. That should be an encouragement to us!

His life was filled with flaws; he was messy and broken. What then, made him a man after God's own heart?

I believe that the Psalms answer this question.

The Psalms are a collection of beautiful songs written to the Lord and easily changed into personal prayers. David's writing encompasses all categories of prayer: adoration, confession, thanksgiving, and supplication. More than that, he bears his heart and seems to understand the attributes and character of God. While his life is not absent of sin, his heart is clearly focused on pleasing the Lord.

Who would not want to model this man's prayers?

This is why I've selected a collection of psalms as the basis for prayers and meditations. Perhaps as you bask in these psalms, your heart will model praise that your child will soon sing, too.

WHAT'S IT WORTH? THE VALUE OF PRAYING FOR OUR CHILDREN

Ephesians 5:15-16 encapsulates the significance of being mamas of prayer:

Therefore be very careful how you live—not as unwise but as wise, taking advantage of every opportunity, because the days are evil.

It does not take long for us to realize that the world in which we live is broken. Terrorist attacks, government upheaval, violence, and abuse have become so commonplace that many individuals try to ignore them completely. Children are educated about ideas and concepts that we would never imagine necessary at ages we would never imagine appropriate. Many people wring their hands and decry the state of our world or look to the government to fix the problems.

The challenges in our world, however, are not able to be fixed by any laws, peace treaties, or campaigns. Our world hurts under the crushing weight of sin, and each person can only be freed from their own sinful heart by trusting in the Lord Jesus to save them.

Being aware, then, of the evil world in which we live, how do we prepare our children to interact with society in a way that pleases the Lord? How do we prepare them for the challenges we know await them?

It starts now, mamas. Redeem the time.

In the Bible, the Greek word translated as the phrase "making the most" can also be translated "to redeem" and literally means to "ransom or buy off." Praying for your children is an opportunity for you to buy back valuable time and invest in the future of your children. With the boom of technology and social media, our generation has lost touch with mindfulness in regards to how we spend our time. While online shopping or watching television, we let hours slip away. Although there is nothing inherently wrong with spending time on these activities, our roles as parents do not allow us to be passive with the way we spend our time.

- Your time with your child is short
- The days are evil
- The world wants to mold your little one into its own image
- The Evil One wants your child's heart

So, how do we redeem the time? I believe that the most important way is by growing in your personal relationship with the Lord and cultivating a deep prayer life for your children. Invest in their future with prayer with the same intensity as you would their 529 plan. If you haven't done so already, allow this to be a starting place for that journey.

HOW TO USE THIS BOOK

This book is merely a tool.

Each of these chapters is a unique prayer opportunity to guide your thoughts as you are feeding your little one. It is my desire that this book will provide you the impetus to daily redeem the time of one of your feeding sessions and help you invest in your child's spiritual future right now!

Each entry is short so that you can finish a chapter in the amount of time it takes you to get your child's tummy full. There are forty-two prayer opportunities, so if you are on maternity leave you can hopefully establish this pattern of prayer by the time you return to your job. If you are a stay-at-home mother, hopefully this book will encourage you to discipline yourself to make prayer a priority before you resume your full load of responsibilities.

To get the most out of each chapter, take a few minutes to read the Scripture and commentary. If you are rushed, focus your attention on the Scripture and skim the rest. At the end of each chapter is a short prayer; these prayers are to help get you started in the practice of praying. If you don't often pray, consider using these suggestions as model prayers. If you would rather craft your own prayers, please do! This is for your growth as well as your child's. Some of these prayers are directed toward your child's needs, but some are for you. I hope that these prayers are a chance for your soul to be ministered to during a season of transition and change.

Please note that all the prayers fall into one of four categories: adoration, confession, thanksgiving, and supplication. These labels are merely a guide to let you know what the focus of the chapter will be. Adoration is a focus on the Lord, worshiping Him for some aspect of His character. Confession is an opportunity to admit our failures and ask the Lord for help to not live in those sins. Thanksgiving is a time of gratitude, where you express your joy over something the Lord has done for you. Finally, supplication is a chance to bring the worries of your life to the Lord and ask for His intervention. It is my hope that as you pray through these categories all four components will be solidified in your personal prayer life.

As you begin, consider writing a prayer list for your child and putting it in a prominent location so you are reminded to lift them up in prayer. I would encourage you to be specific, thinking through exactly what you would like to see them do or their lives to look like. Consider what challenges they might face in their lives and pray for those.

Do you have a little girl? Pray that she sees her beauty the way the Lord sees it. So many girls struggle with body image issues.

Do you have a little boy? Pray that he will be a strong leader and fight for sexual purity his whole life.

Will your child be public schooled? Pray for them to stand up for their faith even if it is not popular.

Will your child be homeschooled? Pray that they will get along with their siblings regardless of the hours they spend together.

Don't forget to pray for their salvation, as well as their physical and emotional development!

Finally, try not to make completing this devotional into a task. My husband jokes that because I am a list maker I put "write list" on my tasks for the day. If you are a list maker, you get it. If not, you're probably laughing right now. The point is, try not to make prayer time something that you are just checking off. If it feels like another chore on your weighty pile of responsibilities, pray that the Lord changes your perspective and that you see the value and necessity of your role as a praying mama.

Are you ready? Let's get started.

Week One

*"No one has greater love than this—that one
lays down his life for his friends."*

JOHN 15:13

Day One

BLESSED: THANKSGIVING

PSALM 113:5-9

Who can compare to the Lord our God, who sits on a high throne? He bends down to look at the sky and the earth. He raises the poor from the dirt, and lifts the needy from the garbage pile, that he might seat them with princes, with the princes of his people. He makes the barren woman of the family a happy mother of children. Praise the Lord!

———

Perhaps you are keenly aware that the birth of your child was nothing short of a miracle. Especially for those who struggle with infertility, conception is an event worth celebrating. Many know all too well the heartache of wanting a child but having that desire unfulfilled.

Such was the experience of a woman named Hannah (if you have some extra time, you can read her story in 1 Samuel 1-2). While she had a loving husband, she was unable to have children, and her husband's other wife had many. To make this grief more acute, this other wife would constantly upset Hannah, making the weight of her infertility a heavier burden to bear. This emotional toil often came to a head during the family's annual time of worship when Hannah would be so maligned by her rival she would often burst into tears and refuse food. During one of the most special times of their family year, Hannah was constantly reminded of her inability to fulfill her deep desire for children.

In one such instance, Hannah departed the family celebration and went to pray. She begged the Lord for a male child and promised to commit him to the Lord's service for his entire life. First Samuel 1:19 says that "the Lord remembered her" and Hannah was able to conceive and give birth to a son. Faithful to her promise, Hannah, at the time of her son's weaning, brought him to the temple and dedicated him to the Lord. Then she left her young child in the care of the priests, and he served before the Lord for the rest of his days. Within this context, Hannah offers a song of praise, one that rings with some of the same offerings as the psalm above.

No one is holy like the Lord! There is no one other than you! There is no rock like our God! Those who are well-fed hire themselves out to earn food, but the hungry no longer lack. Even the barren woman gives birth to seven, but the one with many children withers away. He lifts the weak from the dust; he raises the poor from the ash heap to seat them with princes and to bestow on them an honored position. The foundations of the earth belong to the Lord, and he has placed the world on them. (1 Samuel 2:2,5,8).

Repetition indicates significance, and the concept of the Lord being the One to grant children is found throughout Scripture (Genesis 25:21, Genesis 29:31, Genesis 30:22, Ruth 4:13, 1 Samuel 2:21). What practical insight can we learn from this basic truth of the Lord granting children, as it pertains to this psalm and the prayer of Hannah?

If the Lord has given you a child through pregnancy or adoption, you are blessed. It might sound trite, but your little one is a precious gift, and the Lord has chosen your home to be the one in which he or she is raised. Regardless of how inadequate you feel you are to raise them; you are the perfect person for the job. You are by no means alone in this task, however. You are empowered by the Lord, the One who grants life and who fills our life with good things.

Who else is high and exalted but bends down to hear our troubles? Who else lifts the discouraged from their lowly places? The same Lord who has blessed you with your child attends to your needs and hears your heart. Praise the Lord!

In this season, be sure to thank the Lord for the little one He has given you. Cuddle them close and remind them that they are a gift and that you as their mama are blessed.

Gracious Father,

Who am I that you would fill my life so full of goodness? Thank you so much for giving me this little one. (Insert child's name) is such a precious gift from you, and I am so humbled that you would entrust them to my care to raise them. Thank you for their life and thank you for the plans that you have for them. Please help me to walk humbly in an awareness of my need for you every day as I strive to raise them in a way that pleases you. Please empower me by your Holy Spirit to be the type of mother that you have called me to be.

In Jesus' name, Amen.

Day Two

REPRESENTED: ADORATION

PSALM 96:1-9

Sing to the Lord a new song! Sing to the Lord,
all the earth! Sing to the Lord! Praise his
name! Announce every day how he delivers! Tell
the nations about his splendor! Tell all the
nations about his amazing deeds! For the Lord
is great and certainly worthy of praise; he is
far more awesome than all gods. For all the
gods of the nations are worthless, but the Lord
made the sky. Majestic splendor emanates
from him; his sanctuary is firmly established
and beautiful. Ascribe to the Lord, O families
of the nations, ascribe to the Lord splendor
and strength! Ascribe to the Lord the splendor
he deserves! Bring an offering and enter his
courts! Worship the Lord in holy attire! Tremble
before him, all the earth!

———

Have you ever noticed how media—regardless if it's the movies, social media, insurance commercials, or magazines—often portray dads in a distinctly inferior light to moms? Frequently, the storyline goes something like this: Mom has either returned to work or is out for a girls' night and Dad is left in sole care of the child. After much reassuring that he is fine, Dad is left alone with the child. Less than a minute into childcare, Dad has a dilemma that somehow, he does not have the problem-solving skills to remedy. After multiple unsuccessful attempts to fix the situation, Dad gives up and Mom, returning from her outing, immediately returns order to the home.

While these anecdotes are humorous and oftentimes gratifying for moms to watch, they always bolster the mother's image by destroying that of the father. Suddenly businessmen, electricians, salespeople, medical professionals, and engineers are unable to unscrew a sippy cup or diaper a child. If your husband or significant other were portrayed in such an unflattering light, it is my sincere hope that you would be quick to defend his intelligence and competence. Out of love for him, you would quickly highlight his positive qualities and intentionally divert attention away from his weaknesses.

In a similar way, as mamas who say we love God, we must be careful to represent Him in an accurate way to our children. It is not that the Lord has flaws that need covering up, rather, that many people purport a flawed concept of who He is. People claim that God is loving and accepts all lifestyles. Some assert that God can be pleased through moral behavior. Others live in ambivalence toward God, assuming He exists but in a distant and uninterested relationship to their lives. While there are countless perceptions of who God is, most are far from the truth and have deeply negative implications for our personal lives. How then do we know what God is really like?

The nature of God is revealed in Scripture, so to know God we must know what Scripture says about Him.

In this psalm we learn that God is newsworthy; He has done amazing things that warrant repeating. He is great. He is worthy of praise. He is the Creator of the space that separates the earth from the heavens. He is surrounded by splendor. His sanctuary is firmly established; it is not threatened by impostors. Think about these things. These are claims worth considering.

If you believe these things to be true, then you serve a great God. If you believe He is great, you will be able to bring Him your greatest problems and concerns in prayer.

If you understand that He is worthy of praise, then you will be willing to speak of His glory.

If you believe He is surrounded by splendor and firmly established in his sanctuary, then you will want to warn those that do not worship Him that He alone is God.

As you raise your little one, consider how you represent God to them. If you misrepresent Him, it will not change who He is. If you speak truth about the Lord, you may experience the greatest joy in mothering: leading your child to understand their need for a savior.

Thank you, Father, for who you are. You are amazing and worthy of praise. There is no one else on earth that can demand praise but you, for you alone are majestic and great, and more awesome than all others. Please allow me to know you and represent you well to all that are seeking. As I raise (insert child's name) please help me show them the truth of who you are.

In Jesus' name, Amen.

Day Three

FORGIVEN: CONFESSION

PSALM 51:1-4, 8

Have mercy on me, O God, because of your loyal love! Because of your great compassion, wipe away my rebellious acts! Wash away my wrongdoing! Cleanse me of my sin! For I am ever aware of my rebellious acts; I am forever conscious of my sin. Against you—you above all—I have sinned; I have done what is evil in your sight. So you are just when you confront me; you are right when you condemn me. Grant me the ultimate joy of being forgiven! May the bones that you crushed rejoice!

———

Before we continue with prayers for our little ones and for our own hearts, it is essential that we explore the truth of our need for forgiveness. Psalm 51 is a wonderful reminder of our own sinful nature and our need for the Lord's grace. We all need His forgiveness and His cleansing. We all need the ultimate joy of being forgiven.

Why do we need the Lord to have mercy on us? Each person has done things we know we shouldn't have. From thinking wrong things to having wrong motivations to hurting people with our actions, we have all sinned. This sin makes us completely unacceptable to God and condemns us to eternal death. It is the disease of our hearts.

People didn't always have this problem. In the beginning, God created a perfect world. The residents of this infant earth had one command—to not eat the fruit from one tree in the garden in which they lived (Genesis 2:16-17). Even before the moment that the first man and woman sinned against God by committing deliberate disobedience (Genesis 3:6), God's plan for redemption was already in motion. Their sin spread like a malignant tumor, affecting their countless descendants and destroying their right relationship with God.

The only means for righting this relationship was to have a substitute. God told Adam and Eve that if they ate the fruit they would die (Genesis 2:17) and as God's Word tells us, "For the payoff of sin is death, but the gift of God is eternal life in Christ Jesus our Lord" (Romans 6:23). The Old Testament purification system foreshadowed this substitution with a blood sacrifice offered for the guilt of the people as well as for specific sins. Blood and slaughter became synonymous with sin. As it says in Hebrews 9:22, "Indeed according to the law almost everything was purified with blood, and without the shedding of blood there is no forgiveness." If we are honest in our estimation of ourselves, we—with the writer of this psalm—must recognize our sin and agree that God is just and right to condemn us. Our sin is unavoidable.

There is hope, however, for the ultimate joy of being forgiven.

God the Son, Jesus, was sent to the world as a human. God's plan of redemption was to transfer onto the Son all the sins of humanity through His death on the cross. His perfect life could be the substitution for all of ours, and His sinless death would pay for our wrongs. "Because Christ also suffered once for sins, the just for the unjust, to bring you to God, by being put to death in the flesh but by being made alive in the spirit" (1 Peter 3:18).

Jesus' suffering for our sins was brutal (Matthew 27:11-51, Luke 22:47-23:46) climaxing with the most devastating blow of all, separation from God the Father.

In his moment of death, Jesus cried out "My God, my

God, why have you forsaken me?" (Matthew 27:46b). In his deepest suffering, Jesus mourned his loss of communion with the Father. This suffering and his death were His sacrifice for us.

After his death, however, Jesus rose from the dead (Matthew 28:6, Mark 16:6, Luke 24:33-35, John 20:15-18) and appeared to many eyewitnesses. He then sent His disciples out with instructions to share how to be made right with Him. Now we are all offered this opportunity to have a right relationship with the Lord and to experience His forgiveness.

We must first recognize our need: we need God to have mercy on us. As it says in the book of Romans, "for all have sinned and fall short of the glory of God. But they are justified freely by his grace through the redemption that is in Christ Jesus" (Romans 3:23-24).

We must recognize that nothing we do can make us right with God. It is only by His grace and believing in the work of His Son that we are saved. "For by grace you are saved through faith, and this is not from yourselves, it is the gift of God; it is not from works, so that no one can boast" (Ephesians 2:8-9).

Each of us must make this choice for ourselves. We must confess our sins and believe in His death in our place. As it says in the book of Romans, "because if you confess with your mouth that Jesus is Lord and believe in your heart that God raised him from the dead, you will be saved" (Romans 10:9).

If you have never made a decision to confess your sins to the Lord and believe in Jesus' work on the cross *alone* for being forgiven, allow this to be the time you do! There is a simple prayer below to walk you through the process, but there is nothing special about these specific words. Your sincere belief in Jesus' sacrifice and your plea for forgiveness of your sins is what matters.

If you have already made a decision to trust Jesus' forgiveness of your sins, consider committing to pray persistently for your children to understand and accept God's forgiveness in their lives. These are the most important prayers you can pray, mama.

You are offered the opportunity for forgiveness by a God who loves you. As it says in John 15:13, "No one has greater love than this—that one lays down his life for his friends." That is good news.

Dear God, Please have mercy on me because of your love. Please wipe away my rebellious acts. I know that I have sinned and that my sins have separated me from you. I believe that Jesus' work on the cross is the only way my sins can be forgiven. I ask you to forgive me for my sins and allow me the ultimate joy of being forgiven. I know I have nothing that I can add to this forgiveness. It is through you alone. Thank you for your love for me, demonstrated through Jesus Christ.

In Jesus' name I pray, Amen.

Dear Lord, Please have mercy on my child (insert child's name). Please allow them to realize that they need your great compassion; they need your loyal love. Please open their eyes that they might understand they need your forgiveness and your grace for their sins. Please help them to recognize their need for a savior, and I pray that they will trust in the perfect work of Jesus Christ to save them from their sins. Thank you for your work on the cross, offering each of us a way to the Father.

In Jesus' name I pray, Amen.

Note: If you have prayed this prayer confessing your sins to the Lord and believing in the work of Jesus Christ alone for the forgiveness of your sins, please seek help in understanding how you can grow in your faith journey. You are always welcome to contact the ministry at equippedmama.com to share your questions or comments.

Day Four

RADIANT: ADORATION

PSALM 34:1-6

*I will praise the Lord at all times; my mouth
will continually praise him. I will boast in
the Lord; let the oppressed hear and rejoice!
Magnify the Lord with me! Let's praise his
name together! I sought the Lord's help and
he answered me; he delivered me from all my
fears. Those who look to him for help are happy;
their faces are not ashamed. This oppressed
man cried out and the Lord heard; he saved him
from all his troubles.*

———

Have you ever met a marathon runner? If you have spent time in the distance running world, you have probably heard the joke that you don't need to ask someone if they're a marathon runner— they will tell you.

Perhaps you've never met a happy finisher of this event, but have you encountered the proud mother of an honor roll student? If you have, you likely have heard gushing about their child's academic prowess. How about a new fiancé? Probably you have received an incredibly detailed retelling of the details of her engagement. Regardless of the setting, the principle is the same: People eagerly talk about what matters most to them.

Psalm 34 reminds us that as followers of Christ and as aspiring godly mamas, we must prioritize praising the Lord. In this passage, the writer mentions three specific guidelines for meaningful praise (although by no means limiting to these three). The psalmist mentions praising the Lord *often*, saying he will praise the Lord at all times and continually. He not only praises repeatedly, he praises *specifically* for answering him, for delivering him from his fears, and for saving him from his troubles. Finally, the writer encourages praising *corporately*, encouraging the listener multiple times to join in the worship.

These directions are very simple and clear, but there is one vital element of worship also addressed in this passage that we must practice when praising the Lord in front of our little ones. Our faces. In verse five the writer states, "That those who look to him for help are happy; their faces are not ashamed." Another translation says, "Those who look to him for help will be radiant with joy; no shadow of shame will darken their faces" (Psalm 34:5, NLT).

This radiant countenance brings to mind another instance in the Bible where a man was in the presence of God and his face was radiant. Exodus 34:29-35 describes the physical change Moses underwent after spending extensive time in the presence of the Lord. After receiving the Ten Commandments and seeing the presence of the Lord pass before him, Moses returned to the people of Israel. He alone had been at the top of the Mount Sinai speaking with the Lord in this intimate way, and when he descended from the mountain, "he wasn't aware that his face had become radiant because he had spoken to the Lord" (Exodus 34:29b, NLT).

While the original words used for radiant in these verses vary slightly, we get the general idea. Moses' physical appearance was altered after he had spent time in the presence of the Lord. Similarly, the psalmist writes that those who look to the Lord reflect Him in their faces. Their countenance says it all: the joy they have is clearly from the Lord.

Does your face serve as a good testimony to your little one? As they grow, will your demeanor tell them that you spend time in the presence of God? Is your face radiant from being with the Lord? If it is not, your continual, specific, and even corporate praise might not carry much weight. Perhaps now is a time to pray toward change. Practice smiling and letting your face be a witness to the radiance of God.

———————————

Father God,

Thank you that you are the God who is worthy of all my praise. Thank you that you have delivered me from my fears and failures. Thank you that those who look to you for help are happy and their faces are radiant with joy. Please allow me the grace to model that joy for (insert child's name) that they might grow to know and understand the transformative power that you alone can bring. Please allow my face to shine so that when my little one sees me they can truly see you.

In Jesus' name, Amen.

Day Five

COMPASSIONATE: THANKSGIVING

PSALM 103:1-4, 12-14

*Praise the Lord, O my soul! With all that is
within me, praise his holy name! Praise the
Lord, O my soul! Do not forget all his kind
deeds! He is the one who forgives all your
sins, who heals all your diseases, who delivers
your life from the Pit, who crowns you with
his loyal love and compassion... As far as the
eastern horizon is from the west, so he removes
the guilt of our rebellious actions from us. As a
father has compassion on his children, so the
Lord has compassion on his faithful followers.
For he knows what we are made of; he realizes
we are made of clay.*

If you have been through the infant to toddler transition before, you likely are familiar with the incredible attention that goes into the first tenuous baby steps. Whether you have watched as a proud mama, auntie, or babysitter, you have experienced overwhelming pride and joy in seeing that child put one shaky foot in front of the other. For parents and caregivers, there is support that you likely offered as the little one worked toward walking.

For most little ones, the process of mobility starts with tummy time to encourage muscle development. As they progress, they become slightly mobile, first rolling over, and then making little army-crawl scoots. During this time, the parents primarily ensure that the child is free from dangerous objects and that their exploration does not turn to injury. As they finally start to walk, baby is seldom alone. While the crude mechanics might be present, they are still far too inexperienced to be left alone to totter. They need constant care to stay safe.

In a similar way, Psalm 103 reminds us of the Lord's careful knowledge of our capabilities and what we are able to bear. The psalmist says that the Lord realizes that we are made of clay—this is likely a reference to the first created man (Genesis 2:7), making a very clear distinction between us and God. We are the clay; He is the Potter; we are all the product of His labor (Isaiah 64:8). Scripture delineates this disparity between us and God in nature—we as created, and He as Creator—but it also delineates a Father/child relationship.

God's image here is tender and loving, with His compassion on particular display. He is the Creator of our lives and the forgiver of our sins, yet in His compassion He loves us like a father. He understands what we are able to handle, for He knows what we are made of. After all, He is the one who formed us.

If at times your duties as mama or wife seem too much for you, remember that the God who formed you knows what you are made of. The One who formed you knows what you can handle. In Matthew 11:28-30, Jesus is calling to those who seek to follow Him and says: "Come to me, all you who are weary and burdened, and I will give you rest. Take my yoke on you and learn from me, because I am gentle and humble in heart, and you will find rest for your souls. For my yoke is easy to bear, and my load is not hard to carry."

Nowhere in Scripture are we commanded to muddle through the challenges of life on our own. Here, however, Jesus does promise us a load we will be able to carry. It is the load He gives us. This load is easy to carry because it is given to us by one who loves us and knows every detail of our lives. Jesus does, however, require that we come to Him to be given that release. As you live out your role as mama, do you ask Jesus to give you a load you can carry?

The Lord is compassionate and knows what we can handle. He is kind and ready to forgive our sins. Do you seek Him for these blessings He has in store for you, or are you content to toddle alone?

Gracious and compassionate God,

I thank you that you are merciful and compassionate. Lord, my life apart from you is nothing but sinful and wicked, and yet you forgive all my sins. You are so good and so kind to me. Thank you so much that you know my limitations. I am aware day by day just how limited and finite I am, and am reminded yet again how much I need you. Please intervene in all my responsibilities, that I would take your yoke upon me rather than the one I make for myself. Please help me to understand how you want me to serve you in your power and in your strength. Thank you that you do not leave me alone, and that when I seek you, you are ready to help. Please empower me to love my little one, serve my family, and do all my work in the joy and strength you provide.

In Jesus' name, Amen.

Day Six

SOURCE: SUPPLICATION

PSALM 18:1-3

He said: "I love you, Lord, my source of strength! The Lord is my high ridge, my stronghold, my deliverer. My God is my rocky summit where I take shelter, my shield, the horn that saves me, and my refuge. I called to the Lord, who is worthy of praise, and I was delivered from my enemies.

———

The Mississippi River is one of the most significant water passages in North America. Second in length only to the Missouri River, this massive waterway cuts through ten states and serves as a major North American migration route. According to the Environmental Protection Agency, more than fifty cities rely on the Mississippi River for their main water supply.

At its widest point, this river is over eleven miles wide and moves 593,003 cubic feet of water per second. At the origin, Lake Itasca in Clearwater County, Minnesota, the river is only twenty to thirty feet wide—the narrowest point—and moves water at a mere six cubic feet per second. While perhaps Lake Itasca is the least impressive point of the river, it is the most vital. Without this unassuming lake, there would be no Mighty Mississippi. It is the source.

So often, child raising is focused on results. Bumper stickers on minivans across America loudly proclaim which families raise the merit students, the varsity letter winners, and the members of honors choir. However, you would never see a bumper sticker that says, "My kid isn't that special, but boy she has character!" or "My kid has a reading disability, but he sure loves people!" No, our world values individuals by output rather than source. Often, I believe it is easy for us to do the same. When people ask about my daughter, I am quick to come up with her most recent accomplishments rather than the character that God is creating within her.

By doing this, I focus on what she does rather than her source and risk miscommunicating that her output dictates her value.

Psalms are a great place to be reminded of the importance of source, especially Psalm 18. David called the Lord his source of strength in the context of the Lord rescuing him from all his enemies. How easy it would have been for David to have looked at his safety and success and taken pride in it! Rather than becoming consumed with pride, however, he worshiped the Lord for His power and strength. David understood that his victories were not from his own efforts, and therefore out of gratitude he worshiped. Consider spending some time in this passage. Meditate on the strength and awesomeness of God. It will bless you.

As you raise your little one, transfer this awareness of the Source to your child. Your child's accomplishments and safety are from the Lord's hand. Abiding in Him and drawing strength from Him is necessary, for He is the Source of life. From Him, and only Him, comes all that is needed for every good work. As it says in the Gospel of John, "I am the vine; you are the branches. The one who remains in me—and I in him—bears much fruit, because apart from me you can accomplish nothing" (John 15:5).

———————————————

Great Father,

You are my source of life and the source of my child's life. All that (insert child's name) ever accomplishes is only from your hand. Thank you that you are their shelter. You are their high ridge. Their safety. Thank you that you are worthy of praise for great are your deeds, and great is your character. Please help me never to value my child for what they do but rather for who you have created them to be. Thank you that whatever you call them do, you will supply them with the energy and protection and strength. Please help them, and me, to abide in you and bear fruit in and through you.

In your Son's precious name, Amen.

Day Seven

JUST: THANKSGIVING

PSALM 37:1-6

Do not fret when wicked men seem to succeed! Do not envy evildoers! For they will quickly dry up like grass, and wither away like plants. Trust in the Lord and do what is right! Settle in the land and maintain your integrity! Then you will take delight in the Lord, and he will answer your prayers. Commit your future to the Lord! Trust in him, and he will act on your behalf. He will vindicate you in broad daylight, and publicly defend your just cause.

———

In our world, people—children especially—seem to have a fascination with things needing to be fair. A kindergarten teacher would never give two of her fifteen students candy and skip the others. Why? Because she would be barraged by thirteen loud protests of "that's not fair!" Many parents try to counteract this feeling of injustice by teaching their little ones that life isn't fair, but this abstract explanation often isn't adequate until adulthood.

Psalm 37 offers a strong alternative to demanding fair treatment: waiting for the Lord to act on your behalf. The psalmist acknowledges a problem replete in our world today, "wicked men seem to succeed" (v. 1). How often do we see that around us? Embezzling bosses uncaught. Unreasonable business transactions never righted. Toxic relationships never restored. Evil people seem to get away with whatever they please. This injustice can be so discouraging to hearts that want to see fairness rule.

Numerous times throughout the Bible, the Lord acted on the behalf of another. Perhaps one of the most powerful visuals for divine vindication occurred in Exodus 14, shortly after the Israelites experienced a dramatic freeing from the oppressive slavery of the nation of Egypt. The people found out that Pharaoh sent his army after them. They panicked, convinced they would all surely be killed. In Exodus 14, God reassured the people that He would not only protect them, but completely wipe out their enemies. His fierce promise, spoken through Moses, was this:

Do not fear! Stand firm and see the salvation of the Lord that he will provide for you today; for the Egyptians that you see today you will never, ever see again. The Lord will fight for you, and you can be still (Exodus 14:13b-14).

What happened when the Lord fought for Israel? The Lord sent an angel between the Israelites and the Egyptians so they could not pass. The Lord split the Red Sea open. Dry land appeared, and the entire nation of Israel safely passed through to the other side. Then the watery depths consumed the army of Egypt, and all of them were killed. Without a single Israelite arming himself for battle, the Lord vindicated the people with an absolute, leave-no-survivors victory.

Psalm 37 offers a crucial lesson you must teach your child: The Lord dictates the final say. He determines what fair treatment is, and His judgment is always perfect. As it says in Romans 12:19, "Do not avenge yourselves, dear friends, but give place to God's wrath, for it is written, 'Vengeance is mine, I will repay,' says the Lord." Perhaps rather than just teaching your child that life isn't fair, emphasize that we serve a God who always will, in His good time, deal out judgement justly.

Father God,

Thank you that you are the source of justice, you are just, and that you are faithful to judge all acts of sin. You are good and merciful. I know that I should fall guilty under your judgement were it not for your love in sending Jesus to die for me. Please help my child to trust in you as their righteous judge and to always rest in the promises that you are more than able to execute justice in our world. Please allow them to seek your vindication rather than the cheap replacement of man-made fairness. Thank you, Father.

In Jesus' name, Amen

Week Two

"And my God will supply your every need
according to his glorious riches in Christ Jesus."

PHILIPPIANS 4:19

Day One

OVERWHELMED: CONFESSION

PSALM 42:5-8

Why are you depressed, O my soul? Why are you upset? Wait for God! For I will again give thanks to my God for his saving intervention. I am depressed, so I will pray to you while I am trapped here in the region of the upper Jordan, from Hermon, from Mount Mizar. One deep stream calls to another at the sound of your waterfalls; all your billows and waves overwhelm me. By day the Lord decrees his loyal love, and by night he gives me a song, a prayer to the living God.

———

Have you ever felt overwhelmed by the billows and waves of life? If you have a new little one, you undoubtedly have. Rapidly changing hormones, sleeplessness, busyness, and loneliness could be just a few contributing factors to feeling like your safe space has been completely destroyed. Perhaps you have tried to shake yourself out of it, but you still find yourself trapped in a place you don't want to be. Sound familiar? If so, you're not alone, and this psalm is for you.

It is always encouraging to hear the writers of the Bible articulating their struggles with frustration and depression. While used by God, these men still experienced the same range of emotions each of us have—and that included discouragement and self-pity. Although no one suggests that this psalm was written by the prophet Jonah, verse seven bears strong resemblance to Jonah's prayer for deliverance, which he offers to the Lord from his lowest place.

The account of Jonah reminds us that the Lord uses people who are still in process. When God told this Old Testament prophet to warn a wicked nation about impending judgement, Jonah went in the polar opposite direction. The Bible cuts straight to the heart of Jonah's disobedience when it says he did so "to escape from the commission of the Lord" (Jonah 1:3). Undeterred by Jonah's disobedience, the Lord sent Jonah's escape ship into a violent storm, and when Jonah's sin was found out, the Lord sent a large fish to swallow Jonah alive and bring him to a place of complete repentance. From the literal depths of the earth, Jonah wrote the following prayer:

I called out to the Lord from my distress, and he answered me; from the belly of Sheol I cried out for help, and you heard my prayer. You threw me into the deep waters, into the middle of the sea; the ocean current engulfed me; all the mighty waves you sent swept over me (Jonah 2:2b-3).

The Lord answered Jonah's prayer with a twofold miracle—a second chance at obedience and deliverance from digestion. Regurgitated onto dry land, Jonah completed the mission the Lord had for him, and he saw widespread repentance.

In your own life, both as a mother and follower of the Lord, there are significant truths to apply from the prayer of Jonah and this powerful psalm. First, the Lord is in control even in the midst of your overwhelming tide. Perhaps He has you there so that you call out to Him. Consider asking the Lord to show you that purpose so that you can learn to find joy and reason to worship in your situation.

Second, wait for the Lord to act, and as the psalmist suggests, wait while giving thanks. Praise is a strong anecdote to pessimism, and when you are singing the goodness of God you can hardly be having a pity party. Offer up the song the Lord has given you to sing. Even if you're tone deaf and can't rhyme, sing what's in your heart. As you sing, wait for the Lord's deliverance.

———————————————

Dear Lord God,

I confess that right now I feel depressed and my soul is upset. I feel life billowing and overwhelming me, and I am floundering. But I know that you are faithful to deliver me, and not only to safety, but to a place of rest and singing. Please put a new song in my heart, a song of praise to you. Please allow me to serve you and my family with the joy only you can bring to me. I seek your deliverance, because what I am facing is not something I can change on my own. Thank you for your faithfulness to accomplish more than I can ask or think. You are the living God, and I praise your holy name.

Day Two

FUTURE: SUPPLICATION

PSALM 1:1-3

How blessed is the one who does not follow the advice of the wicked, or stand in the pathway with sinners, or sit in the assembly of scoffers! Instead he finds pleasure in obeying the Lord's commands; he meditates on his commands day and night. He is like a tree planted by flowing streams; it yields its fruit at the proper time, and its leaves never fall off. He succeeds in everything he attempts.

———

When parents are asked the dreams that they have for their children, often the list includes desires for happiness, affirmation, safety, and security. Those of us who had good upbringings want to see our children offered the same opportunities we had. Those who suffered from poverty, abuse, or neglect dream of a better life for their children and often go to great lengths to ensure their children's futures are bright.

In the very first psalm, David comments on the best way to ensure a lifetime filled with good things—as measured by God's standards. The chapter opens with the phrase "how blessed" which literally means, "how happy." This is an exclamation, showing the fervor with which David feels this truth. How happy, indeed, is the one who does not hang out with the wrong crowd, who does not associate with those who do evil, or talk in ways that are wrong or displeasing to the Lord.

As I watch my little girl change and grow, I have begun to recognize traits in her that are mine. It warms this mama's heart to see her eyes sparkle when she makes me laugh or watch her try a sour food and pucker her lips in disgust. While I already have seen good traits develop in her, I have also noticed her fall into behaviors that are clearly a part of her fallen nature. These, too, I have passed to her!

I know that as she grows, she will begin to mimic the behavior of those she spends time with. I want to eternally cover her ears against the criticisms she will hear, the doubts that will be planted, and the seeds of discontent that will be sown. Peer pressure is strong, a truth which is echoed in 1 Corinthians 15:33 which reads; "Do not be deceived: 'Bad company corrupts good morals.'" My daughter will be influenced by those around her. I know that I cannot eternally separate her from everything that could be a bad influence.

How then, does this psalm offer encouragement for us as well as our growing children? The writer offers an alternative to falling victim to evil influences. He says how blessed is the man (or woman) that *does not* follow the advice of the wicked or listen to them or spend time with them. Why would this person turn away from bad influences?

This question is answered in verse two. He *finds pleasure* in obeying the Lord's commands; he *meditates* on His commands day and night. This person is clearly one that loves the Lord and enjoys spending time with Him. His desire to please the Lord outweighs the pressure he feels from those around him. It appears that he is able to overcome temptation because he is in love with the Lord.

What is the result? He is not trapped by the evil of those around him (v. 1), he has a close relationship with the Lord (v. 2), and he succeeds in everything he attempts (v. 3). What a future this would offer our children if the same could be said of them!

Father God,

You know that the world in which (your child's name) lives is evil. Please allow my child to walk with you so closely that they are able to have discernment when in the presence of evil influences. Please help them to love you and your Word so much that they are able to have victory over evil temptations. Please allow them to be successful in your eyes, dwelling in your presence, and abiding in your Word. Thank you, Father.

In Jesus' name, Amen.

Day Three

LOVER: ADORATION

PSALM 63:1-7

O God, you are my God! I long for you! My soul thirsts for you, my flesh yearns for you, in a dry and parched land where there is no water. Yes, in the sanctuary I have seen you, and witnessed your power and splendor. Because experiencing your loyal love is better than life itself, my lips will praise you. For this reason I will praise you while I live; in your name I will lift up my hands. As if with choice meat you satisfy my soul. My mouth joyfully praises you, whenever I remember you on my bed, and think about you during the nighttime hours. For you are my deliverer; under your wings I rejoice.

———

Do you remember falling in love? When my husband and I first started dating, we lived over 400 miles away from each other. He was finishing some post-graduate training, and I was also in school. Our schedules made it difficult for us to spend much time together, but on the weekends when he could fly to central Indiana to visit, I would put away my homework, postpone responsibilities as much as possible, and spend as much time as I could with him. Sometimes we had adventures, sometimes we just made a meal for my housemates. It was not important what we did, rather, we just wanted to be together. Because we dated long-distance for close to two years, nothing felt better than a big hug from Jon after weeks of being apart.

Why is it that so many people celebrate falling in love through romantic movies and romance novels? Simply put, people love being in love. The chemicals in our bodies that make us feel in love are pleasant. No one forces you to spend time with someone you love; it is your pleasure.

After having a baby, time and priorities often get tossed around. Often baby's needs come first, making romantic relationships much harder to keep strong. While the tendency to pour into your child and mate is good, let me encourage you that at this point in your life, you *more* desperately need to develop another love.

Your love for the Lord.

When your life is fueled by a love for the Lord, and all that you do comes from His presence and His love, you can be the mother and spouse you are called to be. As Jesus says in Luke 6:45, "The good person out of the good treasury of his heart produces good, and the evil person out of his evil treasury produces evil, for his mouth speaks from what fills his heart."

So, fill your heart with love for the Lord!

Perhaps at this point you feel like you really don't have time to love the Lord like you love your child. Your baby requires all your time and energy. But it is when you feel like you least have time that you most need to make time to cultivate a deeper love for the Lord. If in this season you are not feeling in love with the Lord, this psalm is a beautiful place to start. Please consider the truths outlined by the psalmist in this love song.

- The love of God is better than life itself.
- The Lord satisfies our soul.
- The Lord is our deliverer.
- The Lord shelters us under His wings.
- The Lord brings us to a place of rejoicing.

Contemplate the goodness of God and His love for you, and pray that your heart will be wildly, passionately, and fully in love with the Lord.

Lord, you are God, and yet you also love me. This is too wonderful for me to consider. I have seen your acts of splendor in my own life (praise the Lord for any acts He brings to memory). In this season of busyness, help me understand the great worth of experiencing your loyal love. Allow me to praise you joyfully out of a full heart. You are my protector and the lover of my soul. Please give me a heart that longs to be with you always. Please allow my little one to love you with their whole heart, too.

In Jesus' name, Amen.

Day Four

FULL: THANKSGIVING

PSALM 23:1-6

The Lord is my shepherd, I lack nothing. He takes me to lush pastures, he leads me to refreshing water. He restores my strength. He leads me down right paths for the sake of his reputation. Even when I must walk through the darkest valley, I fear no danger, for you are with me; your rod and your staff reassure me. You prepare a feast before me in plain sight of my enemies. You refresh my head with oil; my cup is completely full. Surely your goodness and faithfulness will pursue me all my days, and I will live in the Lord's house for the rest of my life.

Have you ever lacked something? Perhaps you lacked money and had a medical bill that went delinquent or you were unable to make your mortgage or car payment. Maybe you lacked wisdom in a decision and lost a valuable friendship. It's possible that a lack of integrity caused you to slip into a situation that you regretted for years. To lack something, or to be without, is a horrible reminder of our frailty as people.

As a new mama, it is easy to want to keep your child safe from all forms of lack. This might result in overspending on items for them, straining your budget. It could also end in overcommitting them to activities. At the time, these things seem to be for their benefit, but instead they drive you into a state of endless guilt, feverish overachieving, and chronic exhaustion.

This psalm, however, gently reminds each of our hearts that it is not our job to meet all the needs of our child; it is our heavenly Father's. From the abundance of His riches the Lord provides for all our needs. Did you notice the action words used by the writer of the psalm? He says that he "lacks nothing, must walk, and will live." He lacks nothing. Walks, but not alone. He is promised an inheritance. Even in his doing, he is completely dependent upon and the recipient of the goodness of the Lord.

In contrast, what is the Lord doing? He takes, leads, restores, leads (yes, again!), reassures, prepares, refreshes, and pursues. These things He does to those who call Him their shepherd. What an image of a tender, compassionate, and loving God and Father.

More than merely noticing the needs of His sheep, however, God is able to meet these needs. The author does not say his needs are simply met; he lacks *nothing*. His cup overflows. His life is characterized by satisfaction and wealth because the Lord provides for his needs. Therefore, his life is full to abundance.

How does the Lord provide for your needs? He supplies all that we need from His riches, His wealth—a wealth that knows no end. As Paul wrote in his letter to the Philippians, "And my God will supply your every need according to his glorious riches in Christ Jesus" (Philippians 4:19).

The Lord takes all our needs and fills them so that we lack nothing. He has infinite resources at His command to give us and our families a life that is full and overflowing. That knowledge should fill our hearts with peace and thanksgiving.

Lord God,

Thank you that you are my Good Shepherd. Thank you that I lack nothing—and neither does (fill in child's name). Thank you that I can trust you to fill our lives with good things, even to overflowing. Thank you that when we walk through the hard times life brings us, we do not walk alone; you are right there beside us. Thank you that you promise your goodness and faithfulness to pursue us—my family—all the days of our lives.

I thank you, Father, that you are rich in love and in compassion and you lavish those things on us. Thank you know my needs and my child's needs, and that you provide for us from your endless wealth. You are great and worthy of praise.

In Jesus' name, Amen.

Day Five

NATURE: CONFESSION

PSALM 36:1-7

An evil man is rebellious to the core. He does not fear God, for he is too proud to recognize and give up his sin. The words he speaks are sinful and deceitful; he does not care about doing what is wise and right. He plans ways to sin while he lies in bed; he is committed to a sinful lifestyle; he does not reject what is evil. O Lord, your loyal love reaches to the sky; your faithfulness to the clouds. Your justice is like the highest mountains, your fairness like the deepest sea; you preserve mankind and the animal kingdom. How precious is your loyal love, O God! The human race finds shelter under your wings.

In Psalm 36, the writer depicts someone we would all rather not see our child become. He is evil, rebellious to the core and does not fear God. Rebellious is definitely not a flattering adjective, conjuring up images of one who cannot submit to the authority of another. A rebellious man (or woman) in this context, would be someone who is in direct opposition to or in defiance of the authority of God. In mainstream American culture, we have lost the concept of what it means to be submissive to anyone—least likely of all, the Lord. We as a people have become rebellious to the core. What does this actually look like? We rename sin with more inclusive labels, so that those who need conviction will not feel it. We numb our guilt with entertainment and satiate our every desire. We surround ourselves with counselors who will condone our decisions, rather than pointing us to the Word of God. These are trademarks of those who are too proud to recognize and give up their sin!

However, if we are to be loving, godly mamas we must teach our children that to be rebellious to the Lord is damaging not only to others but to themselves. We must teach them what the Bible says about man's sinfulness, we must teach them that apart from God, people are not good. In a culture where young people are told to follow their heart, we must remind our little ones what the Lord says about our thoughts and desires: "The human mind is more deceitful than anything else. It is incurably bad. Who can understand it?" (Jeremiah 17:9).

This is our nature. This is your child's nature.

While it is not encouraging to be reminded of our child's sin nature (likely you have already seen it displayed firsthand) this psalm also reminds us of the nature and character of God. While man apart from God is sinful and filled only with thoughts and desires for more sin, the Lord is rich in love and faithfulness. It is out of this love and faithfulness that He sent his Son to die for us and for your child. It is because of this faithful love that we can be assured of the promise for those who believe; "So then, if anyone is in Christ, he is a new creation; what is old has passed away—look, what is new has come!" (2 Corinthians 5:17).

Praise the Lord your child's nature—our nature and all of humanity's nature—can be restored!

Father God,

I confess that apart from you, my nature is desperately sinful. I confess that my child is a sinner, and I pray that one day you will help (insert child's name) to fully understand their need for you. Please help me to be mindful of the culture in which we live and not become dulled to what sin truly is. Please help me gently point my little one to their need for you. Thank you for your faithful and loyal love.

In Jesus' name, Amen.

Day Six

DEPENDENT: SUPPLICATION

PSALM 104:13-14, 27-31

He waters the mountains from the upper rooms of his palace; the earth is full of the fruit you cause to grow. He provides grass for the cattle, and crops for people to cultivate, so they can produce food from the ground. All of your creatures wait for you to provide them with food on a regular basis. You give food to them and they receive it; you open your hand and they are filled with food. When you ignore them, they panic. When you take away their life's breath, they die and return to dust. When you send your life-giving breath, they are created, and you replenish the surface of the ground. May the splendor of the Lord endure! May the Lord find pleasure in the living things he has made!

———

When my first child was born, I assumed I was well prepared for the task of taking care of an infant full-time. I had several siblings and extensive babysitting experience. To help put myself through college, I had worked as a respite caregiver for individuals with special needs. Surely there was nothing this seven-pound child could throw at me that I hadn't encountered before. Yet two days after delivery, after being wheeled to our truck, I was overwhelmed with panic as the nurse walked back into the hospital. How could I be left to care for this child? How would she survive? How would I survive?

In the upcoming weeks and months, I learned that I was substantially less prepared for the task than I had assumed. However, I also learned that I was much more in tune with the needs of my child than I might have realized. When she would cry, I began to differentiate when she was hungry, tired, or uncomfortable. I learned how to provide for her with an intuition that surprised me.

In a very similar way, Psalm 104 praises the Lord for His care in sustaining life throughout the earth. Plants, animals, and people all rely on the provision of the Lord for daily life. At the Lord's instruction the rain falls, the sun shines, and the crops grow. By His command, lives are brought into being and lives end. This Psalm highlights the careful attention that the Lord gives to each of His living creatures, emphasizing that all beings, whether small or mighty, equally depend on the Lord. All of His creatures wait for Him. All of them rely on Him.

Recognizing our complete dependence upon the Lord should be our catalyst for peace. As we are overwhelmed with the task of mothering—whether it be the financial strain, physical challenges, or emotional tension—we can rest in the fact that the Lord hears our infant-like cries. When we might not even know the reason for our discouragement, He understands what we need. In Jesus' Sermon on the Mount found in Matthew chapters 5-7, He says:

Therefore I tell you, do not worry about your life, what you will eat or drink, or about your body, what you will wear. Isn't there more to life than food and more to the body than clothing? Look at the birds in the sky: They do not sow, or reap, or gather into barns, yet your heavenly Father feeds them. Aren't you more valuable than they are? (Matthew 6:25-26).

What a comfort to know that our Father, who knows our needs, places value on us. His provision for our lives is not an idle promise but one that can be seen throughout creation. He sustains all living things, and all things depend on Him. He, through the words of Jesus, tells us not to worry about the basics. He knows already what our needs are. Jesus goes on to say that God, as a good and loving Father, gives good gifts to His children who ask Him (Matthew 7:11). He does not promise to meet every whim or fancy, but He does give what is good because of His love for us.

Perhaps my panic of new mothering was not your experience, but maybe there is another aspect of your life that has left you feeling overwhelmed. Regardless of the type or the depth of your distress, you can be sure that the Lord hears your cries. Just like your little one might not even know why they are crying; your frustration might not be a tidy, pinpointed issue. Still, the Lord understands your torrent of emotions.

Rest in the truths that for those who know the Lord, the Holy Spirit Himself intercedes for you and prays for you even when you cannot pray (Romans 8:26). The Lord cares for you (1 Peter 5:7). The Lord is always with you (Matthew 28:20). You too, with all of creation, must wait on the Lord. But wait in confidence, knowing that He hears your cries and knows your needs.

Lord God,

I thank you and praise you that you hear my every cry. Thank you that you are well aware of my needs and that you go before me, supplying what I need. Please help me in this season, (insert personal situation) that has made me feel very (insert emotion), and right now I do not feel at all equipped to the task to be the mama I need to be. Please help me to wait for you as you provide for my needs. Thank you for the way you provide for all creation. Please help me wait expectantly for your faithful provision.

In Jesus' name, Amen.

Day Seven

REST: ADORATION

PSALM 46:1-5, 10-11

God is our strong refuge; he is truly our helper in times of trouble. For this reason we do not fear when the earth shakes, and the mountains tumble into the depths of the sea, when its waves crash and foam, and the mountains shake before the surging sea. (Selah) The river's channels bring joy to the city of God, the special, holy dwelling place of the sovereign One. God lives within it, it cannot be moved. God rescues it at the break of dawn. He says, "Stop your striving and recognize that I am God! I will be exalted over the nations! I will be exalted over the earth!" The Lord who commands armies is on our side! The God of Jacob is our protector! (Selah)

———

Throughout the Bible, men and women encounter scenarios that would cause anyone to strive or feel out of control.

One such scenario occurs in 2 Kings 6. A famous Israelite prophet had become displeasing to the King of a neighboring country. Each time this King plotted an invasion against Israel, the prophet knew, and so over and over the King was thwarted in his plan. After this scenario repeated several times, the enraged King plotted to capture this prophet so that he could attack freely. The morning of the planned abduction, the prophet's servant had risen early and noticed that their city was surrounded. Warning his master, he must have been surprised by his response. His master said that their side outnumbered the invaders. I would imagine the servant tried again to communicate their dire predicament to the master. But rather than despairing or preparing for the invasion, the prophet prayed, "'O Lord, open his eyes so he can see.' The Lord then opened the servant's eyes and he saw the hill was full of horses and chariots of fire all around Elisha" (2 Kings 6:17b).

The account of Elisha and his servant explains how the Lord rescued them both, striking the invading horde with blindness and allowing the very man they sought to destroy to lead them into enemy territory. What a turn of events for the King who planned this man's downfall! In the face of apparent danger, the prophet Elisha told his servant not to fear and calmly waited for the approaching army to draw near. This is the perfect image of not striving. Elisha was free from striving because he had a thorough understanding of the power of God and the heavenly resources that were available to him. The armies of heaven were waiting to defend him—and he had the eyes to see it.

When do we strive? We strive when we feel a situation is out of our control or when we feel that if we worked hard enough, we could be in control. We strive to avoid lack, we strive to meet our own expectations, we strive to meet the expectations of others. This passage, however, emphasizes the need to *stop* striving because a true knowledge of who God is should calm our worried hearts. As famous theologian A.W. Tozer once said, "What comes into our minds when we think about God is the most important thing about us" (The Knowledge of the Holy).

What do we think about God's power? If we believe God is not strong enough or wise enough or loving enough to handle our problems, our mothering will be characterized by striving. We will need to do all, be all, and handle all. If, however, we recognize the infinite power of an all-knowing, all-loving God, we, too, will recognize that our side outnumbers whatever enemies we face! What an encouragement that should be to the way we face our role as mothers.

Do you feel like you are striving in your parenting? Does

each day feel like a fight? Do you dread making it through the day only to wake up to another set of challenges?

Take time to claim this truth: If God is on your side, you have no reason to strive.

Recognize the wealth of the riches our loving Heavenly Father offers you right now. He is your protector. He will be exalted for who He is and for all He has done. He desires to fight for you. Allow *Him* to win the victory in your life.

Heavenly Father,

You are my strong refuge. I praise you for being my helper in times of trouble. I thank you that you are God and that your name will be exalted over all the earth. Thank you that you command the armies of all the host of Heaven and you are on my side. Please open my eyes that I might see that no matter what enemies oppose me, that with you by my side, I have nothing to fear. Help me to cease from my striving in my parenting. Help me to recognize that all my efforts are only worthwhile in you. Please allow (insert child's name) to recognize that everything I do is only in and through you. I pray that they recognize that for themselves too.

Thank you for being all that I need and for redeeming and rescuing my life. You are my protector, and I praise you that you are able to protect me, and mighty to bring me to safety.

In your strong and powerful name, Amen.

Week Three

"Because he who is mighty has done great things for me, and holy is his name."

LUKE 1:49

Day One

SHELTER: THANKSGIVING

PSALM 62:1-2, 5-8, 11-12

*For God alone I patiently wait; he is the one
who delivers me. He alone is my protector and
deliverer. He is my refuge; I will not be upended.
Patiently wait for God alone, my soul! For he
is the one who gives me confidence. He alone is
my protector and deliverer. He is my refuge; I
will not be upended. God delivers me and exalts
me; God is my strong protector and my shelter.
Trust in him at all times, you people! Pour out
your hearts before him! God is our shelter!
(Selah) God has declared one principle; Two
principles I have heard: God is strong, and you,
O Lord, demonstrate loyal love. For you repay
men for what they do.*

———

From what do you seek shelter? In this season of life, it is incredibly possible that you feel separated from a place of security, hope, and trust. Oftentimes, a new child brings different challenges into a family or relationship. Whether financially, emotionally, or physically, life is changed. Perhaps you've adjusted to your new little one's presence, but your job security feels uncertain. Maybe you're feeling isolated, unsupported, or distant from those who used to offer you camaraderie and friendship. Perhaps you stepped down from a lucrative work position and now you feel as though you have given up your identity. If these situations feel at all familiar to you, you are not alone.

In this brief passage, the writer mentions three times that the Lord is his protector, and twice he confesses that God is his deliverer. He calls God his refuge and asserts the strength of God with absolute confidence. The writer's focus on physical protection suggests that, to this point, he had suffered physical danger and opposition. As you study the life of David, you find ample evidence for this fact. Yet his pattern for worship is far from unique in the Bible. Throughout Scripture, we find examples of those who respond to physically overwhelming situations with unqualified worship.

One powerful example of such worship can be found in Luke 1:46-55. Immediately following a shocking announcement that she would conceive and have a child, Mary left her home to visit her cousin, who had also found herself miraculously pregnant. Although Mary was a virgin, an angel came and told her that she would become pregnant and become mother to the promised Messiah, Jesus. Undoubtedly scared and confused, Mary likely worried that her divine selection for this task to bear the Messiah would result in her fiancé rejecting her. Her parents would undoubtedly not believe her explanation, and in her culture, stoning was the consequence for being an unwed mother. The stresses of her calling were high, and she knew it.

Upon greeting her cousin, Mary was met with a miraculous reassurance of the Lord's hand of blessing upon her. Without having solutions to her concerns, and by no means free of danger, Mary offered a prayer of praise for the Lord's favor.

This prayer of Mary echoed aspects of Psalm 62, praising the Lord for His might and His power, rescuing those in affliction and bringing justice to those who live in sin. These are powerful words to come from the mouth of one called to a seemingly impossible task.

Because he who is mighty has done great things for me, and holy is his name; from generation to generation he is merciful to those who fear him (Luke 1:49-50).

These attributes of God are unchanging. He is still our shelter. He is still our protector, and He who is mighty has done great things for you. This Psalm reminds us of the importance of worship even before deliverance.

Praise before blessing. We do not worship in hope that God will deliver us, but in the confident expectation that God has the strength to accomplish what is best for us. God is strong, and He still demonstrates His loyal love towards us. Will we believe this truth and seek shelter in Him today?

———————————

Strong and Mighty God,

I praise you. You are still the strong and faithful God of the Psalms and the Mighty One who Mary praised. You are unchanging and regardless of my circumstances, you are not surprised by my challenges nor are you overwhelmed by my concerns. I thank you that you know the end from the beginning and you have already determined what is best for my situation. Please help me to praise you even before I have answers and to model a spirit of praise before my child(ren) that they might also see and worship you.

In Jesus' name, Amen.

Day Two

RESOURCE: CONFESSION

PSALM 121:1-8

I look up toward the hills. From where does my help come? My help comes from the Lord, the Creator of heaven and earth! May he not allow your foot to slip! May your protector not sleep! Look! Israel's protector does not sleep or slumber! The Lord is your protector; the Lord is the shade at your right hand. The sun will not harm you by day, or the moon by night. The Lord will protect you from all harm; he will protect your life. The Lord will protect you in all you do, now and forevermore.

If you've ever been outdoors in the middle of a very hot summer, you know the importance of shade. Separated from the protection of air conditioning or sunscreen, we are quick to sunburn and suffer from heat-induced illnesses. If you have tried outdoor activities with your little one, likely you have already explored the many ways to keep them from the intensity of the sun's heat. How fragile our bodies are! We depend on shelter from the sun, yet we require the warmth and light from this star for survival. Aside from these things, we need food and water frequently. As we care for our little ones, we also recognize that we need sleep—desperately!

As we come to grips with our own frailty, we can rest in the truth of this psalm. Our true dependence is on the Lord, our creator and protector. As our creator, He is completely different from us. He knows our weaknesses, yet He is not restrained by human limitations. In Acts 17 Paul says,

The God who made the world and everything in it, who is Lord of heaven and earth, does not live in temples made by human hands, nor is he served by human hands, as if he needed anything, because he himself gives life and breath and everything to everyone (Acts 17:24-25).

We can trust in the God who created everything to be able to meet our needs because He is the One who sustains all things (Hebrews 1:3), He holds all things together (Colossians 1:17), and apart from Him nothing has been created (John 1:3). We serve a God of limitless strength. He is the resource on whom we call.

This psalm praises the Lord as creator, but also reminds us that unlike us, He is unencumbered by space and time. With a little one, you likely are all too aware of your lack of sleep. Middle of the night feedings, reflux, and messy diapers can make exhaustion and frustration all too commonplace. Yet when you are watching those wee hours pass with an unhappy child and a numb mind, how often do you remember that your protector is awake with you? This same protector that created your life never ceases from watching over you. Now. Forever. How perfectly suited is the Lord to being our eternal resource!

When you become weak or tired or emotionally worn, the Lord is present, protecting you in all you do. When you speak from ignorance or unkindness, the Lord is always there to offer comfort and keep you from slipping. When you are unable to control the circumstances of life, the Lord is your shade at your right hand. He is the one who gives you the relief you need.

The Lord is faithful to offer this protection and intervention, yet how often do we forget to turn to the one who made us? It is so easy to forget! When do we turn to the one who sustains us with cries for help? When we are hurting or confused, do we rush towards the arms of the One who knows us completely?

The Lord is our greatest resource for He is not only completely self-sufficient, but He is always present and deeply in tune with our needs. An old hymn writer put it perfectly when he said,

Oh, what peace we often forfeit,

Oh, what needless pain we bear,

All because we do not carry

Everything to God in prayer!

("What a Friend We Have in Jesus" by C. Converse).

As your journey as a mama reminds you of your own limitations, let this psalm encourage you that the Lord is your resource. He is from where your help comes. Let your weakness drive you to your knees, that you might draw from the strength of the One who created you and protects you.

———————————

Father God,

Thank you that you not only created me, but you desire to be involved in the intricacies of my life. I thank you and praise you that you promise to watch over me at all times. I confess that all too often I rely on myself to make it through each day, but I know I lack the strength apart from you. This work that I face as a mother and (insert any other responsibilities weighing on your heart) is more than I can handle on my own. Lord, I need you, and I thank you that you make yourself available to hear my prayers and meet my needs. Please supply me with the strength I need for this day, and allow me to rest in your presence and protection. Thank you, Father.

In Jesus' name, Amen.

Day Three

TETHERED: SUPPLICATION

PSALM 16:5-11

Lord, you give me stability and prosperity; you make my future secure. It is as if I have been given fertile fields or received a beautiful tract of land. I will praise the Lord who guides me; yes, during the night I reflect and learn. I constantly trust in the Lord; because he is at my right hand, I will not be upended. So my heart rejoices and I am happy; My life is safe. You will not abandon me to Sheol; You will not allow your faithful follower to see the Pit. You lead me in the path of life; I experience absolute joy in your presence; you always give me sheer delight.

In the 2016 Boston Marathon, Josh Crary competed as one of the many thousands of runners. His time was impressive, but not fast enough for notoriety. Due to the bombings at the end of the race, Josh was stopped before he even completed the event. The significance of his achievement was not in the pace he ran but rather the obstacle which he overcame. Mr. Crary is blind. Diagnosed with a retinal condition that claimed his sight as a teen, he attempted the race tethered to a guide. Side by side, the two covered the first twenty miles of the course before the emergency caused them to forgo the remaining 6.2 miles. Tied at the wrist to his guide, Crary was able to participate in an event that would not otherwise be possible for him.

What an amazing journey of faith and trust!

As new moms, how often do we feel as though we are blind? We might read a book about parenting, and likely friends from the gym, grocery store, and church offer advice or tips. But when it gets down to the sleepless nights, and the monotonous silence (or the absence thereof), we often feel thoroughly alone. Even if you are blessed with a supportive and loving husband, every man needs rest. Likely, you have found yourself rocking your little one alone in the darkness of night, numb with exhaustion. It is possible you have felt inadequate for the task at hand. Perhaps you have felt desperate, unsure of how to handle this challenge called mothering.

But just as the tenacious competitor in the Boston marathon needed a guide to make it through the race without stumbling, so do we. In this psalm, the writer states that he constantly trusts the Lord. Why? "Because he is at my right hand, I will not be upended" (Psalm 16:8b). This verse paints an amazing image for us to consider. It is as if you, blindly running the race of mothering, are also tethered to the Trustworthy Guide. The Lord runs beside you.

Take a moment to consider that. What a relief to know that you are not alone! You can join the psalmist when he says that his heart rejoices. He is happy. His life is safe.

What promises from this psalm can you glean for your life right now? The Lord grants stability and prosperity. The Lord grants a secure future. The Lord gives inheritance. The Lord guides. The Lord is at your right hand. The Lord will not abandon His followers. The Lord leads in the path of life. The Lord gives delight.

In the darkest, loneliest, longest of nights, the Lord is right there with you. When you fear failure as a mother or a mate, the Lord is there to instruct you. To those faithful to follow the Lord's leading, He is there to lead you along the path of life—not just for this life, but for the life to come. What a blessed promise for us as mothers. We never need to be alone; the Lord is faithful to lead us. And He will be faithful to lead your child, also, if they call on His name.

If you know the Lord, you are tethered. The question is, do you strain under the tether of His leading, or rejoice in the security and safety His guidance brings?

Dear Lord,

Thank you for your promise to give me safety and stability. I know that both of these gifts come only from your hand, and only from submission to the gentle guidance of your instruction through your Word. Please keep me from chafing under your tether, but help me, rather, to rejoice in the safety your guidance brings. Thank you that you would care enough about me and my role as a mother to instruct and guide me in the path of life. Thank you for the life you give, a good life here on earth, and the promise of the best life in Heaven to those who are yours. Please already be working in the heart and mind of my little one that one day (insert child's name) will seek to be guided by your Word and your truth.

In Jesus' name, Amen.

Day Four

MASTERPIECE: ADORATION

PSALM 139:13-18

Certainly you made my mind and heart; you wove me together in my mother's womb. I will give you thanks because your deeds are awesome and amazing. You knew me thoroughly; my bones were not hidden from you, when I was made in secret and sewed together in the depths of the earth. Your eyes saw me when I was inside the womb. All the days ordained for me were recorded in your scroll before one of them came into existence. How difficult it is for me to fathom your thoughts about me, O God! How vast is their sum total! If I tried to count them, they would outnumber the grains of sand. Even if I finished counting them, I would still have to contend with you.

———

No mama prayer book on the Psalms would be complete without a brief jaunt into Psalm 139. Likely, many of you are familiar with this passage of Scripture; perhaps some of you read it while pregnant. Perhaps if you were particularly hormonal and emotional at the time, it brought you to tears. Completely reasonable. It is a sacred and beautiful thing that the Lord knows our unborn child with the intimacy described in this passage. But if your child has kept you awake for a few weeks now, or if you have other little ones vying for your attention, if you feel physically or emotionally exhausted, these Scripture-infused musings might feel very distant from your reality.

If that is you, let this be your refocusing and grounding. This psalm forces us to recognize the masterpiece that is God's crowning creation: humankind. Your child. And you.

More than simply creating your little one, the Lord was intimately involved in their growth and development. He made their mind and heart. Your child's intellectual capabilities, capacity to love others, and feel emotions are all trademark facets of the loving work of an infinitely attentive Heavenly Father. Like a skilled craftsman, He wove the parts of their bodies together, joining neurons to appropriate pathways, attaching ligaments, and filling bones with the stem cells needed to later grow the body's blood supply. He watched as your little one's body took shape and grew. Before their eyes could detect light, He knew what they would see. Before you knew you were pregnant, He knew your child's name and their length of days. That is the intimate love only an all-knowing, all-loving God could have for us! And this is the intimacy the Lord has with your child and with you.

Perhaps your child was not born physically or mentally designed in the way that you anticipated. Maybe you greeted a child with a profound disability or birth defect. Maybe you have wondered on your darker days if your child truly is an awesome and amazing work of the Lord. For an answer to that question, we must visit John 9.

In this Gospel narrative, Jesus and His disciples came across a poor beggar who had been blind from birth. When they saw the man, Jesus' disciples asked if his condition was a result of his sin or that of his parents. While this seems like an incredibly insensitive question to raise, the Lord's answer is perfect. Without berating the disciples for their question or focusing the spotlight on the man's condition he replies to their question at face value.

"Jesus answered, 'Neither this man nor his parents sinned, but he was born blind so that the acts of God may be revealed through what happens to him'" (John 9:3). Jesus did not dwell on the man's disability as a matter of blame but rather of purpose. He knew the man had been born disabled for a very specific reason: the glory of God.

Immediately Jesus healed the man, and as a result, the man believed in Jesus and worshiped him (John 9:38). This man received physical and spiritual healing, then praised God for his release from his lifelong disability.

Perhaps that is not the path God has chosen for your child, but you can rest in the fact that He has a plan for his or her life. In His very capable hands, the Lord can use your child's story for His glory.

In whatever season you read this, remember that the Lord created your child with immense attention to detail. His or her abilities, or even disabilities, never escaped His watchful care. He created them, and His thoughts about your child are more than can be counted. The God of the universe thinks about your child with love, concern, and purpose. That is an immense source of comfort and joy.

———————————

Father God,

I thank you that you are the Master Creator and Designer who created my child just as you wanted them to be. Thank you that you think about my child and that you have good plans for them and their life. You are sovereign over my life and the life of my child, so I know that you will use any hardship my child faces to work into your good and perfect plan. Please help me to understand that and to trust you in the hard process. You have created a masterpiece in my child, and I thank you and praise you for creating their life and entrusting them to me.

In your name I pray, Amen.

Day Five

SPEAK OUT: THANKSGIVING

PSALM 107:1-6

Give thanks to the Lord, for he is good, and his loyal love endures! Let those delivered by the Lord speak out, those whom he delivered from the power of the enemy, and gathered from foreign lands, from east and west, from north and south. They wandered through the wilderness on a desert road; they found no city in which to live. They were hungry and thirsty; they fainted from exhaustion. They cried out to the Lord in their distress; he delivered them from their troubles.

———

There is nothing sweeter than a Cinderella-end to an adoption story. Some dear friends of ours, Josh and Kelly (names changed for the purposes of this book), unable to have their own children, had tried for years to foster to adopt. Fifteen times, the little ones brought into their homes were relocated with a family member on very short notice. With each emotionally-charged departure, their dream of adoption seemed more and more distant. As the pair considered an alternate route of adoption, an emergency case was brought to their attention. Lindsey, a bright, beautiful, bubbly girl of eight had no family members wanting to claim her. After some meetings and proceedings, Lindsey was quickly integrated into their family. Now, their home is filled with vibrant pictures of the three of them, each wrapped in a smile. "I love you, Mom and Dad"—a hand-written sign designed by Lindsey, is proudly displayed on the refrigerator. This little girl is now in a loving home—and she is happy to say it.

What a testimony to a redeemed situation!

The King James Version of Psalm 107:2 says, "Let the redeemed of the Lord say so, whom he hath redeemed from the hand of the enemy." Redeemed. This word carries the idea of being purchased, restored, or given value. Each of us who have confessed our sins and trusted the Lord Jesus for our forgiveness have been redeemed. We have been bought at a great price (1 Corinthians 6:20). We have been chosen to be conformed to the image of Jesus (Romans 8:29). We have been given the Holy Spirit as our advocate and comforter, the eternal presence of God with us (John 14:16). We have been given a new spirit (Romans 8:10-11). These should be reasons to celebrate!

The apostle Paul encourages believers that, not only have we been redeemed, but we have also been adopted. We are brought into the Lord's house as full members of His family.

But when the appropriate time had come, God sent out his Son, born of a woman, born under the law, to redeem those who were under the law, so that we may be adopted as sons with full rights (Galatians 4:4-5).

Do we reflect the gratitude of one who has been redeemed, adopted, and cherished? Do our children know that we are redeemed?

In this psalm, the writer encourages the listener to praise the Lord for His miraculous intervention, for His redemption of an impossible situation. As mamas, our charge is to model praise for our little audience to see. We cannot depend on someone else telling them. If you do not already do so, take the time to model praise in your home and to your family. Praise the Lord for your restoration, your redemption, and your new life.

Give thanks to the Lord, for He is good to *you.*

His loyal love endures to *you.*

Let *you*, the redeemed of the Lord, say so.

———————————————

Lord God,

Thank you so much for offering me redemption and restoration from my life of sin and shame. Thank you that your Word is true and that in you my benefits are endless. Thank you for saving me and giving me a new life, and a new name. Please help me to model a heart of gratitude for my little ones that they might see you and know their need to also experience your redemption.

In Jesus' name, Amen.

Day Six

FEAR: CONFESSION

PSALM 4:4-8

Tremble with fear and do not sin! Meditate as you lie in bed, and repent of your ways! (Selah) Offer the prescribed sacrifices and trust in the Lord! Many say, "Who can show us anything good?" Smile upon us, Lord! You make me happier than those who have abundant grain and wine. I will lie down and sleep peacefully, for you, Lord, make me safe and secure.

————

In a world where solid biblical truth is difficult to find, do you worry that your child will receive error-filled teaching that will lead them away from the Lord? There are countless churches across America, yet not all of them are filled with solid biblical teachers. Some promote teaching social issues apart from Scripture, promising earthly prosperity to those saved from sin, as well as many other inaccurate teachings. In Psalm 4:5, the psalmist reminds the reader that there are not countless appropriate ways for us to worship the Lord. He says, "Offer the prescribed sacrifices and trust in the Lord." This warning heralds strongly back to Leviticus 10 and the first instance that the Lord demanded a specific way of being worshiped and honored.

In the passage in Leviticus, we find that the Lord had just detailed specific instructions for sacrificing for sin offerings, peace offerings, and other various occasions. At the command of the Lord, the priest and his sons were consecrated and their offerings were brought. As a sign of His acceptance of their worship, the presence of the Lord appeared to the people and consumed the offering with fire (Leviticus 9:24).

Subsequent to this holy and awesome experience, the high priest's sons, Nadab and Abihu, took their fire pans and offered "strange fire before the Lord" (Leviticus 10:1) Although they had just been commanded appropriate means of worship, they decided to come before the Lord in the way they saw best. What was God's response to their act of "worship?"

Death.

The Bible says "So fire went out from the presence of the Lord and consumed them so that they died before the Lord" (Leviticus 10:2). It might feel harsh or even cruel that these men were killed for offering the wrong sacrifice. However, they were aware of what God wanted, and they willingly worshiped in a way not prescribed by the Lord. They did not show God to be holy because they did not obey.

In response to their deaths, Aaron the high priest was not allowed to mourn and the sons were carried away to be buried by another (Leviticus 10:4, 6). This event demonstrated to the people the severity with which God takes appropriate worship. God demands obedience motivated by reverent fear.

Out of an appropriate fear for the power of God, for His holiness, and for His ability to give life and take it, may your child understand their need to tremble in fear and to turn away from their sin. The Lord has given us His Son to take away the guilt of our wrongs, but we must teach our children that apart from that forgiveness there is ample reason to tremble before God.

Praise the Lord that that is not where our story needs to end, for we can stand in the forgiveness of our great High Priest, forever free from sin. Let us pray that our children know this and understand the need to turn to the Lord, that they might be given the freedom and security of trusting in Him.

Dear Father,

I pray that you would help (insert child's name) to grow in wisdom and discernment that one day they might understand how to discern between right worship and wrong. Please help them to understand that only through the atoning work of our great High Priest, Jesus Christ, can any of us be saved. Hallelujah! I thank you that your Son is our great High Priest who has passed through the heavens and who is capable of sympathizing with our weakness and yet without sin! Thank you that He was tempted in every way and yet without sin, and so He understands all the challenges and struggles that I face as a mama and that my child will face. Lord, this world is broken, and we so desperately need you to give us the safety and security we so crave. Please do the work in my heart and in my child's heart that only you can do.

In your name I pray, Amen.

(Scripture allusions from Hebrews 4:14-15.)

Day Seven

RESOLUTION: SUPPLICATION

PSALM 39:1-7

I decided, "I will watch what I say and make sure I do not sin with my tongue. I will put a muzzle over my mouth while in the presence of an evil man." I was stone silent; I held back the urge to speak. My frustration grew; my anxiety intensified. As I thought about it, I became impatient. Finally I spoke these words: "O Lord, help me understand my mortality and the brevity of life! Let me realize how quickly my life will pass! Look, you make my days short-lived, and my life span is nothing from your perspective. Surely all people, even those who seem secure, are nothing but vapor. Surely people go through life as mere ghosts. Surely they accumulate worthless wealth without knowing who will eventually haul it away." But now, O Lord, upon what am I relying? You are my only hope!

Have you ever made a resolution to be a better mom? Maybe you have developed a biting tongue. Maybe your mom support group has become a time for you to gossip about your family, husband, or child. Maybe you do everything you need to do, but your heart is unsettled, ungrateful, even resentful. Maybe you desire to change. Often, however, our desires are as successful as New Year's resolutions—lasting only until the urge to cave to temptation is stronger than our desire to overcome.

Do you ever worry that your traits will be passed along to your little one? I have watched as my little girl has started doing things just like me. Meticulously she closes lids on containers, shuts drawers, and rearranges clothing. As I possess a strong trait for orderliness and perfection, I have watched with mixed pride and chagrin as I realize that my precious daughter is copying my modeled behavior. What else is she picking up along the way?

As mothers who love our little ones dearly, we do not want to pass our critical spirits, our laziness, our pride, or our selfishness to them like a genetic trait, but our natural tendency is to do just that! Can any of us relate to the opening few verses of this psalm? I definitely can! How often do we say that we won't do something wrong, but the moment that resolve forms, we immediately feel the sickening pull to that sinful thought or action?

As believers in the Lord, we should understand that we are not doomed to eternal failure. The Lord has not given us a "pull yourself up by your bootstraps" lifestyle to live, but rather he has empowered us to live a life victorious from the sins that call our name. The apostle Paul comments on this same struggle between wanting to do what is right and inevitably failing, concluding with a comment many of us can identify with; "Wretched man that I am! Who will rescue me from this body of death?" (Romans 7:24). What is his conclusion? This is found in the following verses, "Thanks be to God through Jesus Christ our Lord!" (Romans 7:25a) and continues by stating that for the believer:

There is therefore now no condemnation for those of us who are in Christ Jesus. For the law of the life-giving Spirit in Christ Jesus has set you free from the law of sin and death (Romans 8:1-2).

We have the opportunity to overcome our evil tendencies and temptations, but only through the power that Jesus Christ gives us.

In desperation, the psalmist proclaims a need for dependence in Psalm 39: "You are my only hope!" (Psalm 39:7b). He recognized his need.

Do we?

Throughout the Bible—especially in these passages (Romans 8 and Psalm 39)—we are offered hope to overcome the worst of personal struggles or imperfections. But this victory is only offered to those who fully submit themselves to the power and authority of God through Jesus Christ. None of us inherently have the ability to be the type of mother that we want to be, or that we are called to be. But through the life-giving Spirit, given to us through Jesus' sacrifice, we can be divinely empowered to change and to become women that look like Christ. Through submission to the Lord and His Word, we have hope to change. That is not a resolution destined to failure.

Lord God,

I know that apart from your strength and your power, I will never be the type of mother that I know I am called to be. I see such ugliness in my heart that I do not want passed to (insert child's name). But I also know that your Word says that there is no condemnation for those of us who are in Christ Jesus, and I thank you, that as a Christ follower, this promise is true for my life. Please empower me by your Holy Spirit to live a life separate from the evil desires and sins that seem to follow me. Please give me freedom, and help me reflect your love and your holiness to my child today.

In Jesus' name, Amen.

Week Four

*"Day after day he carries our burden, the God
who delivers us."*

PSALM 68:19B

Day One

FAITHFUL: THANKSGIVING

PSALM 22:2-5

*My God, I cry out during the day, but you do
not answer, and during the night my prayers do
not let up. You are holy; you sit as king receiving
the praises of Israel. In you our ancestors
trusted; they trusted you and you rescued
them. To you they cried out, and they were
saved; in you they trusted and they
were not disappointed.*

———

Fear appears to dominate the thoughts and actions of many. According to a study presented by Consumer Health Day, nearly 74% of polled Americans indicated that they were either "afraid" or "very afraid" of corrupt government officials, 61.6% indicated a fear of polluted oceans and lakes, 60.7 % indicated a fear of polluted drinking water, and 57% confessed they feared they would not have enough money for the future ("What Americans Fear Most"). In the guise of responsibility, many make elaborate plans to protect their health, family and assets. While planning ahead is wise, it is important not to transmit a heritage of fear to our children.

Repeatedly, Three hundred and sixty-five times the Bible says, "fear not." This lack of fear, however, is not a mere wishful hope. We are not told to fear without reason nor given trite catchphrases such as "it'll all work out" as self-improvement mantras. Our relationship with the God of the universe should give us confidence in the face of fear.

We can be confident that our lives will be full of struggles and situations that will cause us and our children to be tempted to be afraid. Jesus himself promised challenges in John 16:33 when He says, "I have told you these things so that in me you may have peace. In the world you have trouble and suffering, but take courage—I have conquered the world." We are promised trouble. Being a Christian is not a safety net against struggles and hard times.

However, in this same passage, Jesus also promises peace. This peace is not based on the confidence that the problems will go away but rather in trusting that our loving God will be with us in the middle of our problems. His presence is our peace.

A powerful antidote against fear is recalling the faithfulness of God. This is exactly what the psalmist does in Psalm 22. These verses are the heart cry of someone who has sought the Lord, who wants to be obedient but is starting to despair. Rather than succumbing to fear or dejection, however, he focuses on the attributes of God. God is holy. God is King. God is faithful.

These promises are still true.

As a mother who loves the Lord, it is imperative that you dwell on the faithfulness of God. It is popular to worry about your children—it is even encouraged by the culture—but it is not biblical. Rather than fear, allow rest and peace to dwell among your family. Rest in the faithfulness of the Lord. Recount what God has done. Teach your child that God has been faithful; teach your child they need not fear.

My Lord and my God,

I thank you because even when I do not see my prayers answered, I know you hear them. I am confident that you remain faithful to me and to my family. Please help (name of your child) to know and understand the confident hope that they have in you. Please help them to know that they need not fear because your presence is their peace.

Thank you, Father, for your faithfulness not only to me but to my family. Thank you for your provision and protection over each of us. Thank you that you can be trusted. I thank you that you are holy. I thank you that you use your power to intervene in our lives. You are the King and the world is still in your hands. Please allow my child's heart to rest in your faithfulness.

In Jesus' name, Amen.

Day Two

DESIRE: CONFESSION

PSALM 27:3-5

Even when an army is deployed against me, I do not fear. Even when war is imminent, I remain confident. I have asked the Lord for one thing— this is what I desire! I want to live in the Lord's house all the days of my life, so I can gaze at the splendor of the Lord and contemplate in his temple. He will surely give me shelter in the day of danger; he will hide me in his home; he will place me on an inaccessible rocky summit.

———

In E. Nesbitt's children's book, *Five Children and It,* five siblings encounter the stuff of dreams; a wish-granting fairy called the Psammead. Grumpy, and not particularly pleasant to look at, the creature is not naturally alluring. His strange ability, however, is. He allows the five to make one wish per day, with the mutual understanding that the desired object will turn to stone at the end of the day. With many misadventures, the children return daily, each expecting a new request to be granted. Creating a series of catastrophes, the children finally wish the events to be made right, and the fairy agrees, on the condition they cannot ask for any more wishes.

How often do we approach the Lord with a similar attitude? More often than not, our prayers become little more than a lengthy list of people or situations we want to see healed or needs we desire to be met. These prayers are of course appropriate at times and we know that the Lord is attentive to those who call to him- as it says in 1 Peter 3:12, "For the eyes of the Lord are upon the righteous and his ears are open to their prayer. But the Lord's face is against those who do evil." The point is not that asking for things is wrong. Rather, this passage is a reminder that we must seek the Lord out of a desire to know Him. Desire is key.

This beautiful portion of Psalm 27 reveals to us the heart of one who is deeply in love with the Lord; he clearly communicates a desire to be in the Lord's presence. He wants to gaze upon Him. To know Him.

From before my children were born, I began praying for them to know the Lord. But in reading this passage I was struck with a few questions.

Do I cultivate in *my* heart a desire for the Lord so that my child wants to know Him too?

Do I want to gaze on the splendor of the Lord, or do I simply want to live in the Lord's house?

Do I desire the Lord, or do I just want what He has to offer?

If your child does not see you desire the Lord, likely he or she will not be drawn to him, either. If your child sees you going to the Lord always with a lengthy laundry list but never with a desire to linger, they will take your cue. What you desire matters—both for your walk with the Lord and your child's.

If you realize that your heart has been guilty of approaching the Lord for selfish reasons, you're in good company. We've all been there! But we are so blessed to serve a loving God who knows that our hearts and our motives are fallen and so often prone to sin. There is time—even now—to make the change and allow your heart to desire to be in the Lord's presence. This is a vital example you can give to your child.

How? Start with prayer. Be honest with the Lord, opening your heart to Him. Confess your sins to Him. Allow Him to wash you clean and start again.

———————————————

Lord,

I confess my heart is fleshly and can be so focused on myself. I confess that I often approach you with a desire to see my needs met rather than to simply be in your presence. Please allow me to model for (name of your child) a heart that truly desires you. Please allow me to make the gospel attractive to them so that they love you first rather than the riches you offer. Please allow me to desire you more than anything.

In your name, Amen.

Day Three

INVESTMENT: SUPPLICATION

PSALM 119:9-16

How can a young person maintain a pure life? By guarding it according to your instructions! With all my heart I seek you. Do not allow me to stray from your commands! In my heart I store up your words, so I might not sin against you. You deserve praise, O Lord! Teach me your statutes! With my lips I proclaim all the regulations you have revealed. I rejoice in the lifestyle prescribed by your rules as if they were riches of all kinds. I will meditate on your precepts and focus on your behavior. I find delight in your statutes; I do not forget your instructions.

———

What is the value of purity?

Most all girls dream of the day when a man they love presents them with a beautiful ring and asks them to become his wife. When a famous quarterback proposed to his wife, the ring offered was valued at well over half a million dollars. A staggering 7.25 carat diamond in a simple solitaire setting, the ring was impressive to say the least. But jewel experts commenting on the value of the ring explained that the true worth of the diamond was found in its clarity. This stone was internally flawless, meaning that it had no imperfections within the diamond. Regardless of the angle or the lighting, the stone was perfect—which of course was reflected in its price.

Diamond inclusions are explained by one jewel source as being "imperfections within a diamond that are created due to the extreme pressure and heat that diamond's experience when they form" (*Brilliance.com*). As parents, many of us worry about the imperfections that our child might develop as the world exerts extreme pressure on their little hearts and minds. We know these influences can be destructive, even devastating, but we are incapable of shielding our child from every unbiblical ideology. How then, can our little ones remain pure?

In Psalm 119, a psalm written to celebrate love for the Word of God, David answers that exact question. The great King of Israel emphasizes the need for extreme caution and vigilance for living a life of purity. He says a young person must guard their heart—conjuring up images of a well-fortified castle with archers on the battlements. This is an appropriate image for a successful warrior and king to have used; the heart is a battle ground, and the results of losing the fight are dire.

In these four verses, David offers practical advice for how to gain victory in the arena of the mind. 1. Guard your mind according to God's instructions. 2. Seek the Lord with all your heart. 3. Store up the words of the Lord. 4. Ask the Lord to teach His statutes to you. Although these are simple steps, they require faithful study and commitment to long-term discipline to reap the benefits.

If purity in your life and the life of your child is a priority to you, consider implementing these practices now. Teach your child to pray, using Scripture, that the Lord will guard their heart. Model a love and passion for the Lord that envelops your heart and your desires. Memorize the Word and help your little one also store up Scripture in their heart. Meditate on the Word, asking the Lord to teach you His truth. These four practices are some of the most important skills we can model and teach our children; with these tools, they can protect their hearts. As it says in the Proverbs: "Guard your heart with all vigilance, for from it are the sources of life" (Proverbs 4:23).

A pure heart, like a flawless diamond, has great value. But like all things of value, it comes at a high price. Take the time to invest in the future of your child's heart. Teach them how to have a pure life. Teach them how to guard their lives with the instructions of the Lord.

It starts with you.

Thank you, Father, that your Word is sufficient to guard the life of my child.

Help me to recognize the urgency of fighting for the purity of my little one's mind. Please help me to model a love for your Word and a humility to be taught by your decrees that my child can follow. Please allow my child to grow to love and desire intimacy with you above all else.

Please guard (insert your child's name)'s heart according to your instructions. Please keep them from straying from your commands. Allow them to desire to store up your words in their heart so they will not sin against you. Please teach them your statutes and allow them to live a life pure and holy, pleasing before you.

In Jesus' name, Amen.

Day Four

INDESCRIBABLE: ADORATION

PSALM 68:4-6, 19-20

Sing to God! Sing praises to his name! Exalt the one who rides on the clouds! For the Lord is his name! Rejoice before him! He is a father to the fatherless and an advocate for widows. God rules from his holy palace. God settles those who have been deserted in their own homes; he frees prisoners and grants them prosperity. But sinful rebels live in the desert. The Lord deserves praise! Day after day he carries our burden, the God who delivers us. (Selah) Our God is a God who delivers; the Lord, the sovereign Lord, can rescue from death.

———

In J.R.R. Tolkien's moving conclusion to the *Lord of the Rings* trilogy, the weight of an overwhelming burden brought the protagonist, young Frodo Baggins, to the brink of defeat. Physically exhausted and pursued by seen and unseen creatures, Frodo, on the way to Mount Doom, finally collapsed. The terror inspired by his pursuers, all seeking Frodo's enchanted ring, held little sway compared to the bewitching bauble itself. The ring controlled him and slowly ate away at his sanity as well as his ability to separate from it. At Frodo's moment of despair, Samwise, Frodo's faithful friend, asked him to recall their homeland. Unable to do so, Frodo gave up hope. Mustering his courage, Samwise replied in perhaps the most iconic quote of the saga, "'Come, Mr. Frodo!' he cried. 'I can't carry it for you, but I can carry you'" (Tolkien). Lifting his friend, Sam proceeded to bear Frodo the rest of the way up the mountain to their final destination. He carried Frodo when Frodo could not carry himself.

This moving story is fictional, yet it provides us with a small understanding of the Lord's care as depicted in Psalm 68. In this psalm, the writer praises the Lord for His compassionate and loving protection. God is depicted tenderly, attending to the needs of those who have been abandoned, suffered loss, or been ill-treated. The Lord is intimately acquainted with all of our needs, as verse 19 states: "Day after day he carries our burden, the God who delivers us" (Psalm 68:19b).

Psalm 68 is a beautiful Psalm to remind ourselves of the Lord's love for us, but it is also a rich heritage to share with our children.

There will come a day when your precious little one will encounter personal hardship. When that happens, they need to be reminded of the attributes of God as described in Psalm 68.

- God is worthy of praise.
- He rides the clouds and is ruler over all living things.
- He is an advocate for the poor and mistreated.
- He is a father to the fatherless.
- He settles those who have been deserted and sets the prisoner free.
- He daily carries our burdens.

If we believe these facts about God, then they are truly life changing. If God truly is the ruler of all living things, advocate for the poor, and father to the fatherless, can He not be trusted with our burdens? The story of Sam and Frodo is inspiring because it is completely counterintuitive to the nature of our culture. Precious few people are *willing* to carry the burdens of others, even fewer are actually *able* to. God, however, says that He is able. He is willing. This is proof of His indescribable love for us. This is love worth praising Him for.

In this time, at this early stage in your child's life, set

the precedent of adoring the Lord for His indescribable love for us. He is intimate with our needs and cares deeply for us. Pray that this will be the foundation on which your child builds his or her faith and life.

Father God,

Thank you for this precious little one whom you have given me to love and care for. I pray that as they grow, you will help me to be faithful to share with them the love you have for us. Thank you that you are so intimately acquainted with all their needs and that who you are will never change. Please help them to know and believe that you are worthy of praise. You are worthy of adoration. You are near, and you are intimately acquainted with my child's heart. Please soften their heart toward you and allow their voice to one day sing your praises.

In the precious name of Jesus, Amen.

Day Five

SUSTAINED: THANKSGIVING

PSALM 73:1-4, 17-18, 23-28

Certainly God is good to Israel, and to those whose motives are pure! But as for me, my feet almost slipped; my feet almost slid out from under me. For I envied those who are proud, as I observed the prosperity of the wicked. For they suffer no pain; their bodies are strong and well-fed. Then I entered the precincts of God's temple, and understood the destiny of the wicked. Surely you put them in slippery places; you bring them down to ruin. But I am continually with you; you hold my right hand. You guide me by your wise advice, and then you will lead me to a position of honor. Whom do I have in heaven but you? I desire no one but you on earth. My flesh and my heart may grow weak, but God always protects my heart and gives me stability. Yes, look! Those far from you die; you

destroy everyone who is unfaithful to you. But
as for me, God's presence is all I need. I have
made the sovereign Lord my shelter, as I declare
all the things you have done.

———

Just over fifty years ago, Joni Eareckson Tada, Christian, disability-ministry advocate, singer, author, and
artist, suffered a diving accident that would forever
change her life. Before she jumped, she was an athletic,
strong, seventeen-year-old with the world's possibilities endlessly open to her. During the summer following her high school graduation, Joni went swimming in
the Chesapeake Bay and dove into water that was much
shallower than she anticipated. In her impact, she frac-
tured her spinal cord between her fourth and fifth cer-
vical vertebrae leaving her a quadriplegic.

Joni struggled with a range of emotions following her
accident: denial, despair, doubt, and depression. Finally, returning to the one truth she knew, Joni sought
the Lord to make meaning of her personal tragedy.
Not only did the Lord change her attitude and give
her joy and purpose in her disability, He used her to
be one of the most influential players in disability
ministry worldwide. Now reflecting on her time as an
individual with a disability, Tada says, "I really would
rather be in this wheelchair knowing Jesus as I do
than be on my feet without him." ("Reflections on the

50th Anniversary of my Diving Accident")

These are the words of one intimate with suffering but also acutely aware of the sustaining grace of the Word of God. In her reflections, Tada speaks with joy and as one who has been blessed—which she has indeed, for this situation has brought her into a deep relationship with God. The question then begs to be asked: do you pray for the sustaining grace of the Lord to be sufficient for your child regardless of what challenges they face in their lives?

In the words of this passage we find one wholly absorbed in the Lord. The Lord meets his every need for companionship, as the author says that he desires "no one but you on earth" (v. 25). The Lord grants stability that cannot be found in personal health or youthful strength (v. 26). The writer is aware that the one thing that he needs is the presence of God; God is his shelter (v. 28) but also the object of his desires and adoration. This is not simply a mouthed prayer nor an act of pious religiosity. These are the words of one passionately in love with the Lord. These are the prayers of one who is sustained by the Lord, no matter what situations he might face.

As you pray for your child, aware of the inevitability of suffering in this life, perhaps shift your focus from protection *from* trials to being sustained *through* them. Pray that the Lord becomes their source of shelter, that

His presence becomes all that they need and desire. Pray that they learn to become sustained by the very presence of God, that they can see trials as opportunities for growth and rejoicing.

Dear Lord,

Thank you that you are truly my source of strength and stability. Whom do I have in heaven but you? I do not deserve your protection or provision for me, yet you give it so graciously. Thank you that you also care so much about the needs of my child. Lord, I know that one day (insert child's name) will go through suffering, whether from a physical disability, financial ruin, or loss of a loved one. I know that in this world trouble is guaranteed because this world is broken and needs you. I beg you to reveal yourself to (insert child's name) that they might learn that your presence is all they need. Please allow them to rest in your shelter, and please prepare them with the strength to be sustained through whatever trials you might allow their way.

In Jesus' name, Amen.

Day Six

COVER MY MOUTH: CONFESSION

PSALM 141:1-5

*O Lord, I cry out to you. Come quickly to
me! Pay attention to me when I cry out to
you! May you accept my prayer like incense, my
uplifted hands like the evening offering! O
Lord, place a guard on my mouth! Protect the
opening of my lips! Do not let me have evil
desires, or participate in sinful activities with
men who behave wickedly. I will not eat their
delicacies. May the godly strike me in love and
correct me! May my head not refuse choice
oil! Indeed, my prayer is a witness
against their evil deeds.*

———

Have you ever said something entirely regrettable? Perhaps you gave unsolicited parenting advice, dieting advice, or relationship advice? As quickly as it left your mouth, you wished you had a net to gather it back up and stuff it deep down your throat.

With little ones, it is so valuable to have temperate speech and not allow words to fly unchecked, but how do we do that practically? How do we train our children to be wise with their words when compulsive speech might be a vice of ours?

In Psalm 141 the writer makes specific petitions with regard to speech in the ten short verses. He asks the Lord twice to listen to his cries for help and twice to accept his prayer (vv. 1-2), he seeks discernment in his speech (vv. 3-4), and he asks for correction from the godly, that his prayer might be a witness against the evil deeds of others (v. 5).

It appears that the writer of this psalm understood the gravity of imprudent speech, for he asks the Lord to place a guard on his mouth and to protect what comes out of his lips. This image of a fortified city gate appears a little severe for a man seeking wisdom in his speech. But the writer goes a step further, asking for pure desires and freedom from sinful activities.

Interesting that the writer asks for pure *thoughts* when seeking pure *words*. This theme, however, is repeated throughout the Bible. In Proverbs 4:23-24, the author writes, "Guard your heart with all vigilance, for from it are the sources of life. Remove perverse speech from your mouth; keep devious talk far from your lips." In Matthew 15:19, Jesus emphasizes that the fruit of the heart influences the fruit of the lips when He says, "For out of the heart come evil ideas, murder, adultery, sexual immorality, theft, false testimony, slander."

Again, Jesus highlights the importance of a right heart in regard to pure speech when He says, "For the mouth speaks from what fills the heart" (Matthew 12:34b). Clearly the issue of sinful speech isn't as simple as an ill-thought through comment or careless criticism. Our words reflect our heart.

As we hear our own mouths and those of our children speaking things that reflect a sinful heart, let us model the humility needed for healing and victory. Let us, with the psalmist, ask the Lord to work in our hearts and our mouths, that we might be able to speak freely from a pure heart.

Lord God,

I confess that at times my words and my heart are not pleasing to you. I know that my speech reflects my heart, and I want my heart to reflect your heart. Please help me as I speak in front of my little one, that my talk would be from a pure heart. Please forgive me for when it is far from that. Please help (insert child's name) to one day understand what it means to have a pure heart, and I pray that they would follow you in their thoughts and their speech and their actions. Please redeem the words of my mouth.

In Jesus' precious name, Amen.

Day Seven

OBEDIENCE: SUPPLICATION

PSALM 112:1-4, 7-9

Praise the Lord! How blessed is the one who obeys the Lord, who takes great delight in keeping his commands. His descendants will be powerful on the earth; the godly will be blessed. His house contains wealth and riches; his integrity endures. In the darkness a light shines for the godly, for each one who is merciful, compassionate, and just. He does not fear bad news. He is confident; he trusts in the Lord. His resolve is firm; he will not succumb to fear before he looks in triumph on his enemies. He generously gives to the needy; his integrity endures. He will be vindicated and honored.

———

Replete throughout the Bible as well as the course of human history have been stories of those who have been blessed by living lives obedient to the Lord. One such man was Jim Elliot. Elliot walked with the Lord, writing journals of his quiet times that would put many of us to shame. He read the Bible with voracity and passion. He joined a mission to serve the Waodani Indians, a tribe reputed to be dangerous. Despite the threat of personal danger, Jim Elliot felt the call to serve them and bring them the gospel. And on January 8, 1957, Elliot and his four teammates were murdered under false accusation of ill-treatment toward the native people. Was this man blessed by the Lord? He died young, only twenty-eight years old, leaving a widow and daughter of ten months. He died without seeing a convert from his mission work and without significant financial assets. What made him blessed?

Heralding back to Psalm 1, this passage reemphasizes how blessed is the one who obeys the Lord. Also similar to Psalm 1, the writer articulates that this man takes delight (Psalm 112:1) or finds pleasure (Psalm 1:2) in obeying the Lord's commands. This psalm goes on to explain that such a person is free of fear (Psalm 112:7), he is confident and trusts God (Psalm 112:7), he is resolved in his thinking and he is victorious in what he does (Psalm 112:8). He is generous, full of integrity, and is given a future of being vindicated and honored (Psalm 112:9). This man is not only blessed in material ways but also in strength of character and reputation. He is a man to be honored and revered.

How do we as mothers encourage our little ones to be blessed by God? I believe the answer is found in both Psalm 1 and Psalm 112. There is blessing in obeying the Word of God, and in delighting in and keeping His commands. This can only be accomplished by knowing the Word of God, or in the case of our little ones, being taught the Word of God.

And we must teach them.

This is not to say that our goal as mamas is to help our children establish their viewpoint on the millennial kingdom before kindergarten or understand every aspect of God's grace or the working of the Holy Spirit. We likely do not fully understand all these areas of doctrine ourselves. But it is essential that we are faithful to teach the Lord's commands to our children *anyway*.

How do we do that? Through personal time in the Word. Through study. Through seeking help from a godly spouse. Through asking your pastor. It is crucial that you develop your child's spiritual education so that they know and understand the Lord's commands and what it takes to keep them.

How else are they to understand their inability to keep them? How else are they to know that they need Jesus?

What if your child is called to lead a life like Jim Elliot?

What if you train him or her in the ways of the Lord and your reward is that they suffer for Him? What then? Might I suggest Paul's response to suffering, as outlined in his second epistle to the Corinthian church,

For our momentary, light suffering is producing for us an eternal weight of glory far beyond all comparison because we are not looking at what can be seen but at what cannot be seen. For what can be seen is temporary, but what cannot be seen is eternal (2 Corinthians 4:17-18).

Look to the eternal blessings the Lord desires to give to your child. Surrender them to follow His will whatever it might be. Finally, train your children in righteousness, that they might know what it means to be obedient to the Lord.

Dear Father,

Thank you so much for the gift of my child. Thank you for the good plans you have for them and for their life. Thank you that you desire more than anything that they love you, obey you, and submit to your will. Thank you that your plans for them are good, whether that blessing comes in this life or the life to come. Help me to trust you with the life of my child, and please help me to be faithful to instruct them in your Word with all diligence. Please strengthen me with your Holy Spirit for the task at hand.

In the precious name of Jesus, Amen.

Week Five

"I have told you these things so that in me you may have peace. In the world you have trouble and suffering, but take courage—I have conquered the world."

JOHN 16:33

Day One

HOME: THANKSGIVING

PSALM 84:1-5

How lovely is the place where you live, O Lord who lives over all! I desperately want to be in the courts of the Lord's temple. My heart and my entire being shout for joy to the living God. Even the birds find a home there, and the swallow builds a nest, where she can protect her young near your altars, O Lord who rules over all, my king and my God. How blessed are those who live in your temple and praise you continually! (Selah) How blessed are those who find their strength in you, and long to travel the roads that lead to your temple!

———

There's something so alluring about home-makeover shows. Although they all seem to be variations on a theme, many people love seeing the remodeler transform a beaten down, dumpy house into something that belongs in *Home* magazine. For many years, a husband-and-wife team transformed unassuming, even ugly homes across central Texas into places of beauty. Their projects required substantial work and significant financial investment, but the end result was well worth the effort. Breathing new life into these carcasses of houses, the pair would tear down walls, open spaces, retile, re-grout, rearrange, and emerge with the vision they had foreseen from the very beginning.

People love beauty. Regardless of the space or structure, something within our hearts is *drawn* to that which has beauty. We long to be surrounded with that which charms our eyes and puts our hearts at rest. A place we can call home. Have you ever wondered why? We are meant to long for our future home, knowing this world won't last forever!

The psalmist in Psalm 84 says that the place where the Lord lives is lovely. The Creator of all things beautiful surrounds Himself with beauty. This dwelling place of the Lord is a place of worship, one that brings joy. It is a place of safety and rest for all His children. Those who seek to travel and live there are blessed. Unlike the home-makeover shows, this place does not need renovation; it needs nothing. It is the house of God, and more than being simply beautiful, it is the answer to all our deepest longings on this earth.

Our desires to be known,

to be loved,

to be safe,

to be welcome,

to be at peace all culminate in our future home: the house of God.

Jesus promises that, for those who place their faith in Him, He has set aside a space in the house of God. He speaks directly to this when He says:

And if I go and make ready a place for you, I will come again and take you to be with me, so that where I am you may be too. And you know the way where I am going (John 14:3-4).

More than just a mansion, however, God's home is the place where the curse of our sin is forever removed. All the hurting of the sinful world is removed as we dwell in the presence of the Lord. As it says in the final book of the Bible:

And I heard a loud voice from the throne saying: "Look! The residence of God is among human beings. He will live among them, and they will be his people, and God himself will be with them. He will wipe away every tear from their eyes, and death will not exist any more—or mourning, or crying, or pain, for the former things have ceased to exist (Revelation 21:3-4).

This is the home of one who, as the psalm says repeatedly, rules over all. His supremacy rules over all dangers, offering us safety. His love rules over all accusations, condemnations, and fears. His justice keeps sin far from His home. For those who believe in Jesus and have forgiveness for their sins, this is their home, too.

If this day you are struggling with the weightiness of the world—or perhaps worrying about the struggles that will wear down your little one—take time to worship the Lord for His home in which He has prepared space for you. Thank Him for His beauty and for the desire for beauty that He has put in your heart. Meditate on the beauty of the home that God has promised for those who believe.

Thank the Lord that He has prepared a beautiful home for you: Heaven.

O Lord who rules over all,

Thank you that you sent your Son to go ahead of me and prepare a place for me in your Heaven. Thank you that your home is lovely because you reside there. Thank you that your presence fills your home with glory and majesty and strength and peace. Thank you for your love for me, that you would include me in your home and make a place for me. Thank you for who you are. You are glorious. You are beautiful. You are strong. You are powerful. You rule over all.

I praise your name, Amen.

Day Two

RESOUND: ADORATION

PSALM 29:2-5, 7-8

Acknowledge the majesty of the Lord's reputation! Worship the Lord in holy attire! The Lord's shout is heard over the water; the majestic God thunders, the Lord appears over the surging water. The Lord's shout is powerful, the Lord's shout is majestic. The Lord's shout breaks the cedars, the Lord shatters the cedars of Lebanon. The Lord's shout strikes with flaming fire. The Lord's shout shakes the wilderness, the Lord shakes the wilderness of Kadesh.

———

Of all trite phrases, "Sticks and stones may break my bones, but words will never hurt me" might be the most untrue. If you have ever spent considerable time with an adolescent, you know that words wield weight and power. A catty comment about being overweight can hurl a young teen into an eating disorder. A disparaging comment about someone acting effeminate can cause a young adult to question, doubt, or be ashamed of his or her sex. Attacking someone for a disability or weakness can cause them to isolate and avoid the assistance they need to reach true independence.

Knowing the enormous influence which words can hold, it is necessary that we guide our precious little ones to listen to the words that are strongest and best. We must teach them to listen to the words of our Father. If they grow intimately acquainted with what He says about Himself and about them, they will be defended and prepared to wisely handle the cacophony of life.

Psalm 29 is a perfect passage to meditate on the voice of God because it focuses on the theme of the Lord's shout. In this psalm, we learn that the Lord's shout is heard over the water; it is powerful, majestic, and breaks the cedars. The Lord's voice is a force to be feared and listened to.

How, though, do we have our children learn to hear and understand the voice of the Lord? We must first teach them who the Lord is and what His voice has done.

The voice of the Lord is heard over the water, and it is the voice that shaped the water (Genesis 1:9).

The voice of the Lord promised redemption for a sinful people (Gen. 3:15) and at the words "it is completed" (John 19:30) the Son of God bought our forgiveness.

The voice of the Lord healed the sick (Matthew 15:28, Mark 2:11-12).

The voice of the Lord commanded unclean spirits to be gone, and they obeyed (Mark 5:8,13).

The voice of the Lord resounds like a trumpet (Revelation 1:10).

The voice of the Lord brings condemnation and judgement, as well as commendation and reassurance (Matthew 25:35-45).

The voice of the Lord calms the storms and speaks peace into our weary hearts (Mark 4:39).

People who listen to the voice of the Lord grow in wisdom (Daniel 2:23).

Your children will not be taught to listen to the voice of the Lord by the world, however, so they must be taught by you. As you raise your little one, take time to show them how the voice of the Lord has worked through the history of the world. How better to do that than using the words of God that are available to us in the Bible?

Teach your child the Bible from cover to cover, highlighting the Lord's mighty acts. As you teach, pray for their salvation; pray for it now, pray for it faithfully until you see your prayers answered. For apart from knowing the Lord, how are they to hear His voice? Apart from hearing His voice, how are they to differentiate right thoughts from those of the world?

———————————

Thank you, Father, that in your words there is life and there is true wisdom. Thank you that your voice resounds in power and strength and at your name one day all people will bow. Please help my child to understand the necessity of knowing and hearing your voice that they might walk in your ways all the days of their life. Please allow their heart to be sensitive to your Holy Spirit, that you would allow them to come to a saving knowledge of who you are. Thank you for revealing your words to us through your Scripture. Please help me to be a faithful teacher of your words to my precious little one.

In your mighty name, Amen.

Day Three

REBUILT: CONFESSION

PSALM 147:2-6

The Lord rebuilds Jerusalem, and gathers the exiles of Israel. He heals the brokenhearted, and bandages their wounds. He counts the number of the stars; he names all of them. Our Lord is great and has awesome power; there is no limit to his wisdom. The Lord lifts up the oppressed, but knocks the wicked to the ground.

———

Are you ever tempted to remove the news icons from your search bar on your web browser? I have become so wearied by the political banter, social squabbles, and onslaught of violence that have barraged our world that I seldom check for news updates. Sin is definitely alive and well.

Frequently, I also receive updates on how the Christian church suffers global persecution, and with a precious little daughter to protect, I want to turn off my phone and forget that evil is in the world. Perhaps you have faced these same overwhelming emotions as you read about wrongs you can never personally right. Perhaps you consider what personal persecution your child may have to face, and shudder.

What, then, do the Psalms offer as comfort and direction to a praying mama wanting to shield her child from the evils of this world? Psalm 147 is a perfect place to dwell and glean strength for challenging times. In this psalm we learn that the Lord is in the business of restoration. He brings back exiles from captivity. He is the one who heals and restores those who are emotionally and physically crushed. He comes alongside the oppressed and lifts them up. These statements reveal important truths about our God.

God is acutely aware of our suffering. How else could He know from where to rescue the exiles and where to return them? Who told the Lord when to rescue the brokenhearted and what would be the way to heal their hearts? He does not need to be told because He already knows. The first reassurance offered from this psalm is that the Lord is aware of the suffering in our world—and the suffering you and your child will face. He is acutely aware of all of our needs, and He is more than able to meet them.

Secondly, the psalmist reminds us to meditate on the power of the Lord. He says that the Lord is great and has awesome power. He is not at the mercy of our political system or governmental unrest. He is above and beyond any man-made construct.

Jesus spoke to this issue toward the end of His time on earth. Knowing that His death was imminent, He warned His disciples that He would return to the Father and that their band of disciples would be scattered. Rather than promising them physical ease or deliverance, Jesus encouraged His followers to keep a heavenly perspective when He said:

I have told you these things so that in me you may have peace. In the world you have trouble and suffering, but take courage—I have conquered the world (John 16:33).

These same words of comfort should bring encouragement to our hearts. We have not been promised a life of safety and security; you have not and your child has not. But for those of us who trust Christ as our Lord and Savior, we can join our names to this promise; we have overcome the world in Christ! This is the hope we have and the reason for our lives. This is the hope your child has, and this is the hope you must teach to them. So teach these twin truths to your little one as you see the broken world into which they have been born:

- God knows our suffering.
- Christ has overcome the world, and they can experience this victory as well.

Celebrate the restoration the Lord offers. This world and all its struggles do not escape His notice. Worship Him for that today, and teach the truth of who He is to your little one.

Lord God,

I confess it is so easy for me to look at this world and want to worry. I know that nothing can ever be made right apart from you. There is so much violence and cruelty, and I confess that makes me anxious for my child. Please take away my anxiety and replace it with a confidence in your total knowledge of the world and in your victory over the world. Thank you that through your Son's sacrifice, I might also experience that victory through eternal life with you.

In Jesus' name, Amen.

Day Four

HOLY: ADORATION

PSALM 99:1-9

The Lord reigns! The nations tremble. He sits enthroned above the winged angels; the earth shakes. The Lord is elevated in Zion; he is exalted over all the nations. Let them praise your great and awesome name! He is holy! The king is strong; he loves justice. You ensure that legal decisions will be made fairly; you promote justice and equity in Jacob. Praise the Lord our God! Worship before his footstool! He is holy! Moses and Aaron were among his priests; Samuel was one of those who prayed to him. They prayed to the Lord and he answered them. He spoke to them from a pillar of cloud; they obeyed his regulations and the ordinance he gave them. O Lord our God, you answered them. They found you to be a forgiving God, but also one who punished their

sinful deeds. Praise the Lord our God! Worship
on his holy hill, for the Lord our God is holy!

———

According to a 2016 study conducted by the Barna Group, nearly three-quarters of the United States would identify as being Christians. However, this designation does not seem to influence the faith they claim to have. Based on a metric of several questions about basic Christian beliefs, almost half of Americans polled were considered post-Christian, as the majority of their beliefs did not align to basic Christian doctrine such as Jesus being sinless and the Bible being accurate. Given these statistics, it is not surprising that some polls quote that as little as 17.7% of Americans attend church on any given Sunday.

As you work to provide a physically and spiritually healthy climate for your child, how do you ensure that they do not negatively contribute to these sad statistics?

In Psalm 99, the writer emphasizes the importance of worshiping the Lord for many of His attributes, but the most repeated in this passage is the Lord's holiness. In the nine verses of this psalm, God's holiness is referenced on multiple separate occasions, all within the context of worship and praise. This attribute of holiness reappears often in Scripture, referring to things that are separate, dedicated (to a special purpose), or consecrated. The Israelites' priestly clothing and food, for example, were considered holy because they were set aside for very specific usage. God's name was considered holy and was therefore carefully guarded against being used in idle speech.

God's nature is holy, and many times He is referenced by this attribute. This name implies that He is perfect, sinless, and completely separate from the nature of others. In the Old Testament, the Lord is repeatedly referenced as "the Holy One of Israel" (Isaiah 17:7, Isaiah 30:15, Jeremiah 50:29). Jesus is called "the Holy One of God" during His earthly ministry (Mark 1:24). Finally, the third member of the Trinity is known often by His nature of holiness as part of His title (Luke 11:13, Acts 1:8).

When faced with the holiness of God, people are forced to respond.

Isaiah 6 depicts a snapshot in a dark season of Israel's history. Arguably the last good King of the southern kingdom had died, and the prophet was likely discouraged, assuming that the rise of a wicked king would bring divine judgement on the nation.

In this context, Isaiah saw the Lord. Supernatural beings attended Him, and His glory was revealed in an overwhelming display. Repeatedly, these supernatural creatures called out endless worship: "Holy, holy, holy, is the Lord who commands armies! His majestic splendor fills the entire earth!" (Isaiah 6:3b). This man of

God responded in repentance, assuming his doom was sealed. The reason for his terror? When faced with the holiness of God, his sin was clearly exposed.

This should be our response too. As we begin to grasp the depth of God's holiness, we unwrap how far from His standard we fall. We understand our need for His saving grace, and we, like the prophet Isaiah, seek the Lord's mercy.

Perhaps the decline in church attendance in our nation stems from an apathy for the holiness of God. Do we understand just how holy the Lord is? Do we worship Him for this attribute and praise Him that He is in every way perfect and spotless and "other" from us? This is reason to worship!

As you raise your little one, now is the time to instill in them a knowledge of the holiness of God. Worship Him for His position of power. Praise Him for His nature that is completely different from you and me. Model a fear for the Lord out of an understanding that He is not like us.

He deserves our worship. He is holy.

Gracious and Compassionate God,

You are holy, and your holiness exposes my sin so clearly. Lord, I know that I fall so far from the standard that you set of holiness. Lord, when I begin to understand who you are and your nature of holiness, all I can do is praise you for your mercy that you forgive my sins through Jesus Christ. Please teach me how to model your praise to (insert child's name). Please help me to worship you for your holiness and to teach my child of who you are.

I praise your holy name, Amen.

Day Five

DEFENDED: THANKSGIVING

PSALM 56:4-5, 8,11

In God—I boast in his promise—in God I trust, I am not afraid. What can mere men do to me? All day long they cause me trouble; they make a habit of plotting my demise. You keep track of my misery. Put my tears in your leather container! Are they not recorded in your scroll? in God I trust, I am not afraid. What can mere men do to me?

———

Do you ever wonder what could happen to your child if you could not take care of them? With news platforms constantly telling about bullying and mass shootings, car accidents and abuse, there is much fuel for anxiety! Yet as mamas who love the Lord, it is imperative that we learn not to give in to the temptation to worry. This psalm is a wonderful reminder of our security in the Lord's capable watch care.

The writer of this psalm boasts in the protection of the Lord, repeatedly meditating on the phrase "what can mere men do to me?" Out of context, it might not seem too encouraging that one of the great Kings of Israel had security in the Lord. However, while David experienced greatness, this psalm was not written during a season of prosperity. David had been betrayed by a cruel and jealous King, had several attempts on his life, and had been driven from his homeland to the land of Gath (1 Samuel 21). In enemy territory, David was reduced to behaving like a madman to escape undesired interest from the King. What a low point for such a great man, one that the Lord had called to be King (1 Samuel 16:1) and considered a man after His own heart (Acts 13:22).

This psalm testifies that although David was at a low point in his life, the Lord had by no means finished accomplishing His purposes for David. The greatest blessing God had for David, fathering a child who would be ancestor to the Messiah (Matthew 1:17), was still to come, along with many other accolades, military victories, and political accomplishments. But first, God crafted a man who relied on Him, who understood His heart.

David's trust wasn't based on the absence of things to fear but in a knowledge of the power of God. He understood that despite his personal humiliation and betrayal, the Lord was still sovereign over his situation and life. The Lord still had amazing accomplishments for David, and David trusted the Lord to rescue him.

Considering the life of David should prompt us to ask ourselves the same question he asked. Does your heart echo the confidence of David? With God as your defender, what can men do to you or to your child? Do you trust the Lord to be faithful regardless of what He calls you to do?

- Does He want you in foreign missions? He can be trusted to care for your child.

- Does He want you in the workplace? He can be trusted to care for your child.

- Does He want you in full-time ministry? He can be trusted to care for your child.

- Does He want you to open your home to foster care? He can be trusted to care for your child.

The Lord is trustworthy to accomplish His purposes for your child's life, as well as yours. Rest in the promise that the Lord is trustworthy and that the Lord is on your side.

Lord God,

I thank you that you can be trusted to provide for the life of my child in all situations. I thank you for their life, and I thank you that regardless of what you call our family to, you will be faithful to protect us and give us what is best according to your will and plan. Please help me to trust you with the child you have given to me, and please keep me from the sin of idolizing their safety above obedience to your will. Thank you that you are on our side.

In Jesus' name, Amen.

Day Six

GOVERNED: SUPPLICATION

PSALM 72:1-4

*O God, grant the king the ability to make just
decisions! Grant the king's son the ability
to make fair decisions! Then he will judge
your people fairly, and your oppressed ones
equitably. The mountains will bring news
of peace to the people, and the hills will
announce justice. He will defend the oppressed
among the people; he will deliver the children of
the poor and crush the oppressor.*

———

Less than two weeks after my first child was born, midterm elections were held. Trying to do my civic duty and desiring to vote for a specific state representative, I made my way to our precinct's office. As I scanned my ballot, however, I realized just how little I knew about the candidates listed on my voting card. Sleep deprived and confused, I muddled through, embarrassed at my lack of political awareness. Returning the completed ballot to the worker, I hoped desperately that I aligned politically with the candidates for whom I had just cast my vote.

Likely the last thing on your mind is praying for politics as a ministry to your child. But as you consider the world into which your little one has been born, political freedom is integral to many aspects of how they will live, be educated, work, and worship. My little voting escapade reminded me how ignorant I was about matters of government. Yet this is an arena into which every mama, politically-minded or not, must enter. More specifically, you must enter in prayer, interceding for the world in which your child will live his or her life.

What do you pray for? This psalm, likely written by the great King Solomon, outlines a number of items for prayerful consideration. Multiple times in this short passage the writer asks that God grant the King the ability to make just decisions. This need for discernment in our governmental leadership is just as crucial today as it was in the writing of this psalm. As the president commands the army, deals with foreign policy, and nominates justices for the Supreme Court (among many other duties), his need for wisdom is great. Praying for a fair ruler who makes decisions out of a desire for justice is a fantastic place to start.

The writer describes an almost idealistic vision of the mountains bringing peace and a king who will defend the oppressed and needy. While we know that true peace comes from a personal relationship with the Lord, it is still a good thing to ask for God to allow national peace through a godly leader. Repeatedly throughout the Bible, the Lord offers national security and blessing for nations that follow Him, (2 Chronicles 7:14, Leviticus 26:3-6) so we can join this prayer as we ask the Lord to allow our children to live in a land characterized by peace.

In addition to that prayer, we should seek the salvation of our ruler (1 Timothy 2:1-4), that the way we respond to our government hierarchy may be reflective of our respect and love for the Lord. We also should pray that our children live submissively to their governing authorities, knowing that God has established them in their positions (Romans 13:1). Regardless of whether we agree with the political leanings of our government, Scripture dictates that we should honor these authorities. Therefore, out of obedience to God, we must model this respect for our children to follow.

As you prepare your little one to grow and be secure physically, consider committing to pray for the leaders of the nation in which you live, that your child might enjoy the peace and security of a nation governed by justice and committed to upright standards. Model faithful prayer for the government, and in faith, seek God to change hearts to honor Him.

———————————

Dear God,

Thank you for allowing my child to be born into this country and society. I pray that as they grow up, they might be able to enjoy the freedom to worship, work, and live without fear of the authorities. I pray that you would allow the rulers of our country to have wisdom to govern with justice and righteousness, that this nation might be one that honors your name and your principles.

Thank you that you are the Ultimate Ruler and all justice comes from your hand.

In Jesus' name, Amen.

Day Seven

CLEAN: CONFESSION

PSALM 32:1-5, 7

How blessed is the one whose rebellious acts are forgiven, whose sin is pardoned! How blessed is the one whose wrongdoing the Lord does not punish, in whose spirit there is no deceit. When I refused to confess my sin, my whole body wasted away, while I groaned in pain all day long. For day and night you tormented me; you tried to destroy me in the intense heat of summer. (Selah) Then I confessed my sin; I no longer covered up my wrongdoing. I said, "I will confess my rebellious acts to the Lord." And then you forgave my sins. (Selah) You are my hiding place; you protect me from distress. You surround me with shouts of joy from those celebrating deliverance. (Selah)

Many years ago, when my younger brother was just a toddler, he had a humorous experience that, in a small way, was similar to Psalm 32. My older brother and I were doing something mindless, likely watching a kid's movie, when suddenly my mother realized that Joseph was nowhere to be seen. After a brief search, she located him behind the large leather armchair, clutching a pair of scissors and bearing the marks of an impromptu haircut. Where his bangs used to fall, there was now only a few stray hairs that had somehow been spared the jagged attacks of his child-safe blades. Removing my brother from his hiding place and the scissors from my brother, my mom was met by his ready defense, "I didn't cut my hair."

The jury didn't buy it.

While it can be humorous to see little ones try to avoid punishment for wrong actions, how often do we do the exact same thing? Just as my little brother needed my mother to repair his ill-thought-through actions, so we desperately need the intervention of our Father to heal and restore our sinful mistakes. And yet what do we do? So often we are no better than our original mother and father, pointing at others as the culprits for our sins (Genesis 3:12-13) and fighting the need to confess any personal guilt or wrongdoing. Yet the psalmist encourages us that those who are willing to humble themselves before the Lord are blessed because the Lord will forgive their sins.

As we raise our little ones, we must encourage them to run toward the One who is able to forgive sins and restore wrong actions. While we need enforce appropriate discipline for wrongs done, we must also extend mercy to them when they sin, so they can be pointed toward their merciful Heavenly Father. Just as the psalmist highlights in this passage, God is our hiding place. He is not the one from which we should hide. He is the one who brings restoration in our relationships and healing in our hearts. He is the one who breaks the cyclical patterns of sin and gives us new thoughts and desires.

In our own lives, let us be quick to confess wrongs to our spouses, children, and peers. Let us be eager to tell others of the forgiveness the Lord offers and to show our children that those who are forgiven are those who are blessed.

———————————

Heavenly Father,

Thank you that you offer forgiveness to those who call on your name, and that those who humble themselves before you will find forgiveness. Thank you that you are the one who can offer the healing that we so desperately need. I confess that I often do not come running to you for forgiveness. I pray that I would model that humble and submissive heart, that I might find the blessings that you offer in being forgiven. Please help my little one to grow in sensitivity to your Spirit, that (insert child's name) might understand their need for a savior and their need for forgiveness. Thank you for offering that forgiveness through your Son's death and resurrection for my sins. I confess my need for your forgiveness every day, and I pray for your help in walking in victory in the sin areas in which I struggle. Thank you, Father.

In Jesus' name, Amen.

Week Six

"No trial has overtaken you that is not faced by others. And God is faithful: He will not let you be tried beyond what you are able to bear."

1 CORINTHIANS 10:13A

Day One

SENT: SUPPLICATION

PSALM 67:3-7

Let the nations thank you, O God! Let all the nations thank you! Let the foreigners rejoice and celebrate! For you execute justice among the nations, and govern the people living on earth. (Selah) Let the nations thank you, O God! Let all the nations thank you! The earth yields its crops. May God, our God, bless us! May God bless us! Then all the ends of the earth will give him the honor he deserves.

———

According to statistics from Wycliffe Bible Translators, 2,163 languages do not yet have access to Scripture in their native language. Daily, however, Christians are persecuted and even martyred for their commitment to their faith worldwide. When you consider the need *alongside* the cost, do you desire to see your child participate in the great calling the Lord has for His followers? This calling is found in the Gospel of Matthew, spoken by Christ prior to His return to Heaven. In these verses He says, "Therefore go and make disciples of all nations, baptizing them in the name of the Father and the Son and the Holy Spirit" (Matthew 28:19). This calling is to all believers, not just pastors and those in full-time ministry. We are all called to make disciples of Jesus—to share that He died to pay the price for our sins and that by confessing our sins and believing in His work, we can each be saved.

This psalm focuses on the writer's desire to see the Lord worshiped worldwide. Although written prior to the coming of Christ, the writer understands the beauty of all people coming together and corporately praising the Lord—all nations, all people, representing the entire earth. Can you imagine every nation on the earth worshiping the Lord? What a sight that will be. It is amazing to consider how unified worship of the Lord would bring true peace to broken governments, hope to countries crippled by poverty, and restoration to relationships enslaved by sin.

This can only happen, however, if all people know the Lord. The need for worldwide sharing of the good news of Jesus is echoed throughout Scripture, but one particularly pointed passage is found in Romans chapter 10 where the writer says,

How are they to call on one they have not believed in? And how are they to believe in one they have not heard of? And how are they to hear without someone preaching to them? And how are they to preach unless they are sent? As it is written, "How timely is the arrival of those who proclaim the good news." (Romans 10:14-15).

The desire of our God is to see all people worship Him. His heart is to see hearts turn towards Him in repentance and reconciliation. The question is, however, do we desire to see our little ones involved in the work of the Lord? At what cost?

As we pray for the physical safety of our children, for their growth and wisdom as people, for their futures and educations, let us add to our list that they desire to be involved in the work of the Lord. How beautiful would it be to see your little one help bring this psalm to fruition—seeing all the nations worship the Lord and give Him the glory He deserves.

That would be a legacy.

Dear God,

It is the desire of my heart to see your name glorified and magnified throughout the earth. I desire to see the church become more and more diverse through your gospel going to every nation and people. Please allow me to desire to see my child serve you in whatever capacity you would call them to. Please align my heart with yours that I would want your goodness shared with the nations more than the safety and security of my child. Please let the nations all praise you and thank you in the way that you deserve. Please let your good news go forth and be glorified in the life of my child.

In Jesus' name, Amen.

Day Two

RESTORED: CONFESSION

PSALM 3:3-8

But you, Lord, are a shield that protects me; you are my glory and the one who restores me. To the Lord I cried out, and he answered me from his holy hill. (Selah) I rested and slept; I awoke, for the Lord protects me. I am not afraid of the multitude of people who attack me from all directions. Rise up, Lord! Deliver me, my God! Yes, you will strike all my enemies on the jaw; you will break the teeth of the wicked. The Lord delivers; you show favor to your people. (Selah).

———

To be tempted is an inevitable characteristic of the human experience. Perhaps it is difficult to imagine, but before long your little one will face temptation in many areas.

- Your child will be tempted to lie, deceive, slander, and gossip to make themselves look good.

- Your child will be tempted to manipulate and abuse relationships for personal advancement.

- Your child will be tempted to overindulge in food, alcohol, and spending.

- Your child will be tempted to view pornography and be involved in illicit sexual activity.

- Your child will be tempted to misuse and abuse physical resources or positions of authority for selfish reasons.

Before you despair that your child's life will be ruined by sin, consider the life of David and his journey with temptation. David is first mentioned by name in the Bible in 1 Samuel 16, where the prophet Samuel summoned him from his work tending sheep and anointed him as King over Israel. Although the King in place was not immediately removed from office, the Spirit of God came upon David immediately (1 Samuel 16:13), changing him. David's victory over the Philistine giant Goliath shortly thereafter set into motion his successful military career. It also initiated a relationship defined by conflict between the incumbent King Saul and himself. Over the next several years, David grew in popularity among the people. He was both the military champion of Israel and personal friend of the King's son. Despite David's social advancements, Saul repeatedly made attempts on his life, driving him away from his home and family in desperate self-preservation.

The first significant temptation David faced was recorded in 1 Samuel 24 where, after lengthy periods of fleeing the wrath of Saul, David was presented the opportunity to exact revenge on his enemy. On this occasion, Saul had entered a cave to relieve himself where David and his men were hiding. In a very vulnerable position, Saul was unknowingly at the mercy of his enemy. Despite encouragement from his companions to kill Saul in this presumably opportune moment, David allowed him to live, stating that he would not raise his hand against "the Lord's chosen one" (1 Samuel 24:6).

Several years later, David was living as the King of Israel and Saul was long dead. In a moment of indiscretion, he saw a "very attractive" (2 Samuel 11:2) woman bathing. Rather than leaving the situation and trying to forget the encounter, he inquired as to her identity and had her brought to the palace to have sex with her. As it would happen, the woman became pregnant. Through drastic and cunning measures, the King then arranged for the death of her husband and took this woman as his wife. To many, this would seem like an unsalvageable failure. Yet, in 1 Kings 15:5b David is credited as having "done what he approved and had not disregarded any of his (God's) commandments his entire lifetime, except for the incident involving Uriah the Hittite."

This seems like a strong biblical commendation for a murderer and adulterer. How could Scripture speak so highly of David when he stumbled so badly with these hurtful acts?

A major consideration is David's heart. David modeled humility and true repentance. When confronted with his sin, David was quick to confess (2 Samuel 12:13) and even following a painful divine punishment, David was eager to worship (2 Samuel 12:20). Facing temptation in failure or in victory, David always returned to the source; it was the Lord who restored him. It was the Lord who answered him. Even when he had fallen, he recognized that he needed the Lord all the same.

As you consider this psalm and your child's future struggles, consider the life of David and the encouragement of this passage. Rather than praying that your child never falls, pray that they love the Lord and that when they do experience failure, they seek the Lord to restore them. Pray that your child is also a man (or woman) after God's own heart.

Lord God,

I know that it is not possible that (insert child's name) will never stumble, but Lord I pray that when they do, that you will be their glory and the lifter of their head. Please help them to recognize their dependency upon you, that whatever their failures they will understand their need for you. Please help me to model a humble spirit, help me be quick to confess my sins, and always eager to draw near to you. Thank you that you are quick to forgive and to restore.

In Jesus' name, Amen.

Day Three

TESTIFY: THANKSGIVING

PSALM 105:1-5

*Give thanks to the Lord! Call on his name! Make
known his accomplishments among the
nations! Sing to him! Make music to him! Tell
about all his miraculous deeds! Boast about his
holy name! Let the hearts of those who seek the
Lord rejoice! Seek the Lord and the strength he
gives! Seek his presence continually! Recall the
miraculous deeds he performed, his mighty acts
and the judgments he decreed.*

———

Have you ever noticed how having a child makes you the recipient of more anecdotes and advice than you could have imagined? Often welcoming your baby also includes listening to a host of birth stories, breastfeeding woes, battles with sleeplessness, and other narratives relevant to your new life stage. Frequently, these stories are a means of other people reassuring you that you will survive the upcoming weeks and months. While not all stories women share can be classified as encouragement, there is strength to be found in the testimony of others.

Psalm 105 is referenced by theologians as a historical psalm, written by King David upon the occasion of returning the Ark of the Lord to Jerusalem. This large, chest-like box was very important to the nation of Israel because it had housed the Ten Commandments and was protected by the Lord as holy. Upon this time of great celebration, David writes this psalm as a testimony to the greatness and faithfulness of God. In these opening verses, David encourages the audience to testify to the Lord's goodness by remembering the testimony of the nation. He goes on to recount several significant events in Israel's history which the Lord clearly allowed for the good of His people.

In this psalm we see a simple pattern: Remembering leads to worship, worship leads to joy. We are told to make known His accomplishments (v.1). We are to sing to Him and make music to Him, allowing the remembrance of the Lord's goodness to spur us to worship (v. 2). As those who seek the Lord, we are also to rejoice (v. 3). Thinking about what the Lord has done in our lives should be motivation for our hearts to be happy.

What is the benefit of speaking often of the Lord's goodness in our lives? One significant result is that our testimony will be lived out before our children. Perhaps you have not come from a Christian background. All the more reason to share of the Lord's greatness!

One of the most influential followers of Jesus in the early church, the apostle Paul's helper named Timothy, came from a family of mixed ethnicity and presumably mixed religion (Acts 16:1). Yet, Paul commends this young man for his faith; faith Paul identified in Timothy's grandmother Lois, in his mother Eunice, and also in him (2 Timothy 1:5). What a legacy of faith these women established by testifying of the Lord to their family! Through the faithful witness of these ladies, Timothy was given the model of godliness that set the foundation for a lifetime of ministry. Timothy was immortalized in Scripture for his character and service to the Lord, and his mother and grandmother were also remembered for their faith.

Scripture encourages us to give thanks to the Lord not only to testify to others, but because it is God's will for us (1 Thessalonians 5:18), because it is pleasing to the Lord, and it is fitting for all He has done for us (Hebrews

12:28). Go ahead. Speak of what the Lord has done. Tell the stories that give Him praise. Join the psalmist and give thanks to the Lord, making His accomplishments known. Sing to Him. Remember. Worship. Experience joy. Testify of the Lord's goodness to your family and to the world.

Dear Lord,

Your goodness to me is overflowing, and I am over-whelmed with your greatness. Thank you for the ways that you have shown up in my life when I truly needed you. Thank you for the life you've given me. Thank you for showing me the reality of who you are. Thank you for the situations you've brought me through and the things you've healed me from. Please allow me to testify of your greatness before (insert child's name) that they might also know your strength and power. May my testimony bring you much joy and glory.

In your name I pray, Amen.

Day Four

HURTING: CONFESSION

PSALM 19:1-4A, 7, 12-14

*The heavens declare the glory of God; the sky
displays his handiwork. Day after day it speaks
out; night after night it reveals his greatness. There
is no actual speech or word, nor is its voice literally
heard. Yet its voice echoes throughout the earth;
its words carry to the distant horizon. The law of
the Lord is perfect and preserves one's life. The
rules set down by the Lord are reliable and impart
wisdom to the inexperienced. Who can know all
his errors? Please do not punish me for sins I am
unaware of. Moreover, keep me from committing
flagrant sins; do not allow such sins to control
me. Then I will be blameless, and innocent of
blatant rebellion. May my words and my thoughts
be acceptable in your sight, O Lord, my sheltering
rock and my redeemer.*

―――――

Have you ever looked at your little one and regretted having them? It seems like a horrible idea to admit, but if you haven't thought this yet, you very possibly might. Perhaps after a sleepless night. Maybe when you realize friends are out doing something fun and you are feeding a fussing baby. Perhaps when you look in the mirror and realize that the baby weight isn't just "falling off." Our hearts are full of wickedness, and our nature of evil appears in the most shocking of places. As mamas, it's easy to look at our little ones and blame them for our newly limited freedoms, changed social circles, or unpleasantly modified bodies. It might be easy, but it is not healthy for us nor our child.

Psalm 19 beautifully testifies of the wonders of God's creation. Natural revelation heralds the praises of the Lord. The skies tell of His handiwork. The psalmist highlights how the sunset reflects God's glory. The fading crimson sun washed in the mauve embers of evening sing forth that the Lord is creative and powerful. All of life rejoices in its Creator. Possibly you have experienced this beauty watching a sunset and celebrated the glory of creation.

In his first epistle to the Corinthian church, Paul encourages his readers when he says,

No trial has overtaken you that is not faced by others. And God is faithful: He will not let you be tried beyond what you are able to bear, but with the trial will also provide a

way out so that you may be able to endure it (1 Corinthians 10:13).

Paul acknowledges the very real presence of trials in our everyday life. He, more than most, understood the trials of discouragement, defeat, and isolation. Yet, in his letter to the church in Corinth, he encouraged believers that their trials were not uncommon. Because of the power of God, they were not unconquerable, either.

What does Paul's encouragement and the psalmist's commentary on natural revelation have to do with a hurting mind? Both center on worship. When we focus on the attributes of God, the beauty of His creation, the wonder of His power revealed in everyday miracles, we are able to align our thoughts with His and find a way of escape from our sinful desires.

So, how does this work out practically? Perhaps you will find yourself angry at your child for keeping you awake deep into the night. If this happens, worship the Lord for the beauty of the night sky that He created and has allowed you to enjoy. Take time to consider the constellations, contemplate the perfect conditions of this climate, and praise the Lord for His creativity and design (Psalm 8:4-8).

If you find yourself blaming your child for your apparent lack of importance, worship the Lord that He humbled *Himself* to become a baby and subject Himself to the humiliation of humanity for our eternal redemption (2 Corinthians 5:21). Thank the Lord that your child is a reminder of the love God has for us.

If you are discouraged with your newfound stretch marks and sagging skin and want to blame your infant for your unpleasant physical changes, thank the Lord that this life is not what we look forward to! Worship the Lord that He has provided eternal hope for your fading body and pray for a heart that truly fears the Lord (Proverbs 31:30).

Worship is a choice; it is an opportunity to enter the throne room of God and align our hearts with the King. But as we do so, His thoughts become ours. Our motives come closer to matching His desires. Our sins are exposed and healed. When you identify evil thoughts surfacing, use them as a motivator for worship. Praise the Lord that He has control over your circumstances and your mind. Praise Him, and then look to Him for deliverance from your hurting mind.

———————————

O Lord,

I know that in myself and apart from you my thoughts are wicked and sinful. But I praise you that you are sovereign over my mind and my thoughts. Thank you that you created me and gave me life. Thank you for my child, and thank you for (insert your frustration) because I know that this situation is causing me to see your control over my life. Thank you for your love for me, that in spite of my selfishness, in spite of my humanity, you would love me and send your own Son to die for me. I do not deserve such wonderful love, but I thank you for giving it to me. You are so good and so kind to me.

Please rescue me today from the fallenness of my heart and mind.

In Jesus' name, Amen.

Day Five

DWELL: ADORATION

PSALM 91:1-4, 11-12

As for you, the one who lives in the shelter of the sovereign One, and resides in the protective shadow of the mighty king— I say this about the Lord, my shelter and my stronghold, my God in whom I trust—he will certainly rescue you from the snare of the hunter and from the destructive plague. He will shelter you with his wings; you will find safety under his wings. His faithfulness is like a shield or a protective wall. For he will order his angels to protect you in all you do. They will lift you up in their hands, so you will not slip and fall on a stone.

Therefore since we have a great high priest who has passed through the heavens, Jesus the Son of God, let us hold fast to our confession. For we do not have a high priest incapable of sympathizing with our weaknesses, but one who has been tempted in every way just as we are, yet without sin (Hebrews 4:14-15).

When I became pregnant with our second child, I realized, much to my chagrin, that little ones don't give you a break just because you're sick. Morning sickness the second time included trying to keep both the toddler and the dog out of the bathroom so I could throw up in solitude. I learned that vomiting alone is a luxury rather than a necessity. If you are cuddling your second or third or fourth, you probably can relate.

Regardless of whether you just had your first child or fifth child, you likely are learning that your personal challenges and setbacks also do not take a back seat just because you have a baby. Your carnal cravings are still just as real as they were before you added *mama* to your list of job descriptions. If this is an overwhelming realization that has left you frustrated and discouraged, this psalm is a place for great encouragement.

Interestingly, this psalm does not appear only once in the Bible, verses 11 and 12 are referenced in Matthew 4:6 and Luke 4:10-11 by Satan in his temptation of Jesus. In this context, Satan asks Jesus to prove Himself as the Son of Man by throwing Himself off a building, stating that angels would protect Him and keep Him from being hurt. Clearly this was a scheme on Satan's part to distract Jesus from His true work and mission, and Jesus used Scripture to clarify Satan's misapplication of this passage. This is a passage offering hope to those who live in the shelter of the Lord, rather than a guarantee of eternal physical protection.

So how can we as mamas experience the protection and sheltering spoken of in this passage? How can we know His intervention in our lives as it seems to be promised by these verses? As we look at our personal temptations and struggles, we are wise to consider the model Jesus sets for us in being tempted victoriously. Scripture says He was tempted "in every way just as we are, yet without sin" (Hebrews 4:15b). Clearly, this temptation by Satan was not the only event that challenged Jesus to remain righteous. How, then, did Jesus endure tempting well? He lived in the shelter of the Sovereign One. He resided in the protective shadow of the Mighty King.

When tempted, Jesus responded with Scripture. He knew Scripture and was able to quote it from memory as a means of strengthening Himself against temptation. When He was in the midst of ministry or facing a challenging situation, He would withdraw and pray (Matthew 26:36, Luke 5:16). Jesus modeled a lifestyle of living in the shelter of the Lord—not just in times of chaos—but every day.

As you go about caring for your precious little one, consider what steps you need to live in the shelter of the One who promises to protect you. Take time to dwell in His presence today and every day.

Sovereign Father and Almighty King,

Lord, I know that I do not dwell in your presence as I ought, that I do not draw from your strength as I could. So often I draw from myself and only come to you in times of need. Thank you so much that you are the Sovereign One. You are the Mighty King. You are more than able to handle all my challenges and failures as a mother and as a person. I praise you and thank you for who you are and ask that you keep me constantly aware of my need for you.

In Jesus' name, Amen.

Day Six

CALLED: ADORATION

O Lord, our Lord, how magnificent is your reputation throughout the earth! You reveal your majesty in the heavens above! From the mouths of children and nursing babies you have ordained praise on account of your adversaries, so that you might put an end to the vindictive enemy. When I look up at the heavens, which your fingers made, and see the moon and stars, which you set in place, of what importance is the human race, that you should notice them? Of what importance is mankind, that you should pay attention to them, and make them a little less than the heavenly beings? You grant mankind honor and majesty; you appoint them to rule over your creation; you have placed everything under their authority, including all the sheep and cattle, as well as the wild animals, the birds in the sky, the fish in the sea and everything that moves through the currents of the seas. O Lord, our Lord, how magnificent is your reputation throughout the earth!

———

In a culture that strongly encourages "me time" and "self-care," mothers are fed the lie that our best life begins when our child is no longer our concern. Nap time becomes an opportunity to drink or mindlessly pass hours on social media. Binge watching television becomes therapy of sorts. Children are whisked from activity to activity in a hurried frenzy so moms can get adequate time for "adult" activities.

This is in no way a criticism on taking legitimate measures to physically rest or to emotionally and spiritually recharge. However, in our egocentric society, it all too easy to lose focus of the true calling of being a mother. We are not simply asked to keep a child alive and out of juvenile detention. This view of mothering is what my husband would call being "the eternal babysitter." It is of eternal value that you see your job as a mother is a true calling, with serious expectations and eternal rewards.

We see in Scripture that your little one was created in the image of God (Genesis 1:26-27, Genesis 9:6). As taught in Psalm 8, your little one was created for the glory of God. As a mother, you are responsible to help them understand that their life has a mission, purpose, and value. To do that, you must be willing to commit to full-time mothering. This does not require that you spend all day with your child, but it does necessitate purpose-driven parenting. You must recognize *your* calling has worth and that time is limited to carry it out. You must redeem your time through persistent prayer and accurate application of the Word.

Psalm 8 focuses on the glory of God as revealed in creation. As the natural world heralds the truth of an intelligent designer, some of the chief singers are our little ones. The writer marvels at the honor and dignity with which the Lord has crowned humankind. We are given the attention of the Lord. We are given dominion over the earth. We are granted honor and majesty. From this place of privilege, the Lord seeks our little ones to bring forth His praise.

Recognizing these truths should guide how we speak of our children and to our children and how we view our responsibility as mothers.

When we speak of our children, we must be guarded against negative, slanderous speech. With an awareness that the Lord has placed value on them (Matthew 19:14), we must be careful not to complain about our children (Philippians 2:14) or provoke our children to anger (Ephesians 6:4). When we speak to our children, we must point them toward the truth that they are created to glorify God. Through their discipline, hard work, and character, our children have the opportunity to glorify God. As we raise them, we must look for and seize opportunities to show them the importance of day-to-day worship through their actions.

Our realization of our divine calling should bring urgency to our role as parents. Your role as a mama encompasses helping your child identify and fulfil their God-given mission, too. If we believe that our God *is* magnificent and that He *does* deserve praise, we must teach our children and model the worship that He expects.

Dear Lord God,

Thank you for the inestimable value that you place on my child and on me. Thank you that you have created my child with a purpose. Lord, I pray that as I raise (insert child's name) I would seek to make every opportunity a megaphone for your greatness. I praise you for your kindness toward us as people, that you give us honor and majesty. You are so good and merciful towards us. Please help me to redeem my time and see the value that you have placed on my life as a mother. Thank you, Father, for your love for me.

In Jesus' name, Amen.

Day Seven

LEGACY: SUPPLICATION

PSALM 145:3-18

The Lord is great and certainly worthy of praise! No one can fathom his greatness! One generation will praise your deeds to another, and tell about your mighty acts! I will focus on your honor and majestic splendor, and your amazing deeds! They will proclaim the power of your awesome acts! I will declare your great deeds! They will talk about the fame of your great kindness, and sing about your justice. The Lord is merciful and compassionate; he is patient and demonstrates great loyal love. The Lord is good to all, and has compassion on all he has made. All he has made will give thanks to the Lord. Your loyal followers will praise you. They will proclaim the splendor of your kingdom; they will tell about your power, so that mankind

might acknowledge your mighty acts, and
the majestic splendor of your kingdom. Your
kingdom is an eternal kingdom, and your
dominion endures through all generations. The
Lord supports all who fall, and lifts up all
who are bent over. Everything looks to you in
anticipation, and you provide them with food
on a regular basis. You open your hand, and fill
every living thing with the food they desire. The
Lord is just in all his actions, and exhibits love
in all he does. The Lord is near to all who cry
out to him, all who cry out to him sincerely.

———

Do you ever imagine your child's graduation? It might seem like light-years away, but considering the future has an enormous bearing on the present.

- What scars will they have?
- What successes will they wear as badges of honor?
- What will they look like?
- As they walk, will they meet your gaze with confidence and pride?
- Will they be convicted of their beliefs and morals?

Although it's impossible to dictate the future of your child, your prayers will have an impact on the trajectory set for your child's life. Your beliefs of who God is will make a lasting impression on their lives as well.

In this psalm, the writer celebrates the beauty of continual worship, both in the personal life of the believer and throughout generations. The reason for this worship is founded on the unshakable belief that the Lord is worthy of praise. The writer is intimately aware of the attributes of God; he knows the Lord's greatness. He is convinced that all honor belongs to the Lord. As he meditates on God's character, he is ushered into worship.

This psalm delineates an important truth: true worship is focusing on the character of God and praising Him for who He is. While many faith-based songs focus on how God makes us feel, worship stands in stark contrast to our feelings or desires. Worship is a response which happens when we see the Lord and recognize our unworthiness. When we realize that God is infinitely greater and holier and stronger and more righteous than us, we are forced to fall at His feet in worship (Matthew 2:11, Revelation 1:17, Revelation 4:10-11).

As you consider the godly legacy you desire to leave your children, consider how you worship. Do you recognize how completely different the Lord is from you? Are you in awe of His goodness? Then tell your children (Deuteronomy 11:18-19).

Do you fear the Lord? Do you seek wisdom to be added to your child's life? Then teach your child that the

Lord should be feared (Proverbs 9:10-11). In addition to words, however, let your life speak the goodness of God. Let your worship inspire confidence in the Lord that He *does* hear you and He *does* listen.

- The Lord is great, so come to Him with your weaknesses and ask for His strength.

- The Lord is worthy of praise, so praise Him when He carries you through a dark season.

- The Lord is merciful, so confess your failures to Him and have confidence that He will give you a fresh start.

- The Lord supports those who fall, therefore humble yourself before Him and seek His restoration.

Let this psalm remind you of the legacy you seek for your children to carry. As you raise your little one, keep focused on your goal, your prize. Prepare the way for your child as their prayer warrior. This is the legacy you can leave your children.

Therefore be very careful how you live—not as unwise but as wise, taking advantage of every opportunity, because the days are evil (Ephesians 5:15-16).

As you continue in this journey of mothering, be aware of the urgency of your calling. Yours is a valuable mission. The prayers you offer the Lord for your child have enormous weight and value. Make the most of this opportunity.

Your time is short, mama. Redeem it.

Dear Lord God,

Thank you for the way that you have revealed yourself in Scripture, especially in the Psalms. Please help me to worship you for who you are and see you in a proper light. I pray that I will be faithful to serve my child(ren) as a prayer warrior; please equip me for this task. Please remind me often that the days are evil and that my calling is urgent. I pray that our household will be one of generational worship, that one generation will praise your name to another.

Thank you, Father, for this amazing gift you have given me in this child. I thank you and praise you.

Now what?

It is my sincere prayer that if you have made it to the end of this six-week journey you have committed to growing in the habits of prayer and time in the Word. This is a lifestyle, however, and one that cannot be completed in a single program or plan. Hopefully this book has given you some ideas of how to use Scripture to craft prayers for your child.

As you have worked through the selected psalms, I hope that you have begun to see the nature and character of God in a richer, fuller light. As you have prayed these prayers, I hope you have been encouraged to write your own, adding your own praises and worship as you have considered how great our God is.

I hope you realize how valuable your prayers are. My desire is to see you and me and a whole army of mamas rise up and fight for our children by falling on our knees. I pray that you catch a vision for what this could mean for your child and their future.

So now what? Now keep going.

We must not be merely mamas; we must be mamas that redeem the time. Your battle to redeem the time does not stop with this book or with the weaning of your child or even with them leaving your home. You are their life-long prayer warrior. Your responsibility is great.

So is your God.

It is in His strength that you can accomplish this task of raising your little one. So in the strength He provides, and in the confidence that your labor is not in vain, carry on your good and beautiful work.

.

End Notes

WEEK ONE: DAY FIVE

Information surrounding the subject of toddler development and walking.

Wang, Judy. "How to Encourage Baby's First Steps." Web.

https://nspt4kids.com/parenting/how-to-encourage-babys-first-steps-north-shore-pediatric-therapy

WEEK ONE: DAY SIX

The information regarding the Mississippi River.

"Mississippi River Facts." November 24, 2018. Web. https://www.nps.gov/miss/riverfacts.htm

WEEK TWO: DAY SEVEN

The A. W. Tozer quotation is from:

Tozer, A.W. *The Knowledge of the Holy: The Attributes of God, Their Meaning in the Christian Life.* New York: Harper, 1961. Print.

WEEK THREE: DAY TWO

The hymn referenced in this chapter is credited to the following source:

Joseph Scriven. "What a Friend We Have in Jesus" 1855.

WEEK THREE: DAY THREE
The story of Josh Crary.

James, Steve. "Running blind: 40 sightless runners competing in Boston marathon" *Today*. April 15, 2013. Web.

https://www.today.com/health/running-blind-40-sightless-runners-competing-boston-marathon-1C9347529

WEEK FOUR: DAY ONE
Information regarding the fears Americans most commonly have.

"What Americans Fear Most." *Health Day*. October 19, 2018. Web. https://consumer.healthday.com/mental-health-information-25/fears-and-phobias-health-news-304/what-americans-fear-most-738778.html

WEEK FOUR: DAY TWO
The supporting information for the synopsis of E. Nesbit's children's book. "Five Children and It: Plot Summary." *Wikipedia*. August 6, 2019. Web. https://en.wikipedia.org/wiki/Five_Children_and_It

WEEK FOUR: DAY THREE
Quote about the value of a diamond can be found in the following article.

"What is an Inclusion in a Diamond?" *Brilliance*. Web.

https://www.brilliance.com/diamonds/what-are-in-clusions-on-diamonds

Information about the quarterback engagement. Frey, Kaitlyn. All About the 'Internally Flawless' 7.25 Carat Engagement Ring Tim Tebow Gave His Fiancée. *Yahoo. com*. January 11, 2019. Web.

https://www.yahoo.com/entertainment/apos-internal-ly-flawless-apos-7-151116544.html

WEEK FOUR: DAY FOUR

In this chapter, the reference made to the *Lord of the Rings* book can be found in the following work:

Tolkien, J.R.R. *The Return of the King*. New York: Hough-ton Mifflin Company, 1994. Print.

WEEK FOUR: DAY FIVE

Article on the reflections of Joni Earekson Tada can be found according to the following information:

Tada, Joni Earekson. "Reflections on the 50th Anniversary of my Diving Accident." *The Gospel Coalition*. July 30, 2017. Web.

https://www.thegospelcoalition.org/article/reflec-tions-on-50th-anniversary-of-my-diving-accident/

WEEK FIVE: DAY FOUR

Statistics concerning the American church were located in the following two articles:

"7 Startling Facts: An Up Close Look at Church Attendance in America." *Outreach Magazine*. April 10, 2018. Web.

https://churchleaders.com/pastors/pastor-articles/139575-7-startling-facts-an-up-close-look-at-church-attendance-in-america.html

"The State of the Church 2016." *Barna*. September 15, 2016. Web.

https://www.barna.com/research/state-church-2016/

Additional input for this chapter received from the following work:

McGee, J. Vernon. "Isaiah 6:1" Thru the Bible Radio.

https://www.blueletterbible.org/audio_video/popPlayer.cfm?id=6082&rel=mcgee_j_vernon/Isa

WEEK FIVE: DAY SIX

Information about the duties of the President of the United States was referenced from the following article.

"What are Some of the Duties of the President of the United States?" *Reference*. Web.

https://www.reference.com/government-politics/duties-president-united-states-d19e5bff379fed67

WEEK SIX: DAY ONE

Information pertinent to the work of Wycliffe Bible

Translators as presented in this chapter can be located in the following place: "Our Impact." *Wycliffe*. Web. https://www.wycliffe.org.uk/about/our-impact/

Information and figures compiled within the Wycliffe Global Alliance which can be referenced at http://www.wycliffe.net/en/

WEEK SIX: DAY SIX

Contributing information for understanding the passage in this chapter was retrieved from the following location.

McGee, J. Vernon. "Psalm 8:1-3." Thru the Bible Radio.

https://www.blueletterbible.org/audio_video/popPlayer.cfm?id=5464&rel=mcgee_j_vernon/Psa

KENTUCKY SUMMERS

RED RIVER, JUNIOR, AND THE WITCH

Other Books by Tim Callahan
Sleepy Valley
Come Home, Joe

Kentucky Summers Series:
The Cave, The Cabin, & The Tattoo Man
Coty & the Wolf Pack
Dark Days in Morgan County
Above Devil's Creek
Timmy & Susie & the Bootleggers' Revenge
KenTucky Snow & the Crow
Coming soon:
Nashville Sounds

Kentucky Summers

Red River, Junior, and the Witch

To Pat,
Dream Big.
Blessings,
Tim Callahan
7-7-13

Tim Callahan

TATE PUBLISHING
AND ENTERPRISES, LLC

Published by Tate Publishing & Enterprises, LLC
127 E. Trade Center Terrace | Mustang, Oklahoma 73064 USA
1.888.361.9473 | www.tatepublishing.com

Tate Publishing is committed to excellence in the publishing industry. The company reflects the philosophy established by the founders, based on Psalm 68:11,
"The Lord gave the word and great was the company of those who published it."

Book design copyright © 2013 by Tate Publishing, LLC. All rights reserved.
Cover design by Jan Sunday Quilaquil
Interior design by Jomar Ouano
Cover photography by Tim Callahan

Published in the United States of America

ISBN: 978-1-62746-646-2
1. Fiction / Action & Adventure
2. Fiction / Coming Of Age
13.06.27

This book is dedicated to:

Kids, young and old, who would have liked
to have been a member of the Wolf Pack.

IN MEMORY OF

GREAT AUNT MILDRED COLLINS
9-12-1924 TO 5-13-2013

Acknowledgments

I would like to thank my God and savior, Jesus Christ. I want to thank you for partnering with me to write these books. Without you this is impossible. I thank you for your love, your omnipresence, your omnipotence, and your watchful care for me as I travel the many miles each year.

Thank you for bringing people into my life such as Don and Shirley Jones and Peg Cramer. Shirley designed my new website and she's such a great writer herself. Peg Cramer finds all my many mistakes in my manuscripts and corrects them. Thank you for Traci Jones Nix who has been such a good friend at Tate Publishing.

I thank you for giving up your life as a human here on earth and dying on a cross for me. I thank you for preparing a place for me in heaven where I look forward to spending eternity with you, and loved ones, and those I haven't yet met.

I thank you, God, for letting my books touch others enough that they get enjoyment and a message of love from the stories.

Thank you, Lord, for loving all of us as individuals and caring about us as we struggle in this life. Thank you for your help with this book.

CONTENTS

1

GRAVEYARD FLOWERS

⌒

WEDNESDAY, MAY 30, 1962 – MEMORIAL DAY

I was standing in the Perry Cemetery looking at the names and dates on the grave markers. Most of the last names on the tombstones were Collins, Easterling, Callahan, or Perry. I knew that most of the people buried in the cemetery were somehow related to me. Mom was placing flowers on a few of the graves, along with Mamaw. Janie was making herself a bouquet by picking flowers, some real and some fake, from the arrangements that had already been placed on the graves. Mom was too busy to notice what Janie was doing, and I didn't care. I figured the folks underground didn't really care either.

Being at the cemetery reminded me of my dad who had died nearly two years earlier. Even though he was buried in Ohio, I still thought about him as I roamed the headstones. I hadn't visited his grave since the funeral, mainly because I hadn't been back to Ohio since then.

School had let out for the summer the day before. I was liberated for three months. I was really looking forward to the freedom and the fun I was going to have during the summer. The Wolf Pack was having a meeting the following evening to discuss what ideas we could come up with for our next big summer adventure. If this summer was anything like the summer of 1961, then I was both looking forward to it and dreading it. The summer of 1961 was thrilling and exciting—mixed with danger that almost got us killed. Mom and Mamaw could have been visiting our graves on this day also.

I decided I didn't want to do something that risked my life again. I would vote for a fun, safe adventure. A walk in a park, or a picnic in the woods, building the tree house, fishing the creeks—except for the water moccasins, those were the relatively safe ideas I had for the upcoming summer.

After Mom and Mamaw placed the flowers, we climbed into the car to go back to the store. Mom drove slowly away from the cemetery. Janie leaned forward from the backseat and handed Mom the bouquet and said, "Mommy, I picked these for you. Aren't they beautiful?"

Mamaw looked over at the flowers and exclaimed, "Oh, my Lord."

Mom then focused on what Janie was handing her and started to open her mouth, but she was struck dumbfounded. She wasn't sure what to say at first.

"Thank you. They are beautiful, sweetheart," Mom finally said.

Her next words were directed toward me. "Timmy, you were supposed to be watching your sister. Why did you let her do that?"

I didn't have an answer that I thought she would like. I also wasn't sure why I was getting blamed. I guess it was one of the downfalls of being the older child.

"A bear was chasing me and I didn't have an opportunity to watch her every move," I said and smiled.

"What is wrong with you?" Mom asked.

I didn't think she wanted an answer to that question. I went back to looking out the window at the farms passing by. I saw Homer's farm, blind Uncle Morton's house, the Washington farm, Susie's family farm, and then Papaw's farm. Mamaw rode back to the store with us. Papaw was watching the store while we went to visit the dead. I wasn't sure why it was important to Mom that I went to the cemetery. But she wanted Janie and me to go also, and I kinda liked walking among the gravestones.

Papaw had taken the Wolf Pack to the old cemetery in Blaze so we could pull weeds from around the markers and mow the grass. We wanted it to look good for Memorial Day even though we weren't sure if anyone visited the cemetery. We had found the old cemetery when we had taken an overnight hiking trip and accidently spent the night camped next to it. I had discovered that Carter "Squire" Collins, 1836 -1903, my great, great, great, great grandfather, was buried there. He had fought in the Civil War.

We didn't want our club to be only about fun and adventures, but also we wanted to help do things for people—like community service. I shouldn't say *we* because Purty was all about the fun and adventure. He complained and frowned the entire time at the cemetery. It was too hot he had said—it was seventy degrees! The grass was too tall; it wasn't that bad at all and Randy cut the grass. There were too many weeds to pull and he was afraid he'd get blisters; we found none on his hands. Of course I didn't see him actually pull very many weeds either.

He did drink his share of the pop and eat more than his share of the snacks Papaw had brought. He did complain that he was still thirsty and hungry. Papaw would every so often look at Purty and shake his head, raise it to the skies, and close his eyes. I think he was thanking God that Purty wasn't his grandson.

When we returned to the store after visiting Perry Cemetery, I headed for the lake to take orders from the fishermen who wanted snacks and drinks. A lot of men were off work because of the holiday and were taking advantage of the nice weather and fishing. Mud McCobb, Fred Wilson, and Louis Lewis were fishing from the dam when I stepped onto it.

Mud turned his head and saw me coming. "Timmy, my good buddy, did you have fun walking among the dead?"

"Can't say that I had a lot of fun, but from what I see here from you three, there was just as much action there. It feels as if I'm still walking among the dead." Fred laughed at my comment.

Before they could respond, I heard a commotion on the west side of the lake and saw Sam Kendrick reeling in a nice catfish.

"He's the luckiest fellow I've ever seen," Fred commented. The other two men agreed.

"He must have been holding his mouth right," I told them.

I took their orders and started to walk away when Louis asked, "Did they ever find Billy Taulbee?"

"Not yet. The sheriff has been looking for him in Blaze," I answered.

"I think he headed for the mountains and died up there somewhere," Mud told us.

"Starved to death or maybe bitten by a copperhead," Louis reckoned.

Billy Taulbee and the bootleggers had held Susie and me for ransom last summer. We escaped, and Russell and Silas, the bootleggers, went to prison, but Billy Taulbee got away and hadn't been seen since. Three weeks ago, Susie and I had overheard the boys from Blaze say they could get Billy to help them kill the Oak Hill Gang—that's what they called the Wolf Pack. Therefore, I figured Billy was holed up in Blaze healing from the injuries he had gotten from Silas while we were being held for ransom.

I left them speculating over Billy and headed on around the lake. Sam was adding the large catfish to his stringer as I neared him.

"Those guys having a fit over me catching more fish than the three of them put together?" Sam asked.

"Yep, I told them you knew how to hold your mouth just the right way."

Sam laughed and then twisted his mouth into a weird position and said, "It sumthin' like this," he mumbled. It was my turn to laugh. Sam asked me to bring him a Cola and a boloney sandwich with onions and mustard and a bag of chips.

When I got to the back portion of the lake, a family was spread out on the slanted rock catching bluegills. The two young boys were having a blast. I took orders all the way around the lake and returned to the store. I gathered all the pop, candy bars, and other snacks while Papaw made the sandwiches. I got a can of sardines and a can of Vienna sausages from a wooden shelf. One of the fishermen wanted a cup of raw chicken livers to use as bait, not to eat. I placed everything into a small box along with the sandwiches and headed back to the lake. I made a dollar and ten cents in tips.

James Ernest was working in his garden. Mr. Washington had a small piece of land that he wasn't using and he told James Ernest that he could use it if he wanted to. James Ernest had plowed and disked the half-acre of dirt and planted a large garden. He worked in it constantly, hoeing the weeds and watering the plants. I think it was the first time he had ever had a spot to grow things. He loved it. He was either there working in the garden or making baskets with Raven. I had only learned about his garden in the last week. He said he wanted to share the vegetables with the community folks who were helping him so much.

The leftovers he thought maybe could be sold at the store or at the farmer's market in West Liberty. He loved his garden. It seemed like a lot of work to me.

As I walked back to the store with Coty by my side, I looked up into the sky and searched for Bo, the crow. Bo had disappeared a couple of weeks earlier, and I was worried about him. My blind Uncle Morton told me that Bo was probably off raising a flock of young crows somewhere. He said he expected Bo to return after the babies emptied the nest. I guessed it made sense.

With Memorial Day falling in the middle of the week, none of Mom's sisters made the trip to Kentucky to visit. I was hoping some of my cousins might come. I was going to take them wading and fishing up Licking Creek. Perhaps I could do it during the Fourth of July.

I walked into the store. Papaw was standing behind the counter. Robert Easterling was leaning against the counter cleaning his nails with his pocketknife. He snorted as I walked by and I laughed. I had been up at his home one day last year when he was building a garage. He had dug out a hole for the foundation and then it had rained. When I arrived he was standing in the hole in a slopping mess of mud waiting for a truck to deliver pea gravel. He looked at me and began snorting like he was a hog in mud heaven. It struck me as one of the funniest things I had ever seen. I laughed harder than I had ever laughed before.

Now, every time he saw me he would snort and make me laugh again. Papaw heard the snort and gave Robert a strange look. I held my laughter until I made it out of the store to the living room. Mom asked me what was so funny when I entered the kitchen. I looked at her and Janice and answered, "Robert."

"Yeah, he's a funny one," Janice said, being a little sarcastic, I thought.

I noticed that Mom had placed the flowers that Janie had picked from the cemetery in a vase and placed them on the table. She had the real flowers mixed with the fake flowers all in the same vase. I thought it was strange looking, but I decided not to mention it. I knew I would get blamed again if I brought it up. It was tough being me.

"I need for you to go get a bucket of water from the spring," Mom said.

"Sure. Okay," I said, knowing there was no need to argue.

2

RED RIVER

I walked out the back door with the pail in my hand. I yelled for Coty to come. It wasn't long before he vacated his spot on the front porch and stood beside me. We headed up the gravel road toward the spring. Coty was soon sniffing the ditches and searching the tree line that hugged the road.

I wondered how many times I had made this same trip, how many times had I walked in the same spots on the road. I remembered the day the Tattoo Man walked back to the store with me. He had invited me to come to his cabin for a bite. I wasn't sure who was going to be taking the bite and what was going to be bitten. I had thought it might end up being me.

On another trip to the spring I had Billy Taulbee grab me from behind and cover my mouth with his hand. He begged me to help him, saying he was starving and needed food. After feeding him, he thanked me by kidnapping Susie and me from the store. It didn't seem to me that doing a simple chore such as gathering water from a spring should be so perilous.

The gravel trucks weren't traveling the road because it was Memorial Day. The quarry was closed for the holiday. Mom had told me earlier that we were going to Clayton and

Monie's house for an evening gathering. I was looking forward to seeing Susie. She had been busy helping her parents in the fields and garden and doing other chores. It seemed like the only time I had seen her since our hike to the waterfall was at school or church.

I knew that Susie was excited about our eighth grade year at the Oak Hills one-room school the coming fall. She was also worried about going to high school and what a difference it would be going from a one-room school to a gigantic school with kids from all over the county. I was used to big schools since I had been in so many in Middletown, Ohio. I tried to tell her that she would like it once she got past the first day. I liked the one-room school better also, but we didn't have another choice except to quit school like the Key family kids had done.

Susie and James Ernest were going to continue helping Tucky and his sisters with their reading during the summer. They were going to try to meet twice a week to read. Susie was going to go to the county library to get books for them to read. Miss Holbrook had even let Susie keep one of the reading books from school to help her teach. I was proud of all of them. I was proud that Susie and James Ernest were nice enough to continue helping Kenny, Rock, Adore, and Chero. I was proud that the four Key kids wanted to learn and were willing to continue during the summer.

I walked along looking toward the creek. The tall sycamores grew tall next to the creek. Cottonwood trees also grew along this road. Mom hated them. She hated the white cotton-like material that fell from the trees in the spring. Uncle Morton had told me one day that the cotton-like stuff that fell from the trees was actually the seed that had opened up. The wind would blow the seeds everywhere. It looked like it was snowing some days when the wind blew.

I felt as though the streams and creeks around the store and in the county were the lifeline of the community. They were like the veins that ran through our bodies keeping us alive. The main roads ran along the creeks. Homes were built close to the creeks. Swinging bridges crossed the creeks, and roads to some houses made their way across the creek bottoms. We caught food from the creeks, we played in them, swam in them, and the wildlife depended on the water that flowed in the creeks and brooks.

I felt that much of the county's personality came from the creeks and waterfalls and ponds and lakes that were fed by the water. Many of the communities' names came from the creeks. There was Grassy Creek, Caney, Elk Fork, Lick Branch, Murphyfork, Straight Creek, and Wheel Rim, and probably many more that I didn't even know about.

I knew there was something about this Kentucky County that never left a person who was born here or had spent any fair amount of time here. I had heard men and women say that Morgan County would always be considered their home even when they hadn't lived there in fifty years. It always drew people back. I knew how lucky I was to live here now. I wasn't ever going to take it for granted.

I heard cawing come from the top of one of the sycamore trees. I looked up to see two crows screaming from above. How was I to know if one of them was Bo? All crows looked alike. Even though Bo had sat on my shoulder for many hours, I couldn't tell him apart from another crow. They all were charcoal black. They never varied. I yelled up into the tree, "Bo! Bo!" They just continued cawing.

Coty heard me calling Bo's name. He ran out into the middle of the road and looked around. He then looked up into the sky. He seemed disappointed when he didn't find Bo. I wondered if Coty could tell Bo apart from other crows. I bet he could.

I wondered what the rest of the Wolf Pack was doing. I knew James Ernest was at the Washington's place. Randy and Todd may have gone to visit relatives; since most of their relatives were from Morehead or Ashland, they sometimes would leave to visit them on holidays. Tucky was probably doing something with his brothers and sisters. I hadn't been back to their house since the day James Ernest and I had visited.

Mr. Key had been to the store many times to get stuff, and every once in a while some of the kids would walk to the store to pick up something. They were an interesting family to say the least. I wanted to know them better, but I didn't think I'd be accepting any dinner invitations. I didn't think I'd like possum or groundhog stew.

Mom and Sheriff Cane were still dating. They seemed to really be hitting it off. I figured they would be getting hitched soon. But I still thought Mom might have doubts about marrying a sheriff because of the danger he faced. I thought maybe in some way I was helping by getting Mom used to handling the fear.

I didn't care if Mom got married again or not. It was her choice. I did want her to marry someone who was nice and wasn't a drinker like my dad was if she did choose to get married. I thought Sheriff Cane would be a good stepfather.

I turned right off the road onto the path that led to the spring. Coty ran past me so he could lead the way. As I walked down the trail, I began thinking about James Ernest and Raven. I wondered when they would stop pretending that they weren't boyfriend and girlfriend. I knew how much they cared for each other. I knew they didn't care about the color of their skin, but I also knew that James Ernest worried about the abuse they would take if they were seen together as a couple. I knew he worried mostly about her and her family.

No one in our community cared if they were boyfriend and girlfriend, but if they walked down the street in West Liberty together there was no telling what might happen. It hadn't been that many years before that a sign hung across the main street that read: *If your skin is dark you had better not be in town after the sun goes down.* There were still *No Coloreds Allowed* signs in some of the stores in town. I felt as though James Ernest was trying to protect Raven and her family. I respected him for that.

I wondered when things would ever change. I knew from school that the Civil War ended slavery, but a lot seemed to still be bad. I didn't totally understand the hate some people had for black folks. Why should skin color matter? Even so-called white people had different colored skin and some of the men and women who were in the sun a lot in the summer turned as dark as some colored people I had seen. Not one person I knew got to choose what color they were before they were born. I wondered how my life would have been different if I had been born a black baby. I didn't feel as though I would ever know.

I stooped to dip water into the bucket. I then dipped my hands into the spring and cupped a handful of water and brought it to my lips. It was the coldest, sweetest water I'd ever tasted. Coty drank from the spring.

I picked up the heavy bucket, leaned to my left, and began walking back toward the store. As I struggled with the heavy bucket of water, I wondered what would happen when Raven had to go to the county high school. What would happen to me when I had to go to the high school with the boys from Blaze?

As I walked back toward the store, I came across a box turtle. He had made his way halfway across the road. I placed the bucket on the road and picked up the turtle and looked into his face. He slowly hid into his shell. The bright yellow and black markings of his shell shined in the sunlight. I placed him safely into the grass at the side of the road that he was walking toward. He didn't say thank you, but I felt as though he was thankful. I wondered if he had ever come across a human before. I wondered if he thought about me or was just scared out of his wits. I knew that Randy and Purty had found a box turtle one day and carved their names and the date into the shell. They figured they might see the turtle again.

Coty poked his nose into the turtle's face and sniffed him. Coty decided it was nothing he could eat or play with so he left it there in the weeds. I picked up the pail with my opposite hand and continued on my way home. I saw a pop bottle lying at the side of the road and picked it up. I would collect the nickel for it. I stuck it into my back pocket.

I walked across the backyard and onto the back porch. I opened the screen door and placed the bucket on the sink. I heard everyone talking in the store. Uncle Morton was laughing; it was easy to recognize his laugh—hearty and fun.

He looked up toward the ceiling and said, "Timmy has arrived. I think it's a good day for fishing."

"I was thinking the same thing," I said.

"So then, why don't you boys head up to the lake," Mom told us.

"I haven't been called a boy in a long while. I like it," Uncle Morton told Mom.

Papaw laughed.

Uncle Morton and I spent the rest of the afternoon catching catfish and bluegills. I even caught a two-pound bass. We turned all the fish loose except for a mess of the bigger bluegills, which I cleaned for dinner. Mamaw made coleslaw and cornbread. Fried bluegill was some of the best eating a person could have. We all agreed.

THURSDAY, MAY 31

The Wolf Pack decided to have our meeting at the cabin. We were going to camp out overnight. Everyone was supposed to be there by eight that evening. James Ernest and I arrived early and collected wood and dry moss for the fire. We brought hotdogs and buns and marshmallows for the evening fire. The weather was perfect. By nightfall the temperature was sixty-five. The only problem was we planned the meeting during the dark moon.

I brought my tent and Randy was bringing theirs. Tucky was going to the Tuttle house and coming with Randy and

Purty. We had everything gathered and our tent up before we heard Purty talking on the trail. Coty ran to greet them.

"Hey, dirt sacks," Purty called out when he saw us sitting around the fire. I wasn't sure what a dirt sack was, but I didn't take it personally. I would get even at some point in the night. As soon as he made it to the fire pit, he asked, "Did you bring the weenies?"

"I brought mine," James Ernest said and smiled. "That's awfully personal."

"I've got mine," I joked.

"Purty doesn't have one," Tucky teased and smiled.

"Very funny," Purty said as his comeback.

Randy began unpacking his tent. I walked over to help him put it up. He placed it right at the end of mine. That way we could open the end flaps and make one long tent. Tucky had a large smile across his face as he helped us drive in stakes and helped with the tent. It was near dark by the time we had finished. We stood next to the fire in a circle with our hands together and chanted, "Wolf Pack, Wolf Pack, Wolf Pack, Wolf Pack, Wolf Pack, Wolf Pack—Forever the Pack!" We then howled at the stars above into the pitch-black night.

Suddenly, we heard howling echoing back down the mountainside toward us. It wasn't our echoes.

"What wa-was th-that?" Purty stuttered.

"Well, what do you think that could have been besides coyotes?" Randy said.

"They sounded really close," Purty said.

James Ernest ignored Purty's concern and asked, "Do we want to have the meeting first, or eat first?"

"Let's eat first," Purty said, of course. I knew what Purty would vote for. "Then we can roast marshmallows as we have the meeting."

It wasn't a bad idea, so we all agreed. James Ernest had made five long sticks so we could hold the hotdogs over the fire. I liked my hotdogs almost burnt to a crisp. We had a container of diced onions, a bottle of mustard, and ketchup. Purty didn't have the patience to wait longer than his dog getting warm before he was scarfing down his first one. Purty had poured so much ketchup on his dog that it was dripping over the sides of the bun. The ketchup ran down his chin, looking like blood in the firelight.

I cooked a hotdog for Coty. He ate it and then begged bits from everyone else. We each ate a couple of hotdogs. Purty had four that I counted—might have been more. Randy then called the Wolf Pack meeting to order.

The first thing he said was, "School's out." He got a rousing cheer from all of us. He continued, "And that means that it's summer and time for another Wolf Pack adventure." We all cheered again.

Tucky had heard all about our other adventures during the school year. We had told him about our two-day hiking trip. We had told him about getting trapped in the cave above Devil's Creek. He was told about Susie and me being kidnapped and how the Wolf Pack had rescued us. He had learned about the Washington house being burnt down and, of course, he was part of the treasure chest we had found inside Susie's Cave. We had told him about our fistfight with the boys from Blaze.

"We are now open for suggestions on what we should do this summer," Randy said.

We all looked into the flickering flames of the fire as we thought about the coming summer. I knew that we still planned to build the tree house, but that wasn't an adventure.

"We can build a tree house," Purty said as though he had just come up with the idea.

We all just stared at him. A pebble hit him on the side of his head. "Ow," he said.

Then a dirt wad splattered onto his chest.

"Hey!" he yelled again. Soon everyone was pelting him with rocks and pebbles and dirt clods. He snuggled himself into a big ball, trying to protect himself from the arsenal attack.

"We could do another overnight hike, maybe even longer. Maybe at the Red River Gorge," I suggested.

"That's a great idea," Purty said as he unrolled himself.

"I like that idea," Tucky offered.

"One idea that I had was to take the longer four-day hike that was on the map that goes up around Blaze," Randy suggested.

"That would be fun too," Purty said.

I frowned.

"What?" Randy asked when he saw my expression.

"Remember that the boys from Blaze said they would still kill us. I don't like the idea of going anywhere near Blaze," I explained.

"I think he's right. There's no use stirring up trouble when we don't have to. I'd rather have fun this summer," James Ernest said. I wholly agreed.

"Any other ideas? Tucky?" Randy asked.

Tucky just shook his head side-to-side.

"I had an idea that I think could be fun," James Ernest began. We all focused on what he was going to say. The bouncing flames lit up his face as he leaned closer to the fire to stir it and place another log on the burning embers.

"What?" Purty asked with anticipation.

"We could canoe a river," James Ernest said.

My heart began to race. My head filled with the possibilities of the adventures that could be awaiting a river excursion. I thought of Daniel Boone. I thought of Lewis and Clark. I thought of Huckleberry Finn. I thought of the Kentucky Indians who had used the rivers of Kentucky to travel from place to place.

"That's it! That's what I want to do. C'mon guys, let's vote on it." I was so excited I could hardly hold the thrill inside me.

"What river?" Randy asked.

I knew it was a good question, but who cared what river! Any river. A big river. A little river. The great Mississippi River, the Amazon, the Nile, any river. Let's go!

"We'd have to study it. But I was thinking about either the Cumberland River or the Kentucky River. We would have to rent canoes. We could catch fish to eat. We could swim and float. It would be a blast," James Ernest explained.

I was ready to go home and start packing my stuff, and then Purty asked the stupid question, "You think our parents would let us go on a river canoe trip?"

There it was—the pin that burst the balloon. I wondered if he was right. I wondered if Mom would let me go on a long canoe trip. I was going to be thirteen in July and I felt as if I was old enough and mature enough for the trip.

"We'll have to ask," James Ernest said.

"You're lucky, you don't have any parents to tell you no," Purty said.

We all looked at Purty. No one said anything. No one knew what to say. Tucky buried his head into his hands. Randy stared at Purty. How do you say anything to something so stupid and inconsiderate, to someone who was such an idiot? Purty had a stick and was playing in the fire with it. Silence fell upon the campsite. Purty looked up and saw us staring at him. I saw tears forming in the corners of James Ernest's eyes. They were ember orange.

Purty suddenly sensed the change in the mood and saw that most everyone was shooting daggers at him. He then realized what he had said. He looked into James Ernest's eyes and saw the tears trailing down his cheeks.

"I-I-I am so-so sorry. I wasn't thinking. I'm so stupid." He rose from his log and moved over beside James Ernest and placed his arm around his shoulder. "I'm sorry. I know how much you must miss them. Please forgive me. That's the dumbest thing I've ever said. I didn't mean it like I said it."

James Ernest wiped the tears from his face and said, "You've said dumber things."

I wanted to laugh but held it in. After leaving James Ernest behind last year, his parents had died in a car crash in West Virginia and Mom had taken him in to live with us. I knew that he still mourned the loss of his mother.

"It's okay. We're still friends." He wrapped his arms around Purty and held back more tears.

Purty had certainly dampened the mood around the campfire. Coty rose from the ground at my feet and moseyed over to James Ernest and sat beside him. James Ernest reached down and petted his head. It amazed me how dogs knew which humans were hurting and needed comfort. I sometimes thought dogs were more in tune with human feelings than other humans were.

Suddenly, we heard howling again deep in the woods. This time it sounded like more than one coyote screaming in the wilderness. It became violent in its sound. We then heard yelping and growling. Coty stood and looked out into the trees like he was trying to interpret the sounds. Looking into the woods was like opening your eyes under the bed covers in the middle of the night. It was totally black. All I saw were the shadows our bodies casted on the trees around the fire. Coty then lifted his head and howled with all that he had.

I knew the coyotes were making a kill on their hunt. I wondered what they were killing. They were known to kill other dogs who had ventured into their territory. In the store one day a farmer told Papaw that he happened upon a cow giving birth and a coyote was gnawing on the calf as it was being born. It gave me the willies. I liked knowing that the coyotes were around me in the woods. I knew they were doing what came natural for them. But I also didn't like that they were such killers.

The hair on my arms stood on end. I looked over at Purty and he was literally shaking on his log. The log was moving on the ground. I figured we were safe. The fire and our numbers gave us protection, but it still didn't stop the fright inside of me. I needed to be sure that Coty stayed near.

"What about Red River?" Randy asked.

I couldn't think of what Randy was talking about. My mind had been captured by the coyote howling.

"What?" I asked.

"A guy at school told us about the Red River and it's not that far from here. It flows through what some people call the Red River Gorge. It might be a good choice," Randy suggested.

"We could start at one end and paddle the entire length of the river. We can camp out at night. It would be great fun," James Ernest added.

"Can we invite girls on the trip?" Tucky asked and smiled.

"Not Bernice the Skunk," Purty answered.

We all laughed.

None of us liked Bernice except Tucky—and he only liked her because she pulled him into the school's outhouse and kissed him.

"I could invite Rhonda though," Purty excitedly said.

"There's not a parent in the county that would let their daughter go on a long canoe trip with us," Randy said and shook his head.

"What are we going to do, have three guys in one canoe?" Purty asked.

That was going to be a problem now that we had an odd number of members. It wouldn't be much fun for a guy to have to sit in the middle of the canoe.

"I don't think we could teach Coty to paddle a canoe," James Ernest said.

"If we can teach Purty, then we could teach Coty," I said and everyone laughed.

"We could invite another guy to go on the trip," Randy suggested.

"Who?" Purty asked. Then he said, "Daniel Sugarman?"

"There's no way his mom would let him go with us after he shattered his arm with us last year," James Ernest reasoned. He was right. His mom was very protective. I guessed that was the right word.

"Who else could we ask?" Purty asked again.

We all sat looking into the fire. Each of us was thinking about our friends in the community and in our schools.

"We could ask Hiram," I blurted out. Four rocks pelted my body.

"Okay, okay, bad idea," I cried out.

We were quiet for a few minutes while we thought about it. A long, wet-sounding fart broke the silence. We knew who had done it. Coty lifted his head and looked at Purty and then barked. Even he knew rudeness when he heard it.

Finally I said, "How about Junior?" I really liked Henry Junior, and he was almost ten years old now. He would love the trip.

"Junior?" Tucky asked.

"Henry Washington, Henry Junior, Raven's brother," I answered, looking at Tucky.

"You think it would be safe to take a colored kid on a canoe trip with us? There's folks out there who wouldn't look on us too kindly if they saw us with him. It could be dangerous for him and us," Tucky told us.

"Would anyone even see us on the river?" I asked.

"Probably not many," James Ernest answered.

"It only takes one maniac," Purty said as he leaned to his right. I knew what was coming, and I got up and ran as he ripped another fart from his body.

After giving the air a couple of minutes to clear, I settled back onto my log and belted out a large belch. Purty said, "I can beat that." He then belched, but it collapsed quickly as it left his mouth. Randy belched next. I didn't think it was as good as mine. James Ernest tried, but it was weak. But then Kentucky let out a belch that probably scared the coyotes, bears, and ghosts away. I think it circled the campfire four times. He was the winner, the champ—the belching guru.

3

In Case of Bear Attack

We stayed around the campfire late into the night. We talked and laughed, told jokes, farted and belched, told Tucky some tales he had never heard, and talked about girls. We had tremendous fun. We voted and passed the plan to canoe the Red River. We decided to ask Susie to go on the canoe trip. We thought she would be the most likely girl who would be allowed to go on the trip with us. She got along with all of us. We also decided that Henry, Jr., would be the next one to be invited to join our canoe trip if Susie couldn't go.

A couple of skunks roamed into the camp searching for food. Purty had learned his lesson and left the skunks alone. They foraged for a few minutes and left.

"Bye, Bernice," Purty said as the skunks walked away. We laughed.

Tucky dropped his head but grinned.

After eating two packs of hotdogs and a bag of marshmallows, we were bushed, and full, and ready for sleep. It was around two in the morning before I slipped into my sleeping bag. James Ernest, Coty, and Tucky slept in my tent. Randy and Purty were in their tent. We kept the flaps open between our tents. Within minutes I was sorry we did. Purty farted again, driving me deep into my sleeping bag.

Friday, June 1

I awoke during the night to a strange noise. Something was moving outside my tent. I could hear sniffing and pawing at the dirt. I wanted to say something, but I also didn't want whatever was making the noise to know that I was inside the tent. My body shook as I lay there listening to the animal. I just knew it was going to rip the side of the tent and drag me away into the deep, dark Cumberland National Forest.

Coty lifted his head and then barked. I heard a loud snort come from the animal outside the tent. James Ernest frightfully told Coty, "No, Coty."

"What is it?" I whispered. Tucky was awake by then.

Tucky answered before James Ernest could, "It's a bear. We're all gonna die!" He didn't whisper it.

The bear roared with all his might. I went deeper into my sleeping bag than Purty's farts had driven me. I wanted to hide at least long enough until the bear drug someone else from the tent first. Following the bear's roar was Purty's shriek. I stuck my arm out of the end of the sleeping bag and quickly zipped up the end of the tent, separating us from Randy and Purty.

Coty began barking and growling. Neither I nor James Ernest could shut him up. He was protecting us the best he could. I wondered what the bear thought about a cloth tent barking at him. Or maybe the bear wasn't that dumb. Whatever he was, he decided we needed a side entrance to our tent because one swipe from his paw left four long rips in the side of the tent. He was coming in after us. I wondered why James Ernest and I hadn't brought our rifles.

James Ernest unzipped the other end of the tent and scrambled out of the tent. Coty and Tucky followed him. I was hidden deep in my sleeping bag alone in the tent. I rolled to the opposite side of the tent as far as I could get from the bear's claws. I heard Randy and Purty unzipping their tent and I knew they were also running. Maybe hiding deep in my sleeping bag wasn't the greatest idea I'd ever come up with. I was the only person left in the tents for the bear to eat. I then heard Coty barking and growling at the bear. I heard something hitting the side of the tent other than the bear.

Through the slits I saw a flickering light coming toward the tent. The bear's next growl was directed away from the tent and toward the glowing flames. I slipped out of the sleeping bag and rolled out of the tent and hopped to my feet. I looked to my right and saw James Ernest holding a large stick with flames. The flames were gleaming on his determined face. The bear stood on his back two legs and was flailing his arms as though he was trying to keep the fire away. Coty stood next to James Ernest, barking his head off.

I saw the other guys throwing rocks and sticks at the bear from forty feet behind James Ernest and Coty. James Ernest then glanced toward me and yelled, "Let's get out of here! Come, Coty!" We ran down the trail toward the other guys, who turned and ran. I looked back to see nothing but darkness. I couldn't tell if the bear was following or not. James Ernest still held onto the flaming stick and sparks flickered from it as he ran. We made it to the logging road and stopped. We were all stooped over holding our knees looking down the trail.

I couldn't hear anything and, more importantly, I didn't see a bear lumbering after us. I looked down to see that all of us were barefooted, except Purty. It was nothing new to Tucky, because he never wore shoes in the summertime and seldom any other time.

"Did you take time to put on your shoes?" I asked Purty.

"I never took them off." Purty struggled to answer, trying to catch his breath.

"Why?" I asked.

"In case we were attacked by a bear, or coyotes, or a mountain lion," Purty explained.

How could I argue his reasoning? It had happened. So, all I said was, "Good idea."

"I know," he said.

"Now, what do we do?" I asked.

"Man, is it dark out here." Tucky said what everyone was thinking.

I looked up to see that clouds had covered up the stars. It was pitch black. The only light came from the stick that James Ernest held.

Randy finally said, "We could go sleep in the barn or we can wait a while and then go back to the tents."

"Do you think if the bear leaves he might come back tonight?" I asked.

"He won't come back once he leaves. They typically continue on the path they're on. They usually are heading somewhere and won't double back," James Ernest answered.

We had learned to trust in James Ernest's knowledge. Tucky stared at him for a minute and then said, "How do you know that?"

As we stood there waiting until we thought it would be safe to head back to our tent, we told Tucky about James Ernest and how he had always roamed the woods at night and studied different things and animals. He acted as though we were making everything up.

"It's no lie," I said.

After standing at the intersection of the path and the logging road for nearly a half hour, we decided to cautiously return to the camp. James Ernest led the way with his flaming stick, which was beginning to die out. Coty wasn't barking, which was a good sign that the bear was gone. When we got back to the tents, Coty went over and began sniffing the ground and following the scent. It led him into the woods, which led us to believe the bear had left the campground by going into the woods.

James Ernest went to the fire pit and began stirring the embers and placing more wood on it to burn. It seemed like a good idea to me. I went to the tent and put on my socks and shoes and went back to the fire. Randy did the same. James Ernest and Tucky stayed barefooted. Tucky hadn't even brought shoes with him.

Randy looked at his watch and saw that it was almost five. The sun would be lighting the sky within an hour. I knew I wouldn't be getting any more sleep that night. As we went over the bear's visit, we decided not to tell our parents about the black bear's attack. We knew they would freak out about it, and we then might as well kiss the canoe trip farewell. We could repair the slashes in the tent as good as new with duct tape.

We began making a list of the things we needed to take on the canoe trip. Randy had his pad and pencil and wrote everything down. We weren't sure how many days we would need to be gone. We needed a map to figure out how many miles it was and how many miles we could canoe in a day. We figured sometime in July would be best. There was less work around the farms then, and the heat would keep the fishermen away from the lake, and it would be a great time to be on the water canoeing.

By the time we had rehashed our plans for the trip and the bear attack, it was getting light enough to see around the camp. I was so tired. I wanted to slide into the sleeping bag and get some sleep, but I knew our parents expected us back early to do our chores. It was one of the conditions that allowed us to camp out for our Wolf Pack meetings. We quickly tore down the tents and gathered our things and headed for home. Despite thinking I was going to be eaten by a bear, I had a great time. I loved the Wolf Pack.

4

CANVASBACK DUCKS
AND A WET HEN

⌒

SATURDAY, JUNE 2

One of my favorite things about Kentucky was waking up on a beautiful day and hearing the early morning sounds and feeling a cool breeze fluttering the cloth curtains in my bedroom window. I heard the birds singing outside my bedroom. I awoke to the rooster's crowing and then just lay there listening to the sounds and the smells of the country outside. There was an earthy aroma that drifted into my open window—a mixture of dirt, gravel road dust, flowers, and fish. The smell here was unlike any other I had ever experienced, and I loved it.

I jumped out of bed and hurried outdoors to water the nearest bush. Coty crawled out of his doghouse and came to greet me. His tail wagged as I petted him. I filled his food and water bowls and then went through the house to the store. Papaw had already opened the store and was waiting on a fisherman. We figured there would be a large crowd at the lake due to the perfect weather. The forecast was for a high of seventy-five and clear skies. We had stocked the lake a couple of weeks earlier and fishermen were champing at the bit to catch their share.

Fred Wilson had walked through the screen door just as I walked into the store.

"Good morning, Papaw."

"About time you got out of that bed. It's a beautiful day and you're sleeping it away," Papaw told me. I looked at the clock and saw that it was seven-thirty. I figured I hadn't missed too much.

"When I was your age my pa would have had me be up by five every morning to start on chores," Fred Wilson added to our conversation.

I gave him a frown and said, "I guess things were a lot different in the Dark Ages."

Fred stammered a start to a reply and Papaw laughed. Fred never finished before laughing himself. Fred paid for his fishing and a dozen night crawlers. I met him at the back of the house and handed him the cup of crawlers.

"Come up and join me later if you get the chance," Fred offered.

"I'd love to, but I think I'm going to be busy today," I answered.

"I think you're right. I'd better go claim my spot," Fred said and turned toward the lake.

James Ernest had spent the night with Homer and Ruby. He was going to help them in the garden and a few small jobs around their farm before heading to Raven's farm for the rest of the day to make baskets. We still hadn't mentioned our plans for the canoe trip to Mom. We were waiting for the right time.

I also hadn't talked to Susie since the Wolf Pack meeting to ask her if she wanted to go on the trip with us. I was excited to ask her. I was hoping she would go.

In the next three hours, I ran through the house to get bait so many times that I couldn't keep track. I had never seen so many fishermen at the lake at the same time. The parking lot was full and men were parking on the side of Morgan Road and walking to the store. Regular store customers were having to park behind vehicles in the lot.

At ten o'clock, I ran up to the lake and began taking orders from fishermen for pop and snacks. I got orders for moon pies, banana flips, snowballs, fruit pies, lunchmeat sandwiches, sardines, Vienna sausages—one man said he was going to try them as catfish bait—and pop and candy bars. I made more money in tips during the day than any day ever before. I was hoping to save enough money before the canoe trip to buy a new tent. I didn't want to use a tent held together with duct tape.

I still had most of the money from selling the coins we had found in the cabin. I figured I could tell Mom that I would pay for the canoe trip myself. Maybe it would sway her to let us go on the trip. I had never been more excited about Wolf Pack plans than I was about the canoe trip. I loved being in a boat. I loved fishing. I loved water and I loved camping out. So how could I not be excited about it? I had to do everything I could to go on the adventure.

Janie was playing in the backyard with her dolls. I walked past her and into the kitchen around noon. Mom was standing against the sink drinking a glass of iced tea. Papaw was still waiting on customers, and I was ready for a break from constantly going back and forth to the lake.

"Hi, sweetie, it's been a busy morning."

"I can't ever remember a day this busy. I've been run ragged," I said. I took a drink from my RC Cola and took a seat at the table. Mom sat down opposite me and said, "Hagar and I are going to Morehead tonight for dinner and a movie. Janie is spending the night with Delma and Thelma."

"You think that's a good idea?"

"You don't think I should go out with the sheriff?" Mom questioned.

"That's not what I meant. I was talking about Janie spending time with the brat twins."

Mom laughed and said, "I've let you do some crazy things. I guess I can't say no to her."

"But my things have never been as crazy as spending the night with Delma and Thelma."

"Are you going to be okay here alone?"

"Sure."

"What is James Ernest doing tonight?"

"I don't know. You're supposed to be his guardian," I said and grinned.

Mom rolled her eyes, knowing it was tough controlling James Ernest, or even keeping up with him, not that she worried. She knew James Ernest would obey anything she told him. The problem was finding him to talk to him.

"Can I invite Susie to stay with me this evening?"

"I'm sorry, but I don't think so. I remember what happened the last time you and her were here alone."

That was the day Susie and I were kidnapped. Mom was still scared to leave me at the store by myself, and I knew she didn't want to put Susie in that position again.

"You can go to her house and spend the evening if you want to. Papaw is going to stay and watch the store until closing time."

"I'll call her," I said as I got up to go to the phone.

After being assaulted with verbal insults from Delma, I finally got to talk to Susie. She said she was glad I could spend the evening with her.

I made a final trip to the lake to take orders and then Mom dropped Janie and me off at Susie's house around five-thirty. Sheriff Cane was picking up Mom at a quarter till six for their date. Susie was so cute when she bounced out the front door and ran toward the car when we arrived. Her strawberry-blonde hair was pulled back into a ponytail and it swung from side to side as she ran. Her freckles glowed in the evening sun. Her smile showed off her dimples. She was my girlfriend. I could hardly believe it. I wondered when she was going to smarten up and dump me like her sisters kept wanting her to.

Janie ran with her overnight bag to meet Delma and Thelma.

Delma looked at Susie and said, "We get the princess and you got stuck with the ugly toad."

Janie smiled at being called a princess. I didn't argue. I knew it wouldn't do any good. Monie came out of the farmhouse with her apron still on and spoke to Mom before she drove away. Susie and I ran toward the field that held Mr. Perry, her horse. We stood on the wooden gate and petted the

Mountain Pleasure horse and fed him some oats and grass. The goats were soon there looking for handouts. We fed them and then went for a walk.

We walked along the curvy lane toward the main road. I saw a flock of bluebirds flying from one tree to another to another, as though they were trying to stay with us on our walk. I loved bluebirds. Their blue feathers glistened in the sunlight. Their orange underbelly shone brightly.

"They are so beautiful," I told Susie.

"They seem to hang out around this area," Susie said.

"I wished they hung out at the store," I said. "It's been a great day. I've never seen the lake as crowded as it was today. It was unbelievable how many fishermen were there."

"It was a perfect day for anything. Brenda and I helped Dad around the farm. We strung some barbed wire fence and replaced some rotted fence posts."

When we got near the main road we saw canes shooting up on the other side of the fence and berries that were beginning to ripen. It wouldn't be long before the raspberries and blackberries would be ripe for picking. You could usually find some type of wild berries to pick the entire summer. This year I was going to have Mamaw fix blackberry dumplings. I loved blackberries and knew that adding them to the dumplings that Mamaw made would be as good as the cherry dumplings I loved.

When we reached the road and turned around, I asked Susie the question I had been waiting to ask her.

"Would you want to go on a canoe trip with the Wolf Pack?"

"Sure, I'd love to. That would be so much fun," Susie said excitedly.

"We're planning to canoe the Red River in July. We're not sure how many days it would take."

"What? I didn't know you meant an overnight canoe trip. I don't think Mom and Dad would let me go."

"You don't?" I said, acting surprised, although I wasn't.

"Who else are you asking?"

"Just the Wolf Pack and you," I answered.

Susie turned toward me and her mouth flew open. "I'd be the only girl?"

"Yeah, we only have five guys in the Wolf Pack and need an even number for canoeing. So we debated on who else to ask and we decided on you. Everyone likes you," I explained.

Susie thought for a minute and then said, "It's really nice that everyone wants me to go, but I don't think there's any way I could go. I first thought you meant a day canoe trip down the Licking Creek, or something like that."

"We could do that also, I guess," I said.

"I could do that."

"It still wouldn't hurt to ask. I mean, if you want to go. They may surprise you," I suggested.

"I guess it wouldn't. We'll ask them later," Susie told me.

On the way back to the house, we crossed the fence and headed toward the pond. Deer were already in the field feeding for the evening. A couple of fawns were running and chasing each other. We could see their white spots as they jumped and played. It was *the* perfect evening. I so hoped Susie would be allowed to go on the canoe trip. Of course, I hadn't even asked Mom if I could go. Maybe I should have gotten permission from Mom first before asking Susie.

The bluebirds had flown into the trees around the pond. As we neared the small pond I heard the frogs jump from the banks into the water making splashes.

"I'm so glad summer is here," I stated.

Susie nodded in agreement as she began taking off her shoes. I knew what she was going to do. Two minutes later, we both were dangling our feet in the pond water. We saw small fish come up close to check out our wiggling toes, perhaps thinking they were worms. A few would even nibble quickly and then back away.

I looked over to the other side of the pond and saw a pair of Canvasback ducks swimming along the bank. The male had a chestnut red head and neck, a black breast and rump, and a blackish brown tail. His body was white. It was beautiful. The female was not nearly as pretty. She was mostly grayish with a black chest. I wondered why the males were always so much more colorful in nature. I pointed toward the ducks and Susie's eyebrows lifted with excitement.

As she watched them, she whispered, "Maybe they'll lay eggs and have babies here."

"That would be neat," I whispered back. I guessed we were whispering not to scare the ducks away.

The ducks stayed along the edge of the pond searching for food by bobbing under the water, their tails twitching up toward the sky. Suddenly we noticed the shadow of the hillside behind us creeping across the pond. We knew that meant the sun would soon be setting so we got up and dried off our feet the best we could and put back on our shoes. We headed for the house.

It was so great to spend time alone with Susie. I loved being with her. My heart pounded in my chest every time she touched my hand. As we walked from the pond, we heard flapping behind us and looked back to see the Canvasbacks flying off to somewhere unknown. I was a little sad that Susie wouldn't get to watch the babies hatch and grow up at her pond.

It was twilight as we neared the barn. I looked down into the valley and saw movement along the edge of the woods. I stopped and watched, trying to make out what it was. I then saw the coyote come out in plain sight. He was looking straight ahead toward something and then he sniffed the air and turned his head at us. We were watching each other. I liked watching animals, what they did, how they reacted to things. I knew why James Ernest studied them. It was a world I longed to visit. I wanted to see things through the eyes of a bear, a deer, a coyote, or even a crow.

I wanted to smell what they smelled, hear what they heard, and taste what they tasted. I wanted to hunt like they hunted, sleep where they laid their bodies down at night. I wanted to fly and swoop in the air and be able to land in trees like Bo. Maybe that was why the Wolf Pack adventures were so much fun. We slept in caves like the bears, we hiked the trails that deer and coyotes used, and now we wanted to float the rivers like the ducks, the fish, the minks, and the otters.

Susie looked toward the coyote and let out a small gasp. The coyote finally lost interest in us and headed toward where he had been looking. We watched him walk away in a quickened gait.

"It looked a lot like the same coyote that we met on the road," Susie said.

"You mean James Ernest's coyote?" I said.

"Yes."

"I guess so," I said.

"Maybe he recognized us," Susie said with enthusiasm.

"Maybe he was looking to see if one of us was James Ernest," I said.

We made it back to the house as the sun dipped below the trees. We walked into the kitchen where Clayton and Monie were sitting at the kitchen table. We took seats at the table. They were sitting opposite each other; therefore Susie and I were also—one of us at each side of the table.

"So what have you two been doing?" Clayton asked.

When he asked us that kind of question, I always assumed he was asking if we were off kissing somewhere. I then wondered why we hadn't kissed. We were alone for over two hours and never once kissed. How stupid was I?

I started to say we weren't kissing, but Susie saved me from being embarrassed when she simply answered, "We went for a walk down to the pond. There were two Canvasback ducks swimming in the pond."

"Really?" was all Clayton said.

"Yeah," she replied.

"I wanted to ask you something," Susie said next. She was going right to it.

"Okay," Clayton said. Monie hadn't said a word except "hello" when we walked in.

"The Wolf Pack is planning an overnight canoe trip down one of the rivers this summer. They need another person so they can have two in each canoe. They asked me to go with them. I'd really like to go. Please," Susie said this all very fast, so as to not give them a chance to answer before she could say her piece. She reminded me of Mrs. Tuttle.

Monie finally decided to speak, "There is no way I'm letting you go on an overnight canoe trip with the Wolf Pack. Are you out of your mind? Five boys and one girl and every single time they have an adventure they almost die. You almost died with Timmy without going on one of their crazy adventures. You can forget it, missy. I can't believe you even asked us to go. I would think you would know better. Hmmp!"

Monie all of a sudden had plenty to say. I had never heard her so absolute and positive about something since I had known her. I could tell that Susie knew better than to add anything except: "Okay, thanks for your consideration."

I wasn't quite sure how much Monie had considered it. Perhaps she didn't need very long to consider it. Clayton knew better than to say anything, and Susie knew better than to turn to him for a different answer. Monie had answered for both of them. She had made up their minds. I was hoping Mom didn't have the same reaction when James Ernest and I asked her about going on the trip.

The twins walked into the kitchen.

Delma started to say something to Susie, "I can't believe you would…"

"You two get out of here immediately, and mind your own business if you know what's good for you," Monie warned with starchiness in her voice.

The twins did a U-turn and headed back into the living room to resume their abandoned game of jacks with Janie. It was the smartest decision I'd ever seen them make.

The kitchen became eerily quiet. Three of us were looking at the top of the table. Monie was looking at our fright. She then got up and hurried to the sink.

"I think I'd better head back to the farm. Thanks for letting me visit," I said as I got up and headed out the door.

"It was good having you," Clayton said as I stepped off the porch in my hasty departure.

Before I was out of the yard, Susie had caught up to me. I saw Clayton heading for the barn even though it was dark. I knew that he knew it was a good time to be alone.

Susie grabbed my arm and held on as I walked up the gravel lane. "I'm sorry about that."

"You didn't do nothing wrong," I said.

"Mom wasn't very happy about it," Susie stated the obvious.

"I've never seen her so upset. I guess she had a right to be worried."

"I knew it was a long shot, but I didn't think she would get that mad. Who are you guys going to ask now?"

"We talked about seeing if Henry Junior could go if you couldn't," I told her.

"He would love it. He would have the time of his life."

"I think so too. But Mr. and Mrs. Washington might also think it's too dangerous for him. I thought about asking them before I asked him."

"That way he wouldn't be disappointed if they won't let him," Susie finished my thoughts.

"Yep."

"I sure would love to go. It would be so much fun."

"I'm not even sure Mom will let me go."

"You haven't asked her yet?"

"We'll probably ask her tomorrow, depending on how her date goes tonight," I explained.

I heard a truck coming around the ridge and we heard it turn down the lane. We stepped to the side of the road, and I saw that it was Papaw's truck. He slowed to a stop beside us.

"I came to pick you up," Papaw said through the open window. "Get in, Susie Q. I have to go down to the barn to turn around anyway. I might as well give you a ride."

We both slid into the passenger door and soon we were turning around at the barn. The truck stopped to let Susie out. Clayton came out of the barn to greet Papaw. I opened the door to let Susie out. She kissed me on the cheek and then walked over beside her dad.

"It's awfully late to be working in the barn," Papaw said.

"A good place to hide out for a while, if you know what I mean."

I knew what he meant. I knew no one wanted to be near a woman who was madder than a wet hen. A smart man would get as far away as possible. Children also had learned that fact, usually by the time they had gained any common sense.

"The warpath is not a good place to squat," Papaw added.

Everyone laughed and agreed.

Papaw and Clayton continued talking for a while about normal things men talked about—the crops, weather, gardens, and fishing.

It wasn't long before Papaw started up the truck, and I slipped back into the door and we headed to the farm.

As we started, I said, "Papaw?"

"Yes?"

"The Wolf Pack has decided that we want to canoe down the Red River this summer for our big adventure."

Papaw turned his head and looked at me surprised. He then said, "That sounds like a fun trip."

"We need a sixth person and we asked Susie to go. That was why Monie was on the warpath."

"I can understand why. I thought you were going to ask me to be the sixth man," Papaw said. I laughed.

"Is that funny?" Papaw said.

"No. I would love for you to go. I thought you were joking."

"I would love to, but your Mamaw would throw a fit and I don't think I could keep up with you guys. You'd wear me down. Are you talking about an overnight trip?"

"Probably, we thought it might take three or four days."

"Have you asked your mom yet?"

"No. I was hoping you might help me with that."

Papaw pulled into the spot he always parked the pickup in at the farm. He then leaned back on the seat and rubbed his chin before saying, "I think you might be on your own on this one. If I talk her into letting you go and something happens, she'd never forgive me."

"What could possibly happen?" I knew it was a stupid question as it was coming out of my mouth. I knew we could drown, be bitten by a cottonmouth snake, bushwhacked, and just about anything else a person could think of. But any of those things could happen any day I went down to the creek to play. I wouldn't bring that up though.

"It has to be your mom's decision. Sorry. But I hope you can go."

5

PICKY

⌒

I ended up spending the night with Mamaw and Papaw. Mom had called around eleven when she got home from her date, and I was already asleep, so they decided to leave me there for the night.

Papaw woke me early, around five, because he expected a big crowd of fishermen again at the lake. Mamaw was already up and had bacon frying and eggs in a skillet when I walked into the kitchen sleepy-eyed.

"Good morning," Mamaw greeted me.

"Morning," I said sleepily.

"How did you sleep?"

"Did I sleep at all? It sure don't feel like it."

"You must have had a busy day yesterday. Martin said it was real busy at the store and lake."

"The busiest I've seen it," I answered.

"Where's Papaw?"

"He went out to the barn to feed that danged, old, fool mule of his."

Papaw had bought a mule named Honeycomb two weeks earlier. When Mamaw had asked him what in heaven's name made him buy an old mule, Papaw simply answered, "Wanted one since I was a boy."

Besides chickens and hogs and Leo, the yellow lab, Honeycomb was the only other animal on the farm. Papaw had talked about getting a couple of milk cows, but thought they might be more trouble than they were worth. I had been trying to get him to buy a Mountain Pleasure horse like Susie had. I thought it would be fun to ride them together. I still held out hope of getting one.

Mamaw continued, "That old mule is just as hard-headed as your Papaw. It won't do anything it's told. It has a mind of its own, just like its owner. It's of no use a'tall. All it does is scream like a banshee. *Hee-Haw! Hee-Haw!*"

I began laughing at Mamaw as she stood at the stove imitating a mule in a deep voice. She was waving her arms in the air. I wasn't sure what her arms represented. I knew the mule couldn't fly, and I knew the mule didn't wave his front legs above his head.

Papaw walked through the kitchen screen door as Mamaw was finishing her mimic. He stopped and stared at her and decided against commenting. I had a huge grin on my face. Papaw took a seat at the table and waited for breakfast to be served. Mamaw carefully placed my plate of bacon, eggs, and biscuits in front of me. She plopped Papaw's plate down, the contents jumping a couple of inches into the air and landing back down on top of one another. Papaw rearranged his plate and ate his food without saying anything.

It was still dark outside when we finished eating and headed to the truck. Leo came out of his doghouse to greet me. I petted him before jumping into the cab of the truck.

"Mamaw isn't very happy about Honeycomb," I said as we drove around the ridge.

"I figured that was what she was all worked up about. She'll get over it. I guess she's about as stubborn as the mule," was all Papaw said.

Within two minutes we were pulling into the parking lot. It was still empty except for Mom's car. Coty ran around the side of the house when he heard the familiar sound of Papaw's engine. When I walked into my room I found James Ernest sleeping in my bed. I slowly closed the bedroom door behind me, trying not to wake him, and went back into the store where Papaw was getting the cash register ready for customers.

As soon as daylight came, so did the fishermen. For the next two hours I was running back-and-forth from the store to the back porch to get bait.

When Mom got up she asked if we wanted breakfast.

"James Ernest might. Papaw and I had breakfast at the farm," I answered.

"Is James Ernest here?"

"He's asleep in my room," I informed her.

"We need to get him his own bedroom."

"We could get bunk beds," I suggested.

"That's not a bad idea."

Later that morning we were sitting in our wooden pews at church. James Ernest and I were sitting with Raven and Susie. I told James Ernest that Susie couldn't go on the canoe trip.

"It was a long shot, at best," he said and shrugged his shoulders.

"I guess we should ask Mom today. She was in a good mood this morning."

"Do you think it would be better to get all the parents together and explain our plans like we did the last time?" James Ernest asked. When we had planned our two-day hiking trip a couple years earlier we had gathered everyone together to ask permission, and it had worked.

"Maybe," I said.

Pastor White then prayed and introduced Coal who sang an old Negro spiritual that everyone seemed to enjoy. Some women were even wiping tears from their eyes and cheeks. Pastor White then preached about the pending second coming of Christ. I didn't totally understand it, but I thought it was pretty cool.

That afternoon we called Randy and talked to him about our plans to get the families together. He liked the idea. He said that he and Purty hadn't asked their parents yet. He said he would walk down to see Tucky and let him know about the meeting that we said would be held at seven that evening. James Ernest was going up to Raven's house for the afternoon. He was going to invite the Washington family since we planned on asking Junior to go.

We walked into the kitchen where Mom was preparing Sunday dinner.

"Mom?"

"Yes, dear," she answered.

"The Wolf Pack needs to have a meeting this evening and we want to have it here. Is that okay?"

"I guess so."

"The parents are coming also." I started to walk out of the room, but I had an idea we weren't getting away that easily.

"Get back here," Mom said. James Ernest and I turned around to face her. She then asked, "What is this all about?"

"Can't this wait until this evening when everyone is here?" I said.

"It's nothing bad," James Ernest assured her.

"It has to do with an adventure you guys want to do, doesn't it?"

"Yes," we both answered.

"Tim, you and your friends are going to worry me to death, I just know it. Then you're going to have to raise your sister by yourself," Mom said, while throwing chicken into the hot grease.

We turned back around and left the room. I hollered back, "Everyone is coming at seven."

James Ernest headed to the Washington house, and I headed for the lake to pick up debris from the day before and to take orders from the fishermen.

When I got back from the lake, Mom was in the store talking to Papaw. I was sure they were talking about the meeting and what the Wolf Pack was up to. They quit talking when I walked into the store. I wasn't sure if Papaw told her about the canoe trip or not. She didn't say anything.

Around six-forty-five the Tuttle family drove into the parking lot. Mrs. Tuttle walked through the front door and began talking in her nonstop hurried way before the door closed behind her. "Hi, Martin, I'm not sure what these boys are planning, but I can tell you I'm not thrilled that we're having a meeting about it. Do you have any idea what it is?

They wouldn't tell us anything until we got here. Did they tell you anything?"

She walked on into the living room and then into the kitchen where Mom was. She talked the entire way even though no one was in the living room. "Betty, I sure do worry about these boys, no telling what they have up their sleeves this time. Did they tell you anything? They haven't told us a thing. I wonder who else is coming. I know Kenny's family isn't coming because we picked Kenny up at his house. I like his Mohawk a lot better than that thing he hung from his head before. What is a mother to do? What are you going to do?"

Mom jumped in before Loraine could finish getting her next breath. "I guess we'll have to listen to them and then make up our minds."

"You're so reasonable. I like that about you. You always think before you go and do something. I'm the one who does something and then thinks, 'Why did I do that?' Have you always been that way? I remember marrying Forest and then thinking, 'Why did I do that?'"

"You did not," Mom said as she laughed.

It wasn't long before James Ernest arrived with the entire Washington clan. Mom was surprised to see them. She gave Coal a welcoming hug and said, "I'm surprised to see you."

"I'm surprised myself. James Ernest wouldn't take no to us coming."

"Well, you know you all are always welcomed here," Mom told her.

The Wolf Pack met in the backyard to go over our plans. James Ernest brought Henry Junior with him. He introduced Henry Junior to Tucky.

"Why am I here?" Junior asked.

Randy quickly told him our plans and then said, "We want you to go with us." So much for asking his parents first.

His eyes lit up. A smile spread from ear-to-ear. "Really?" he said.

"Do you want to?" I asked, already knowing the answer.

"Yep, of course I do. I'd love to, but I've never been canoeing. I don't know how," he said worriedly.

"It's easy, we can teach you in ten minutes," James Ernest assured him. "That's why we invited the parents here, to ask permission."

"Where are we going to canoe, Licking Creek or Devil's Creek?" Junior asked.

"The Red River," Purty blurted out.

Junior's mouth dropped open even though he had never heard of the Red River. But the thought of canoeing a river was overwhelming to most of us, especially Junior.

We then went about gathering the parents into the living room. Papaw stood at the doorway between the store and the meeting.

We had decided to let James Ernest give the parents our plans. We thought maybe he could play the sympathy card a little. It was harder for them to say no to James Ernest and we knew it. The women were seated and the men stood around the room watching all the commotion.

James Ernest began, "We brought you here to discuss the Wolf Pack's next adventure. I figure you have already guessed that."

"Why are we here?" Mr. Washington asked.

"I meant to ask you before now, but you were busy. We want Junior to go on the next adventure with us," James Ernest answered.

Henry and Coal looked at their son and saw the excitement all over his face.

"What dangerous adventure do you guys want to do this summer?" Forest asked.

"We would like to take a canoe trip…"

I could hear and see everyone let out a sigh of relief. Mom actually had a smile on her face.

James Ernest then continued, "…down the Red River on a three- to four-day trip."

"No way," Loraine objected first. "I'd be worried about you drowning or being attacked by wild animals or crazy hillbillies. We would have no way of contacting you or keeping track of where you are. You guys can forget about this idea, no way! No how! No way!"

So much for the thought that they couldn't say "no" to James Ernest. He was being treated just like the rest of us.

"Watch what you say about crazy hillbillies. I think we all fit into that mold," Papaw said.

The women gave no never mind to Papaw and kept complaining. "I don't like the idea either." Mom finally was able to voice her displeasure with the trip.

"I've thought about some of your concerns. Each day we would be passing towns in which we could stop and call you to check in and let you know that we were okay. There will be others on the river that could help us if something happened. There are also houses built along the river where we could get help. We'll wear life vests to keep anyone from drowning and all of us are good swimmers."

I didn't know James Ernest had thought so much about the trip. It shouldn't have surprised me though. He was always prepared. The parents weren't so quick to voice their objections after he was done this time. It only took ten seconds before Loraine said, "I still don't think so. You can take a canoe trip in our pond, or the pay lake, or down Licking Creek. You don't need to go away for days."

Papaw jumped into the conversation. "The boys aren't my sons, but I think they would have tremendous fun, and it's a lot safer than climbing around in caves or being kidnapped."

"There's no question it would be fun. I would have no objection if they promised to call every day and give us the locations of where they will camp each night," Forest said.

"We could do that. We may have to take a drive over to check out the spots, but I think we could do that," James Ernest said.

"I'd be willing to drive them down there one day," Papaw said.

"Why didn't your parents come to the meeting, Kenny?" Mom asked.

"I already told them about it and they said it was okay with them. They aren't as picky as y'all," Kenny said.

I could tell that Mom and Loraine, especially, were taken aback by Kenny's observations that they were picky. But they kept their cool and didn't respond.

Mom looked at Coal and asked, "What do you and Henry think?"

Henry Senior spoke, "I trust the boys and I think Junior would have the time of his life. But I think they will need to be extra careful around strangers. There may be some folks on the river not too crazy about white boys being with a colored boy. But I do appreciate him being asked."

"We won't let any harm come to Junior," Randy said.

"Junior is like a brother to me. I'll take real good care of him," James Ernest added.

"When y'all want to go on this here trip?" Mr. Washington asked.

"Probably the end of July or the beginning of August. We need time to get everything for the trip and take a drive down to the river to check it out," James Ernest answered.

Mom spoke first, "I'll agree to it if you can do everything you said you would do."

Loraine was next. "I will if Betty will, but I won't sleep a wink while you're gone. I'll worry myself sick, but I guess you two can go. I'll just go without sleep for a few days. I hope you appreciate it."

Purty pumped his fist into the air like he had just won the World Series. Everyone laughed.

"Junior can go," Coal said and smiled at her son and rubbed the top of his tall, full, Afro black Mohawk.

Junior's face glowed. I worried whether we could keep our promises and keep him safe.

6

Go Pound Sand

Monday, June 4

The lake was silent as I walked around it picking up garbage from the busy weekend. Even though the weather was great, the lake was empty of fishermen. Apparently, they had caught all the fish they wanted during the weekend. Papaw said it was such a good weekend he might have to order another load of fish to be delivered.

I had started around the east side of the lake and made my way to the back bay. I carried a burlap sack with all the stuff I had picked up. I stood next to the slanted rock and wondered if the family I had seen had caught all the bluegills around it. A cooling breeze came from the cliffs that stood behind the bay. It was the perfect June morning until I walked over the rise and met the boys of Blaze standing on the path ahead of me.

I started to turn and run. I started to scream. I started to poop my pants. But I did none of those things and just stood there with a surprised look on my face.

"We've been looking for you," Hiram said smiling.

"Here I am," was all that I could think of to say. There were lots of things I wanted to say, but not when I was outnumbered five to one. I pondered why they were there. Did they come to kill me? It would be easy for the five of them to do that. They could drown me. They could beat me to death. They could even shoot me if they had their gun. There were no witnesses around to stop them. I suddenly came to the realization that running wasn't a bad idea.

"We came to warn you and your stupid friends," Hiram began. "Don't let us ever find you guys in Blaze again. We never want to see you on the west side of Licking Creek again or you guys will have a hard time breathing."

"Yeah, because you all will be dead," a snotty-nosed kid behind him said. I thought it was the same kid I had fought with on the mountain. The others shook their heads in agreement. I thought I heard rattling as they shook.

"I don't think you guys own everything west of Licking Creek. So you can go pound sand," I countered.

"We don't own it, you dumb butt, but we claim it, and you'd better stay away. I think we'd better make sure you remember it and tell the others. I think we'll pound you into the sand." Hiram then took a big step toward me and I did what I thought I should have done in the first place. I turned and ran. Hiram's step turned into a run also. His gang followed him in hot pursuit of me. I knew the path like the back of my hand and I scampered and jumped over all the familiar roots and stones on the path. I heard some of the boys scream and cuss and I knew they were tripping and falling over each other.

I glanced back to see Hiram gaining on me. He was only around ten feet from me. I took the burlap bag I was still carrying and opened it up and threw it over my shoulder as I ran. The bag emptied in the air and flew into Hiram's face. He fell face-first onto the trail.

"You…" Hiram yelled. His string of cuss words followed me as I ran up the stream. I was glad it wasn't him. Words didn't hurt as much as fists. But before I knew it, he was up and running after me again. Others had joined him. It wasn't long before I had made it to the swimming hole. I knew he would catch me soon, so I knew what I had to do. I dived into the swimming hole and went as deep as I could and swam underwater to the Indian cave opening and swam inside. I popped up to the dark coolness of the cave. I thanked God again for showing me the cave. Three times I had escaped death because of the cave.

I wondered what they were doing outside the cave. Were they dumbstruck as to where I disappeared, or did they think I had drowned, or did they dive in to try to save me? Or did they dive in to search the swimming hole to see where I had disappeared? I sat there on one of the stone benches and prayed that Hiram's head wouldn't poke up out of the water inside the cave. I quickly found a big rock that I could hit him in the head with if it did appear.

It never did.

I wasn't sure how long to wait before I swam back out. I definitely didn't want to swim back out and have them standing at the edge of the pool of water waiting for me. I laid back on the bench and breathed in and out deeply for a while. It felt good to breathe. I was glad I was still able. I thought about Coty. He wasn't around this morning when I got up. He could have gone with James Ernest, or he could have been out roaming the woods by himself.

I could hear my heart beating as I laid there in the quiet of the cave. It felt as if it was trying to get out of my chest. I put my hands over my heart to try and keep it from popping out. I could see my hands moving to the fast beating that was happening inside me. I wondered if anyone's heart had actually ever popped out of their chest. Or would I be the first.

After an hour, I began worrying about whether or not Mom was worrying about me. She probably had other chores for me that needed to be done. I didn't think I should tell her about my encounter with the boys of Blaze. I'm sure it would result with me being confined to the store again. No, this was something the Wolf Pack would have to take care of. The thing was, I wasn't sure what the Wolf Pack could do about it.

I decided it was better for Mom to worry a little longer than for her to have to go to my funeral, so I stayed in the cave for another hour. I knew that Hiram and his gang of hoodlums had to have thought I drowned. There was no other explanation for my disappearance. But I also figured they had to have wondered where my body was. Or maybe, they got scared when I disappeared and hightailed it back to Blaze, figuring they might get blamed if I had died. I had no way of knowing which was true and which wasn't.

I carefully walked into the pool of water and submerged myself without making a wave and swam underwater back out into the beams of light shining down into the swimming hole. I held my breath and looked through the water to the sides to see if I saw any dark shapes standing around the pool. I couldn't hold my breath any longer and I popped up into the sunshine. They were gone. I climbed out of the water and headed back down the trail toward the lake.

I picked up the same garbage for the second time once I had found the burlap sack in the lake against the west bank. I continued my route around the lake and noticed that some fishermen had arrived. Uncle Morton sat in his usual spot on the dam, whistling. I walked up to him and he said, "Good morning, Timmy. Betty is worried about where you went off to."

"Good morning. A lot of garbage from the weekend," was all I said, as I turned toward the store.

"I'll come back to give you a fishing lesson as soon as my chores are done," I said over my shoulder.

"Unless you're grounded for lying," Uncle Morton added.

How did he know I wasn't telling the whole truth?

I walked into the store and Mom stood behind the counter. She stared at me as I walked in. It was almost as if she could see the lies before they even came out of my mouth.

"Any other chores you need me to do? Uncle Morton wants me to fish with him for a while." I tried to be as casual as I could. Mom just looked at me. The look that told me she knew something was up and that I was trying to look as though there wasn't. Every kid knows that look that moms give them.

"What happened up at the lake?" she questioned me as though I was standing trial.

"I picked up all the garbage and cleaned up the trails. I talked to Uncle Morton. You can ask him."

"You've been gone almost three hours and I saw a group of boys come running down from the lake and head up Morgan Road. Who were they?"

Mom had heard of the boys from Blaze, but she had never seen them. She didn't realize who the boys were. I wasn't sure what to say. I didn't want to lie to Mom.

"What did they look like?" I asked Mom.

"I don't know. There were five of them. Looked like hoodlums."

Mom and I agreed on something. I wasn't sure what hoodlums looked like, but the boys from Blaze fit my description.

"Sorry, I can't say for sure who you saw unless you could describe them," I said and quickly walked away. I heard Mom huff. I wasn't sure why I didn't want to tell Mom that they were the boys from Blaze, maybe so she wouldn't worry.

I found Janie on the back porch playing with her dolls. At the side of the porch I saw that the Hollyhocks had June bugs covering them. I went into the kitchen and opened the junk drawer and found a ball of string. I went back outside and caught one of the bugs.

"Timmy, what are you doing?" Janie asked.

"I'm making you something to play with."

"I don't want to play with a bug. Are you crazy?"

I tied the end of the ten-foot string around one the June bug's legs and then threw the bug into the air. The June bug began flying around in circles as I hung onto the other end of the string. Janie soon decided she did want to play with a bug and she took over the controls of the string. She then had me tie the other end around the arm of her Barbie doll. She had her doll flying the June bug.

Mom opened the door and walked onto the porch and watched Janie turn in circles. Janie saw her and said excitedly, "Look what I've got, Mommy."

"I haven't seen that done since I was a child," Mom said and smiled.

I broke off another ten-foot section of string and caught another June bug and soon Mom was circling with Janie in the backyard. They laughed and teased each other that their June bug was faster than the other. Mom seemed to forget about the five boys and that I was gone so long. She never did ask why I was wet from my head to my toes. She must have figured it was nothing unusual. Mom had me watch the store for the next hour while she did some of her own chores, and then I went up to the lake to fish with Uncle Morton.

As soon as my line was in the water and I had settled next to Uncle Morton, he asked, "Well, did she buy the lie?"

"I didn't exactly lie to Mom," I answered.

"So what didn't you exactly lie about?"

I gulped and said, "You've heard us talk about the boys from Blaze."

"Yes. Mean bunch, from what I gather."

"They cornered me this morning at the back of the lake and I had to hide from them until I was sure they were gone. I didn't want to tell Mom and have her worry."

"What do you think they would have done had they caught you?"

"I'm not sure, but I knew for sure I didn't want to find out. Probably beat me up good," I explained.

"What did they say to you?"

"The leader told me to tell the Wolf Pack to stay out of Blaze and not to cross over to the west side of Licking Creek. It was theirs, he said."

"That's going to be hard to explain to the Tuttle family since they live on the west side of Licking Creek. I think you'd better tell the sheriff."

"I've already told him about the threat they made to kill us. There's nothing he can do to them until they do kill us. We're kind of stuck between a rock and hard place."

"What did you tell them when they said to stay east of Licking Creek?" Uncle Morton asked.

"I told them to go pound sand."

Uncle Morton laughed.

"I'm not even sure what it means. I heard it once."

He laughed again and said, "I think it means that you don't care much about what they have to say."

"Well, they told me they were going to pound me, so I ran."

"That seems as though it was a good choice."

"I thought so," I said and smiled along with Uncle Morton. I then told him, "I think it's time for your fishing lesson."

7

MOUTH-TO-MOUTH

FRIDAY, JUNE 8

James Ernest was walking with me to the spring. We carried three buckets with us to fill. Coty was walking by my side. I had told James Ernest Monday evening about the run-in with the boys from Blaze. He was really upset and mad that they had cornered me. It looked like he was ready to go to Blaze and take them on himself.

We then had a meeting with the Wolf Pack Wednesday evening to fill them in on what was said and done. We tried to figure out what to do. Nothing we came up with made any sense. I suggested we let Purty stand naked in front of Hiram and his gang. I figured that would stop them from wanting to come around us. But all I got was a laugh out of it. We ended up figuring the best way to deal with it was to stay as far away from Blaze as possible and avoid any contact with them.

We were beginning to collect the things we needed for our canoe trip. Papaw and Mom asked me if I'd like to have a canoe as my birthday gift, which was coming up on July the twenty-first. What boy wouldn't? When I told Randy and Purty the news they asked their parents if they could get one for their birthdays during the coming year. They were told "yes." That gave us two canoes. We only needed one more. We would probably have to borrow or rent the third one.

I used some of my money from the sale of the coins to buy a new tent. With Randy's tent, we had the tents covered. We already had canteens and a cooler for food. Forest had a green Coleman metal cooler that he said we could take with us. We figured we needed to buy a camp stove and we would be pretty much set for the trip. We decided to take as little as possible. We figured we could survive three days in the same clothes. The only other things we needed were fishing poles and tackle boxes. James Ernest was making a list of everything so we could check it before we left on the trip. It was still over a month away, but I could hardly contain myself. It was all I thought about: three or four whole days and nights in the wilderness, on the river. This was what boys dreamed about from the first day they were born.

"I can't wait for the canoe trip. It was the best idea ever," I said to James Ernest as we walked down Morgan Road toward the spring.

James Ernest said, "You act like you're 'bout ready to burst at the seams. I've never seen you so excited."

"Aren't you excited?"

"Yes. But I know it is still a month away and I don't want to wish my life away. I'll enjoy this month and then enjoy the canoe trip."

"You're weird," I said.

"People have said that many times before," James Ernest told me.

"Well, I can't wait."

James Ernest rolled his eyes and laughed at me.

We turned off the road and walked on to the spring. We filled the three buckets and began the long trek back to the store. We placed one of the buckets between us and picked it up together and then each of us carried another bucket with our outside hands. It was a good way to balance the weight. As we neared the road, a gravel truck sped by leaving dust in the air. We waited for the dust to settle and then turned onto the road.

I knew when we returned to the store a surprise would be waiting. We were fortunate not to have a truck pass by before we made it to the store. We placed the buckets on the kitchen sink. I yelled from the kitchen that we were back. Mom came walking through the house to meet us. Mamaw, Papaw, and Janie came out of my bedroom and stood in the living room waiting for the moment to arrive.

James Ernest saw everyone staring at him and said, "What's going on? You guys look like you've swallowed a canary."

"James Ernest, honey, we wanted to make sure you knew you're part of this family so we got you something to prove it," Mom said as she moved the palm of her hand toward my bedroom. She looked like one of those pretty ladies on the TV game shows showing the viewers the prizes.

James Ernest looked at everyone and began to choke up even though he didn't know what the surprise was. Just knowing he was considered part of the family was enough for him to show his emotions. He slowly walked to the door and looked inside and saw the new cedar bunk beds. Janie was jumping up and down with excitement.

Tears filled his eyes before he could even say anything.

I yelled out, "I get the top bunk!"

"You can have whichever bunk you want." James Ernest then turned and hugged Mom and then Mamaw and Papaw.

"The bunk beds were Timmy's idea," Mom told him.

James Ernest then hurried over to me and began hugging me.

"Get off of me!" I said as James Ernest wrapped his arms around me and wouldn't let go. We ended up rolling around on the floor. I couldn't get out of his grip. Janie was leading the laughter.

"It probably won't be the last time they'll be wrestling on that floor," Papaw said as everyone laughed at our antics.

"No more sleeping on the couch," Mamaw stated.

"He ain't sleeping in here with me!" I screamed out from under the weight of James Ernest's body. He was smashing me into the floor.

"It was your idea to get bunk beds for the two of you," Mom said again.

"I take it back." The muffled words came from my squished body.

"Can we get bunk beds, Mommy?" Janie asked. Everyone laughed except me. I was dead.

James Ernest left to make baskets. I was free to do whatever I wanted. It was nearly two in the afternoon and the day had turned warm. I decided to go down to the creek and goof around in the refreshing water. I asked Janie if she would like to go with me. She frowned. She had spent way too much time with the twins.

Coty and I headed below the bridge where the two creeks came together. I was going to relax in the water, look for crawdads, and clear my head. I was tired of being afraid of the boys of Blaze. I wanted to think about what could be done about them. I wondered why some boys always wanted to find trouble. What was wrong with having fun?

I took my shirt off and wore only my cutoff jeans and old sneakers into the water. I began searching under some of the flat rocks for crawdads when I saw some tadpoles swimming in a pool of water. I had heard some folks call them pollywogs. They were funny looking. They looked like a large head with a tail attached. They would turn into frogs. I started watching them closely. I saw that some of them were beginning to grow back legs. When I picked one up it felt weird—kind of like holding tapioca in my hand, squishy and slippery. I placed it back in the water and went back to finding crawdads.

Coty began to bark. I looked to see what he was barking at. I saw three girls walking down the creek. I couldn't tell who they were at first, but then I recognized Rock. I then saw that she was with two of her sisters, Sugar Cook and Chero. Rock waved when she noticed me looking at them. I meekly waved back.

All three of the girls were pretty, but Rock was really pretty. Sugar Cook was the oldest, fourteen or fifteen, and a lot more maturely built. I found myself staring at her as the three girls got closer. They all wore skin-tight, cut-off t-shirts that were tight against their bodies and wet from splashing each other as they neared.

"Hi, Timmy," Rock said when they got close enough to be heard above the water that rushed over the rocks.

"Hi," the other two girls echoed.

"Hello, where's Kenny?" I said, not sure of what else to say.

"He went hunting for supper with Monk and Chuck. They'll either shoot something or find something along the road," Rock answered.

I began to gag.

"What's wrong?" Sugar Cook asked as she rushed over to smack me on the back.

After coughing and getting my breath back, I said, "Nothing, I'm not too sure what happened. What are you three doing this afternoon?"

"We wanted to cool off and decided to wade down the creek and kill the day," Sugar Cook explained.

"What are you doing?" Chero asked. Sugar Cook plopped down into the water beside me and proceeded to lie back in the water, letting the water run over her body.

"I – I – I'm lookin…looking for crawdads," I said as I stared at Sugar Cook in the water.

"I like doing that," Chero said.

"What?" I asked; my mind on something else.

"I like looking for crawdaddies also," Chero said, trying to get my attention.

I snapped out of it and said, "There may be one under this rock. Can you catch them?"

"Of course," she said.

I slowly lifted the rock without stirring the mud and Chero snatched a large crawdad up in one swoop of her hand. The crawdad never had a chance. She then ripped off the tail's shell and all at once bit off the tail and sucked down the insides of the crawdad's body.

"That was a good juicy one," she said, as I fell backward into the water.

That was the only time in my life that I remember fainting. To me, she might as well have picked up a possum from the side of the road and began gnawing on it. It grossed me out so bad that I passed out. The girls thought something was still going on from when I was gagging before. They rushed over to me and picked me up out of the water to keep me from drowning and carried me over to the bank. I awoke in time to realize they were trying to give me mouth-to-mouth resuscitation. At the time though I wasn't sure what they were trying to do. I was still kind of out of it, but I could swear that all they were doing was kissing me. And they took turns saving my life by doing it.

"What in the world is going on?" I heard being yelled from somewhere behind Sugar Cook who was taking her turn saving me with her lips pressed to mine. I thought I recognized Susie's voice.

"Timmy is dying!" Rock yelled.

"He's drowning!" Chero bellowed.

By then Susie was standing there looking down at me. I kept my eyes closed, but I knew she was there. I could feel the heat of her anger.

"How could he be drowning? He's not even in the water! And he's grinning! I've never seen anyone actually die with a smile on their face."

I slowly opened my eyes to see my angel standing above me.

"Maybe this will get the water out," she said. She quickly raised her foot in the air and stomped down hard onto my stomach. If I needed the water removed, the stomp definitely would have done the trick. I moaned and rolled to my side, grabbing the place it hurt, and then rolled back down the bank and into the water.

Susie never looked back to see what the splash was.

That night I went to bed and thought about Susie and the day's event. It was the first night in the bunk beds. I knew Susie was really mad at me. I tried to figure out how it had happened, and how it wasn't my fault. I knew I had to stay away from the creek. Bad things happened with girls in the creek. But I didn't go to the creek to see girls. I went to see tadpoles and crawdads and fish and ducks, and for getting away from everything. It seemed to never work out that way. If I went looking for pretty girls in the creek, I'm quite sure they would never show up.

I was in the top bunk feeling sorry for myself, and James Ernest was in the bottom bunk reading a book. It was a book about little women. I guessed it was about female midgets or dwarfs. I wasn't sure why he was reading it. Maybe it was interesting.

"Susie is mad at me," I said out loud.

"I know," James Ernest announced.

"How did you know?"

"She came over to Raven's while I was there. She went on and on about it for a half hour while we made baskets."

"Why didn't you ask me about it?"

"I figured you would talk about when you were ready," James Ernest told me.

"I don't know if I'm ready to talk about it or not," I said.

"Okay." James Ernest went back to reading his book.

Thirty seconds later I said, "I didn't invite the Key girls to go to the creek with me."

"I'm sure you didn't."

"I was trying to catch a few crawdads to sell for a little extra money for the canoe trip."

"I'm sure you were."

"And then I guess I fainted when Chero bit the tail off a crawdad and sucked the guts from it and swallowed it all right there in front of me."

"I've heard of people in the South doing that."

"Really? In southern Kentucky?"

"No, stupid. I mean in the South, like Mississippi, or Louisiana, in the Bayou."

"A guy can't help it that he faints and falls into the water."

"I'm sure you couldn't."

"The girls were just trying to save my life."

"I'm sure they were."

"That's all that was happening."

"Sounds like it."

The more I talked to James Ernest about it, the more I realized it wasn't my fault. I was in the wrong place at the wrong time with the wrong girls. My head was hurting as I justified the events in my mind.

As I was falling asleep I could still almost taste the kisses on my lips from the three girls. I didn't think they were doing the mouth-to-mouth the right way—at the time I wasn't even sure what mouth-to-mouth was—but they were trying their best. They were trying to save my life. I guess if I could remember their actions I probably wasn't really in danger of dying.

Finally I said, "I reckon I'm in big time trouble with Susie."

"I reckon," James Ernest said as he turned off the lamp.

8

A Girl Magnet

Sunday, June 10

I hadn't seen or talked to Susie since I almost died, mostly from the stomp to my belly. I wasn't as anxious to see her at church as I usually was. Mom was going to pick up Kenny and Rock for church. I knew that wouldn't help my cause, but I couldn't very well tell Mom not to take them to church. I didn't want God mad at me also. Although I did think that maybe that's why this all happened. God was mad at me and decided to send trouble down on me in the form of three tempting Key girls, and, of course, He got me.

I walked into the kitchen in my pajamas and told Mom, "I don't feel well this morning."

"Don't be silly, go get dressed for church."

"But…"

Mom turned and walked into her bedroom to get dressed, leaving me and my "but" alone. James Ernest was already up and gone. I figured he went to water his garden before church. He carried water from a small pond that was on the farm to his garden anytime he thought the plants needed it. I had never seen anyone take care of a garden like he did.

I went into my bedroom and plopped down on James Ernest's bottom bunk. I tried to think up a plan to skip church. Faking being sick didn't work. I heard Papaw in the store waiting on fishermen. Maybe I could tell Mom that Papaw needed help. I slipped on my shirt and pants and went into the store. Mom was talking with Papaw.

"I think I should stay and help Papaw. It will probably get really busy," I interrupted.

"I think I can handle it this morning," Papaw said.

Mom stared at me. I knew that she knew that something was up and she had figured that I didn't want to go to church for some reason. I gave her my pouty face.

"Go put on your church clothes," Mom ordered.

The pouty face didn't work either. I was running out of ideas. I turned slowly and limped out of the store toward my bedroom.

"Why are you limping?" Mom asked.

I turned and said, "I think I hurt my leg yesterday at the creek."

"I think you'd better get in there and get dressed or you won't be seeing the creek or a canoe anytime this summer. I didn't notice any limp last evening or this morning."

My leg suddenly healed itself and I hurried to change clothes. Nothing was going to keep me from going on the canoe trip.

"You want to tell me why you didn't want to go to church this morning?" Mom asked me as she was driving to the Key house.

I looked over at Mom and confessed, "Susie is mad at me, and I didn't want to face her."

Janie laughed in the backseat.

"Well, I'm sure if you just apologize everything will be all right."

Why did Mom assume that I had done something wrong? I started to ask her but decided it was useless, and Mom was pulling into the Key driveway.

Tucky and Rock came bouncing out the front door. Then Chero and Sugar Cook opened the door and followed them. Oh no!

"Is there room for two more?" Sugar Cook asked.

"We can make room," Mom said.

Tucky got in the front with me and the three girls squeezed into the back with Janie. She ended up sitting in Rock's lap. I quickly introduced the two new girls to Mom and Janie.

Mom backed out of the driveway and drove away. As Mom made her way up the winding hillside toward church, Chero asked, "Are you feeling better, Timmy? You weren't looking so good yesterday."

Mom turned her head toward me.

"I'm feeling a little better," I said, trying to make Mom feel a bit bad for thinking I was faking sickness, even though I was. I was suddenly anxious to get to church and out of the car before the girls said too much.

"And what was wrong with Timmy?" Mom questioned. I squirmed in my seat.

"He passed out and fell into the creek. We had to save his life," Chero explained.

"Was Susie there?" Mom asked while glancing sideways at me.

"Susie came as we were saving him and she got pretty mad," Rock told Mom as she was pulling into a parking spot. I scrambled over Kenny and opened the door and ran through the gravel lot and inside the church as Mom listened to the girls tell their story.

James Ernest and Raven weren't there yet and neither was Susie. I sat down in our usual pew and waited for them. A few minutes later the three Key girls and Kenny walked into the church and headed straight for me. Kenny, being a gentleman without any shoes, let his sisters slide into the pew first. Rock ended up sitting next to me. I saved enough room on the end of the row for Susie.

She strolled into the church a minute later and saw me sitting with the three girls and she ended up sitting with James Ernest and Raven in the row in front of us. I waved as she made her way down the row, but she ignored the attempt to smooth things over.

After songs were sung and the collection plate was passed down each row, it was time for visitor introductions. Could this morning get any worse? Yes, was the answer. I was called on to stand and introduce the two new faces.

"This is Kenny and Rock's sisters, Chero Key and Sugar Cook Key." The congregation began to laugh and murmur.

Pastor White tried to settle the congregation down by saying, "We are so happy you came to worship with us today. It's nice having you here. After the service today we're having a small social greeting time. Soft drinks, tea, and cookies will be served."

I lowered my head as though in prayer.

After the service was over, I went searching for Susie as everyone was lining up for refreshments under the shelter. I found her talking with Rhonda Blair under a tree.

I strolled over and nodded hello. They both stared at me.

"I saved you a seat," I said to Susie.

"Looked like you saved a lot of seats," Susie countered.

"Can I talk to you alone?" I asked her.

"No," was all she said.

"I'm sorry, but I didn't want any of this to happen," I spouted.

"You didn't seem to mind it very much," Susie said.

"Chero ate a crawdad and I passed out and fell into the water. The girls thought I was drowning and were trying to save me. I'm not sure what they were doing. When I came to, you were standing there. That's all that happened," I half-lied.

All Susie said in response was, "Don't save me a seat ever again." She and Rhonda turned and walked away.

I stood there watching Susie walk away. I thought my guts would blow up. I felt terrible. I was hurt and sad and mad at the same time. Susie was the only girl that I had ever cared about. I loved Susie. And I stood there thinking she would never love me again. I didn't even think she liked me at all. I collapsed to a sitting position on the grass where we were standing.

The congregation of folks were laughing and eating cookies and drinking lemonade, iced tea, and they were happy. The sun was shining brightly on that beautiful day. I knew birds were singing as they waited for everyone to leave so they could find the cookie crumbs. I could see kids running and playing games with cookies in their hands. Mom was talking and laughing with Miss Rebecca and Coal. I was as sad as a stupid boy could be.

Later that afternoon I went to the slanted rock and fished for bluegills. I laid on the rock and thought of ways I could get Susie to not be mad at me. I remembered that flowers worked once before. I didn't think they would work this time. I wondered if maybe I just gave her some space for a while that maybe she would miss me and then forgive me. I wondered if she was mad at the three Key girls. She was teaching two of them to read. Would she still help them?

I began thinking about my future. I always thought about it with Susie in it. I couldn't think of my future life without her in it. I couldn't think of marrying anyone except her. My bobber went under the water and I watched it disappear. I didn't feel like jerking the pole. I let it lie at my feet. I felt like the worm that was hooked on the end of my line that was being eaten by a fish.

I laid on that rock until the sun dipped below the western hillside. I had fallen to sleep in my misery. I heard someone running up the path toward me. I finally saw a shadow on the rise above the rock. I couldn't make out who it was.

"Timmy," Henry Junior called out.

"Hi, Henry, what are you doing here?"

"We all came to the store and Mom decided to stay and visit a while. I was wondering where you were."

"Good, come have a seat."

"How many have you caught?" Junior asked excitedly.

"None."

"Nothin'?" Junior said disappointedly.

"I just wanted time to think," I explained.

"Can't ya think and catch fish at the same time?" Junior asked.

"You're probably right. I just didn't feel like it."

Junior grabbed the pole and began reeling in the line. "Hey, there's a fish on your line!"

"Yeah, I thought there might be. Reel it in."

Junior reeled the large bluegill in. He unhooked it and put another worm on the hook and cast it back into the water. He put the fish on my stringer. Within seconds he was catching another. He fished until it was so dark we couldn't see the bobber. Junior ended up with a stringer full of bluegills. Watching him have so much fun made me forget about my heartache and pain that had enveloped me. It made me look forward to the canoe trip again.

We walked into the backyard. I had told Junior to take the fish home with him. There were enough to make a meal for the family. Junior hurried inside to tell his parents. I walked around the house to the front porch. James Ernest and Raven and Samantha were sitting on the porch. James Ernest and Raven were sitting together in the porch glider. I moseyed over to the empty rocker next to Samantha and lowered myself into the seat.

"I see that you're moping around," Raven said.

"How mad is Susie?" I asked Raven.

"I ne'er seen her this mad at you. Sometimes you are so stupid."

"I know, but it's not my fault. It seems like every time I go to the creek girls just appear. It's like I'm a girl magnet," I said. James Ernest began laughing.

Raven looked over at me and gave me a strange look. She then rose from the glider and slinked toward me. "I know how it is. I don't know how any of the girls can resist you."

She stood in front of me and then plunked down into my lap. She began running her fingers through my Mohawk.

"You are so irresistible. All of the girls talk about how they want to kiss you and be your girl." Raven began kissing my face. Samantha was having a hissy fit with laughter. James Ernest watched with amazement and a big grin at Raven's act.

At that moment the screen door opened and Mr. Washington and Coal walked out, followed by Mom and the other kids.

Raven kept running her hands through my hair. Coal exclaimed, "What are you doing, girl?"

"I can't help it, Mom. I can't resist this girl magnet. He's so handsome and masculine. I don't know how you can resist. I can't," Raven explained.

"He is awfully cute," Coal said. "But I'm going to have to pull you away. We need to get home. Your Pa has to get up early for work."

"I just can't make myself go," Raven said as she wrapped her arms around my head.

Mr. Washington walked over and wrapped his big arms around her waist and lifted her out of my lap, but Raven didn't let go of my head and so I was pulled across the porch and down the steps toward their truck.

"Please, Daddy. I can't let go. We're stuck together like magnets. I can't let go." Her arms finally popped off and Mr. Washington lifted her over the tailgate into the back of the truck.

"I'll miss you so much! I'll see you at the creek! I'll be countin' the seconds!" she screamed as the truck pulled away. Everyone on the porch was laughing and pointing at me. I finally had to start laughing at myself.

9

FORGIVENESS—HARD TO FIND

⌒

FRIDAY, JUNE 15

The drizzle of raindrops fell gently on the tin roof of my bedroom. It would have been daylight if the clouds weren't hiding the light from my window. I was cozy in my top bunk. I could hear large water drops dripping from the roof to the puddles below my windowsill. It made me need to pee. I jumped off the top bunk and landed with a plunk on the wood floor next to James Ernest's head.

I hurried to the open window and began peeing out the window. Our window faced to the east and the rain almost always came from the west so the rain hardly ever came through the window.

"Are you doing what I think you're doing?" came a deep voice from the bottom bunk.

"I don't know what you think I'm doing."

"I think you're peeing out the window," James Ernest continued.

"You're right then. That's what I'm doing, and it feels great," I said as I finished and climbed back up to my bunk.

"What are you—an animal?"

Nayyyyy, I said.

James Ernest laughed and slipped out of bed and hurried to the window and did the same thing I had done.

"And what kind of animal are you?" I asked.

"A baaaad one," he said and we laughed.

We lay there in the dim morning light. I felt like staying in bed all day. I had been in a bad mood all week. I did chores and pouted around the lake and house.

Tuesday evening Sheriff Cane took Mom for a walk to the butterfly field. Mom came back in such a cheerful, fun mood. She told me and everyone else she could think of that it was the most beautiful thing she had ever seen. It just made me think of Susie. She was still not talking to me. I didn't think she would ever forgive me and like me again. I felt like my heart was dragging on the ground everywhere I went.

"When are you going to apologize to Susie and stop moping around?" James Ernest whispered from beneath me. It sounded like the devil was talking to me.

"I've apologized almost every day. She won't even talk to me now. The twins tell me she's not accepting calls from me and they hang up. Delma told me once that Susie had realized the wrong of her past and is out to find a better boyfriend. Thelma said that most any boy would fit that description."

"Timmy, you know that you two will end up back together as boyfriend and girlfriend," James Ernest assured me.

"This time, I don't know," I said.

"What did Rhonda say when she called?"

"She said that Susie told her that she wouldn't have a boyfriend that went around kissing all the other girls. I never kissed anyone! I can't help it if girls are kissing me when I'm passed out. It wasn't my idea. I didn't tell them, 'Hey, I'm going to pass out now. You girls can take turns kissing me if you want to.' She's being stupid."

"I guess it might take a while for her to get over it. She stopped teaching the girls to read," James Ernest said.

"She did?" I questioned.

"Yep. Raven and I are helping them now. Susie is still helping with Tucky though," he explained.

"You think she'll be Tucky's girlfriend?" I asked, not wanting to hear the answer.

"I don't think so, not after he kissed Bernice in the outhouse." We laughed.

Last week my life was perfect. I lived where I wanted to live. I loved the store and the lake and the people I saw every day. I had the sweetest, prettiest, most wonderful girlfriend in the world until this happened. I was now miserable. I couldn't wait to get away. I wanted to go on the canoe trip even more now. I wanted to leave every minute I was awake. I listened to the quietness of the rain falling, looked out the dreary window, and felt sorry for myself as I pulled the bed sheet over my head. What a difference a week makes!

For some reason the rain made me feel lonelier than I usually felt. Being without Susie as my girlfriend was awful.

Around eleven that morning Rhonda and her mom, Mary, came to the store. I was sitting in the glider on the front porch when they drove up. James Ernest had gone to the Washington's. I said hello to Mary and she went on into the store to talk to Mom. Rhonda sat beside me in the glider.

We watched the rain continue to gently fall on the gravel lot. I wasn't sure what to say to Rhonda. I had never been good at having a conversation with any girl except Susie. I never knew what they liked to talk about.

"Are you looking for a new girlfriend?" Rhonda said, breaking the silence between us.

"Why would I be doing that?" I asked.

"Since Susie is done with you, I thought maybe you were looking for a new girlfriend."

"I didn't know Susie was done with me," I said.

"She's looking for a new boyfriend."

"Did she tell you that?"

"More or less."

More or less? What does that mean? I thought. She either is or she isn't. Why was Rhonda asking and telling me this? Did she want to be my new girlfriend? I liked Rhonda as a friend, but I could never be her boyfriend. I would never do that to Purty. He loved Rhonda and had always wanted to be her boyfriend.

"I'm not looking for a new girlfriend," I said.

"Then why are you kissing other girls?" Rhonda asked.

"I wasn't kissing other girls," I said. I was tired of defending myself. I got up and went into the store. Rhonda followed me.

"You can now," Rhonda said as I walked behind the counter.

"I can do what now?" I asked.

"You can kiss other girls. You could kiss me if you wanted to," Rhonda said as she walked closer to the counter.

"I don't want to kiss any girl," I said.

"Good. I was just testing you, anyway," Rhonda said.

I thought she was trying to save face, but maybe Susie sent her to see if I was looking for a new girlfriend and whether I would want to kiss Rhonda. I figured Susie would call me by evening and say she forgave me for what I didn't do in the first place.

SATURDAY, JUNE 16

I was wrong.

She didn't call. I did chores and waited on fishermen all day.

SUNDAY, JUNE 17

I saved a seat for Susie at church. She sat with Rhonda three rows behind me. The Tuttle family walked into the church just before Pastor White greeted everyone and Sadie saw the seat beside me and hurried to take the spot. I couldn't very well tell her to go away since the service was about to start. I scooted as far away as possible. She took it as a sign that she was supposed to move over also.

In the middle of one of the songs being sung, she whispered in my ear, "Are you ready for a real girlfriend now? I'll teach you to French kiss."

I bowed my head and asked God, "What have I done to deserve this? Forgive me for whatever I did. Please."

Sadie tried to hold my left hand during the service. I ended up sitting on my hand the entire service.

SATURDAY, JUNE 23

Nothing had changed between Susie and me. In fact, I hadn't even seen her since last Sunday at church. It was a nice Saturday; the weather was warm, but nice. The lake was crowded with fishermen and families fishing, teasing each other and laughing. I was walking through the backyard after delivering orders of drinks and snacks. Coty was by my side. I fell to my knees so I could pet him and spotted a four-leaf clover near his right paw. After petting and playing with Coty, I pulled up the clover and put it in my pocket. I knew that I could really use some luck.

When I walked into the store, the three Key sisters were there talking with Mom. It must have been a flawed four-leaf clover. I nodded hello and kept walking through the house to the kitchen. I heard Mom say to the girls, "I wonder what's wrong with him. He's been acting different for a week or so."

"I think he's mad at us," Sugar Cook said.

"Why would he be mad at you girls?" Mom asked them.

I heard Rock say, "We need to talk to Timmy alone if you don't mind."

"I'll get him," Mom said and walked into the kitchen as I was drinking a glass of water.

"The girls want to talk to you. Do you know what this is about?" Mom whispered.

"Will you watch the store? I'll take them for a quick walk," I said without answering Mom's question.

I could tell that Mom wasn't satisfied with what I had to say, but she didn't object, so I left.

When I walked into the store, I said, "Let's go for a walk."

I led them through the door and down the steps and down Morgan Road. Finally I said, "I didn't want to talk where Mom could hear us."

"We came to apologize," Rock began.

"We are so sorry. Forgive us," Chero begged.

Sugar Cook then said, "We know that Susie is really upset with us and we know it's our fault, mainly mine. We really were trying to save your life, but once I realized you were okay I took it too far. We were just having fun."

It was hard for me to admit, but I said, "It was partly my fault also. I knew I was okay, and I didn't try to stop you. I should have stopped you."

"Susie broke up with you?" Rock asked.

"Yeah. She's pretty mad. She won't even talk to me," I told them.

"She won't teach us reading anymore," Chero said.

"I know. I'm sorry about that. I'm hoping she'll get over it and forgive us."

"We're going to walk up to her farm and apologize to her when we leave here," Rock said.

"Are we okay?" Chero asked me.

"We're okay. I like ya'll," I told them.

We turned back toward the store and casually talked as we walked. When we were standing in front of the store, Sugar Cook said, "Anyway, if Susie never forgives you, you know you can always kiss on us. We're tired of kissing our brothers."

I know that I must have made a terrible face. Rock then added, "She's teasing you about kissing our brothers; we ain't from that far back in the hollers."

"You had me going on that one," I said and laughed. I then added, "Let me know what Susie says."

"We'll stop on our way back home," Sugar Cook promised me. The three girls turned and walked up the gravel road toward Susie's house. I hoped it would work.

SUNDAY, JUNE 24

It didn't work.

Susie said she would help them with their reading and writing again, but she was not going to forgive me. She told them she was tired of always finding me with other girls. I was tired of always having her mad at me for things that weren't my fault. I wanted a girlfriend who trusted me and didn't dump me at a moment's notice. I was over it. If she didn't want me as her boyfriend, fine, I'd move on.

Mom picked up the Key kids on the way to church again. I walked into the church and saw that Susie was sitting with Rhonda, Raven, James Ernest, and Purty. I slipped into a pew in front of them with Tucky, Rock, and Chero. Rock was sitting next to me. She was pretty with her flowered sundress on. I turned around and waved to the group behind me. Everyone waved, except Susie. My heart broke a little more.

I didn't hear one word that Pastor White preached. My brain was going back and forth as to what I was going to do. I needed to know if Susie was ever going to forgive me or if she would be like the twins and hate me forever.

Pastor shook my hand as I walked out of the church. He stopped me and said, "Your mind seemed to be somewhere else during the service."

"Yeah. I'm sorry. Seems like I'm always apologizing," I said to him.

"Remember that God loves you," Pastor White said and rubbed my head.

I wondered if that was really true. Did God really love me? It seemed as though nobody loved me. Perhaps I was unlovable. "Thanks," was all I said as I walked away.

Monie was talking with Mom in the parking lot. Susie was standing with Raven and James Ernest. I walked over and stood next to Susie. She stopped talking and looked my way.

"Can we talk?" I asked. Raven and James Ernest slunk away.

"What is it?" Susie said.

"Are you ever going to forgive me? I'm tired of begging you to forgive me. Do you not lo…like me anymore?"

Tears began welling up in Susie's eyes and she shook her head from side-to-side and ran toward Clayton's pickup.

I walked out of the parking lot and down the road toward the store. Tears were streaming down my face. I felt like lying on the road and letting all the trucks and cars use me like a speed bump they had in Ohio.

After a few minutes, Mom stopped the car beside me. "What are you doing?"

"I need to walk home," I cried out through the tears.

"What is wrong?" Mom said with worry on her face.

"Susie hates me," I said. I turned and ran into the woods.

I heard Mom drive away. I fell over a log and lay on the forest floor and cried my eyes out. I knew I wasn't over her.

10

I'm a Teenager

⌒

July 21, 1962

Almost a month had passed since I last talked to Susie, other than to say hello or nod to each other. The twins gloated every time they saw me. I tried my best to leave when I got within earshot of them. Mom and Monie had talked endlessly about the two of us. I heard them say that they couldn't stand the moping around that we both constantly did. I had been given advice from everyone. It must have been the talk of the county. So far, I hadn't found any articles in the county newspaper about our breakup.

Papaw, Clayton, Uncle Morton, Roger Smuckatilly, the mailman, and most of the fishermen had all given me advice from buying her expensive gifts, giving her flowers, writing her a love letter begging her forgiveness, reciting love poems to her, and singing a love song to her. I tried explaining to them that I was over her and that I was on the search for a new girlfriend. None of them believed me. Louis Lewis told me, "No one else will have ya." Fred Wilson told me I should fry her some chicken and take her on a picnic. There was a lot wrong with that idea.

Strangers would come up offering advice. How did they even know about it?

Bo returned a couple of weeks earlier. I was cleaning the paths at the lake when he swooped down out of a tree and landed on my left shoulder. I was glad to see him, happy that he was okay, but his blackness did nothing to cheer me up. The only thing that cheered me up was the fact that the Wolf Pack was leaving on our canoe trip on Monday, July 30th. We had all of our supplies and three canoes. Papaw had taken us to scope out the area and where we would be camping. It was so exciting. The days crept by as I waited for the day to come.

It was my birthday and that didn't excite me at all. It just meant it was another day closer to the trip. I told Mom I didn't want a party. She was worried about me. She even had Pastor White come to the house to talk to me one evening. I assured Pastor White that I would be fine—I was fine. Rhonda Blair was having a big birthday party. I was invited but decided not to go. Susie was one of her best friends, and I knew it would be awkward going with her there.

For my birthday I wanted to go for a hike with Bo and Coty. Mom said I could if I made sure to be back by seven. Mom said that Mamaw and Papaw were coming for birthday cake and ice cream at seven. We would have a family celebration for my birthday since I wasn't going to Rhonda's party.

I wasn't sure where to go on my hike. The afternoon was turning warm so I decided to go wading up Licking Creek toward the tunnel. I entered the creek at the bridge and walked into the water. It felt good. The creeks almost always made me happy unless girls showed up. Bo was with me and Coty was searching the creek banks for smells. Coty didn't like being in the water. He hated it when I took him to the creek to give him a bath. But Mom wouldn't let him in the house unless he was clean.

Breaking up with Susie had made my summer miserable. It seemed as though I went through the motions. Nothing was as much fun. Everything I did reminded me of her. Even wading in the creek made me think of her—the day she stomped me in the stomach, the day she got the crawdad stuck to her pigtail, the day she had the big fight with Sadie. It brought back the memories of the night we escaped from the kidnappers by wading down the same creek. I had professed my love to Susie and told her how I was going to marry her while kidnapped. It now seemed impossible.

An hour into my wade, I came to the creek tunnel. Bo flew off my shoulder and went over the mountain to the other side. When I came out on the other side, I heard Bo cry out, *Caw, caw.*

Coty went through the road tunnel and came down to the creek to get a drink. I began petting him and then I heard splashing. I turned my head to see Rock wading down the creek. Apparently she hadn't seen me yet. She was really cute. Her long sandy hair glistened in the sunlight. She had on cutoff jeans and a sleeveless, checkered blouse that was tied in a knot showing off her flat stomach. Bo began crying out again, *Caw, caw, caw.*

Rock was looking down at her steps and she looked up when she heard Bo. She saw me standing there looking at her. She waved and called out, "Hi, Timmy." I waved back and began wading toward her.

Rock began running toward me through the water. When she got to me, she slipped and began to fall. I caught her, but her momentum took me with her and we both ended up under the water. When we surfaced we both were laughing. It was my first laughter in days.

"What are you doing down here?" Rock asked me.

"I wanted to explore this afternoon, so I decided to wade the creek and here I am," I explained.

"I'm glad you're here. Hey, isn't today your birthday?"

"Yep, how did you know that?"

"We were invited to Rhonda's party and it was mentioned that it might be for both of you. Then we heard you weren't going, so we decided not to go."

"How come?"

"We like Rhonda, she's really sweet, but we don't know her very well."

"You would have had a good time," I said.

"I guess I know why you're not going," Rock stated as we continued walking toward her house.

"I wasn't in a party mood, and I knew Susie would be there. I didn't want to ruin Rhonda's party with people talking about me and Susie."

"I understand. Do you think she'll ever forgive you?"

"No. I've quit trying, and I'm not worrying about it," I said.

"Well, I think you're sweet, and I think she's foolish for not forgiving you," Rock said.

"Why are you out here wading the creek?"

"It's about my favorite thing to do. I wade the creek almost every day that I find time. I love finding the little animals and seeing the small waterfalls in the rapids. Everything about the creek makes me happy, from the coolness of the water to the creatures under it," Rock said.

Everything she said was exactly the same way I felt about the creek, but she said it a lot better than I could have.

"Do you ever fish the creek?" I asked.

"Sometimes, but not very often. The boys fish it all the time. They always bring home a stick full of fish."

I looked over as we were wading up the creek and saw Bo riding on Coty's back on the edge of the road. I pointed toward them and Rock laughed.

She then asked, "What are you doing for your thirteenth birthday? It is thirteen, isn't it?"

"Yep, becoming a teenager. Mom and my grandparents are having a cake and ice cream for me this evening. That's all. When do you and Kenny turn thirteen?"

"August the ninth."

"Really? That means that we'll be back from the canoe trip by your birthday."

"We never do much for birthdays anyway. With ten in our family, we would be celebrating all the time."

"What's wrong with that? " We both laughed.

"I want to show you something. It's right over here. I've never showed it to anyone else." We waded over to the far bank of the creek. A rock wall came straight out of the creek and up thirty to forty feet. A ledge stuck out from the wall at the water's level.

"Follow me under the ledge for around ten feet then you can stand up."

The water depth was nearly four feet where we stood at the ledge. I wondered if she had found another Indian drawing cave. I guessed it was possible, but not very likely. She lowered herself under the water and I followed. She pushed the water with her arms and I did the same and then she stood. I stood up next to her. It wasn't dark. I was surprised. There were rays of light going everywhere. What in the world was it? My eyes began to adjust to the light.

"Wow," was all I could say at the moment.

"That's exactly what I said when I found it."

I saw the jagged sharp points that shot out toward the center where we stood. The rounded walls were entirely a light purple color. I estimated that the sidewalls were close to ten to twelve feet apart. The one wall must have been eroded away over the years allowing us to enter.

"What is this?" I asked.

"I don't know. But it's the neatest thing I've ever found."

"You haven't shown this to anyone else?"

"No. It's a secret between us."

"Why did you show me?" I asked her as I turned to look in her face.

"Because I like you," she said as she moved toward me and kissed me quickly, but gently, on the lips.

I didn't know what to say or do. I was frozen in that spot. It was the first time I had let someone properly kiss me other then Susie. Was I truly over Susie? Could Rock become my new girlfriend?

"I like you too," I said. Rock grinned.

I finally said, "It's like we're in the inside of a rich woman's giant ring."

"It's some kind of crystal-like thing, isn't it?" Rock asked.

"I've seen small ones like this before, but I forget what they're called."

"How big?"

"Maybe nine to twelve inches," I answered.

At the time, I didn't know that we were standing in the middle of a giant geode. Kentucky was known for its geodes. This one was one of the biggest.

Rock and I left the geode and spent the rest of the afternoon swimming, catching crawdads, watching Jesus bugs, and talking. We found some tiny frogs, no bigger than a nickel. They were adorable. It was the best time I had had since Susie and I broke up.

Around five I decided I needed to head home and then a thought hit me. "Why don't you and Kenny come to the store around seven and help celebrate my birthday, and we can celebrate you and Kenny's birthday? It will be fun."

"You sure? Your mom won't mind?"

"Not at all, besides, it's my birthday; I can invite anyone I want."

"I'll try. I'll see if Kenny will come," Rock said and then kissed me on the cheek before turning toward her house. I turned away after watching her skip along in the water. I could tell she was happy. I was happy. I began to skip as I waded. I soon fell on my butt in the water after skipping on a slippery rock.

After gathering myself out of the water and climbing to the road, Bo landed back on my shoulder and we hurried toward the store. I now looked forward to my simple party.

I walked into the store around six-thirty. Mamaw and Papaw were already there. I was smiling as I entered the store and the kitchen.

Mom was in the kitchen with Mamaw. I walked in and Mom said, "You seem awfully happy. I haven't seen you smiling like that in days. The hike must have done you some good."

"I had fun," was all I said.

"You had better change out of those nasty clothes and get ready for cake," Mom told me.

Mamaw said, "Happy birthday! A teenager now, how time flies."

I turned toward my bedroom and then remembered, "I invited Kenny and Rock to my party. That's okay, isn't it? I'm not sure if they're coming or not."

"That's fine, but I thought you didn't want a party?" Mom said.

"Just a small one," I said as I walked away.

I quickly changed and then Papaw asked me to go with him to the farm to help him do something.

When we got to the farm, we stopped at the barn and I followed Papaw as he gathered some oats into a pail. I followed him to Honeycomb's stall and Papaw fed the oats to his mule. Why was I needed for this simple chore? All I was doing was watching. We then walked to the house and Papaw had me pick up a wrapped package that I knew was my birthday gift. We then walked back to the truck and slowly drove back to the store. When we arrived it was ten after seven.

I walked into the store and people began yelling, "Surprise! Happy birthday!" They then began singing, "For he's a jolly good fellow," led by Uncle Morton. Homer and Ruby were there. Robert and Janice and Tammy were there. Dana and Pretty Idell were there. Pastor White, Miss Rebecca, and Bobby Lee were also there. I was surprised to see Clayton, Monie, and the twins there, since Susie and Brenda went to Rhonda's party.

Then I noticed Kenny and Rock in the corner of the store smiling and waving at me. I heard steps on the porch and looked around to see the Washington family coming through the door with James Ernest. "We really sorry to miss the grand entrance, but we's here now," Henry Washington said with a big grin and everyone laughed. The party couldn't be better. Everyone that was there were people I really loved. Raven and Samantha gave me big hugs in the middle of the store and then Rock came over and did the same thing, plus she kissed my cheek and said, "Happy birthday."

"I hope we don't all have to do that," Robert joked, causing laughter to fill the store.

The women headed for the kitchen to ready the cake and ice cream. The men settled out on the front porch to spit and swap tales. The twins, Janie, Mark Daniel, and Bobby Lee headed off somewhere to fight and argue. We other kids hung out in the store talking and laughing. I asked Raven, "Why didn't you and James Ernest go to the big party at Rhonda's?"

James Ernest answered, "I wouldn't miss my best buddy's birthday party for anything."

"Me neither," Raven and Samantha echoed.

Rock walked over next to me and slowly grabbed hold of my hand as we stood there and didn't let go. I noticed the surprised look on the others' faces. I guessed she was serious about being my girlfriend.

After singing "Happy Birthday" to me, I blew out the thirteen candles. Mom then announced that it was going to be Rock and Kenny's birthday on August the ninth and everyone sang "Happy Birthday" to them and then we all ate cake and ice cream and other desserts women had brought.

Mamaw made cherry dumplings, which I had two servings of after eating the cake and ice cream. I was stuffed. After everyone was nearly done eating, I opened the cards and gifts. I got a new pocket watch from Mom, which was really neat. It had a howling wolf on the front.

Mamaw and Papaw got me a set of camping cookware for my canoe trip. We needed that. I received cards and money from some of the families. The twins each wrote me a birthday card.

Thelma's card read: Roses are red.
Violets are blue.
You're so stupid
For being you.

Delma's card read: Happy Birthday to you.
Happy Birthday to you.
You're such a moron.
Happy Birthday to you.
Second verse:
Happy Birthday to you.
Happy Birthday to you.
Susie finally dumped you.
Happy day for us.

I didn't expect anything less from the twins. I laughed. The party wouldn't have been complete without getting insults from the twins. It turned out to be a great party. I felt as though I was finally over Susie and I could go on with my life. I had found out during the day that there were other great girls other than her. I knew that Susie was wonderful and cute and sweet, but maybe she and I weren't meant to be after all.

I was dead tired after everyone left that evening. Clayton gave Rock and Kenny a ride home so they didn't have to walk in the dark. I climbed into my top bunk and collapsed. James Ernest turned off the light and slipped into bed.

"Tell me about Rock and you," came out of his mouth as soon as his head hit the pillow.

I knew he had wanted to ask me the question all evening. I had seen him and Raven whispering about Rock and me as I was opening gifts with Rock sitting beside me on the couch. I also noticed a lot of the adults doing the same.

During the evening the twins walked over to us and Delma asked Rock, "So you're going to make the same stupid mistake our sister made, huh?"

Rock simply told them, "Get lost." They huffed and walked away muttering to each other about how rude Rock was and how stupid her name was.

"I was wading up Licking Creek this afternoon past the tunnel when I met Rock in the creek. We kind of hit it off. The next thing I knew she kissed me, and I guess she's my girlfriend now."

"Wasn't it her and her sisters kissing you in the first place that got you in trouble with Susie?"

"I'm not in trouble this time though."

"Not unless you want Susie back some day. Or the fact that you might not want to eat roadkill possum during your life," James Ernest said seriously.

"Don't knock it unless you've tried it," I said and laughed.

"I don't think I want to eat seconds after Bo."

We laid in silence for a few minutes. I could hear the sounds of night outside our window. I was now thirteen. I felt older, more mature. My life was changing. Since coming to Kentucky, Susie had been my girl. Maybe it was time to change. I felt good about it. She had made her choice and I was now okay with it. I was making mine.

"Are you really going to eat dinner at the Key house?" James Ernest whispered in the darkness.

"Not if I can help it," I whispered back.

James Ernest was asleep within minutes. I wondered what Susie would think once the twins told her about Rock being my new girlfriend. She would probably think, 'I knew it. I was right.'

I soon fell asleep myself, feeling better than I had for the last few weeks.

11

CANOEING

⌒

MONDAY, JULY 30, 1962

I was up and got dressed as soon as I heard the rooster's crow. Bo had begun pecking on the window like he knew it was a big day. Mom made me keep the window barely open. She didn't want Bo nesting on my bed. So I had to keep the window closed except for around two inches at the bottom. Papaw and Clayton were going to drive us to the Red River. Our gear and the canoes were already loaded and we planned to leave at daybreak so we could get on the river early.

I was so happy I couldn't stand it. I had been marking the days off on the calendar that hung in the store. I had July 30th circled in red and it was finally here. I heard Mom and Mamaw in the kitchen preparing breakfast. They had invited all of the boys to have breakfast here before we left. Mamaw told us that it might be the last good meal we would have for three days. She could be right. They were frying bacon and sausage. Mamaw scrambled eggs and made biscuits and gravy.

Mr. Washington dropped off Henry Junior on his way to work at the quarry. Forest picked up KenTucky on his way to drop off Randy and Purty. The house was filled with excitement and adrenaline as we couldn't wait to shove off and begin our next adventure. Junior was beside himself; he was nervous and anxious at the same time. He looked like a small child on Christmas morning standing in front of Santa Claus. We were shoving our breakfast into our mouths as quick as we could.

"You boys look like the hogs at the trough gobbling up the food as fast as you can," Mamaw said.

"Listen, can you hear that?" I said as I held my hand cupped to my ear.

The room got quiet and Junior said, "What do ya hear?"

"I hear the Red River calling us. Don't you hear it? We'd better hurry." Everyone laughed and we continued shoving gravy into our faces.

"I hear it now!" Purty screamed with his mouth full and gravy running down his chin. He scooped it up with his fingers and stuffed it back into his mouth.

Breakfast ended a few minutes after it started and we waited in the parking lot for Papaw and Clayton to finish their breakfast. When they finally walked out the front door, Papaw said, "You think the boys are ready to go, Clayton?"

"I reckon they might be," he answered as he looked at us standing there champing at the bit to go.

Papaw yelled into the kitchen, "We're leaving."

Mamaw and Mom and Janie came out onto the porch to say good-bye. I ran up the steps and hugged all three of them.

Mom told me, "Be careful."

Mamaw told me, "Be a good boy," as she always did.

Janie told me, "Don't drown on the river, Timmy." She had been around the twins entirely too much.

I squeezed into the cab of Papaw's truck with James Ernest and Junior. Coty jumped into the back of the pickup with the canoes and supplies. Randy, Purty, and Tucky squeezed into Clayton's cab. I was glad to not be in the same cab as Purty after rushing our big breakfast. I knew some of his breakfast would come out somewhere, somehow, in some form. I didn't want to be there when it did.

The drive to the Red River starting point seemed to take forever, even though it was only a little over an hour's drive. We were told by some men when we visited before that the first section of the trip was the worst for rapids and that we would probably turn over in canoes. We thought about skipping that part and then Papaw suggested we leave our supplies at our first campground and only take the canoes and paddles and life vests. We also packed a small feed poke with drinks and snacks that we could tie inside the canoe in case we did flip. So our first stop was at our first campground.

Clayton and the rest of the boys emptied quickly out of their cab when we stopped. "That boy has got to have something dead inside of him," he said as he coughed and gagged. We knew exactly who 'that boy' was he was talking about. We quickly put up the tents and stored our stuff inside of them.

We were told that the rest of the trip down river from the first campground would be calm, flat water that we could paddle or drift down the river. We figured the fishing would be easier in those sections. Our tents were pitched around a hundred feet from the river. The deep pool at that area excited me even more to begin the trip on the river—three whole days on the river.

Our put-in spot was twelve miles farther up the river. I was so excited and nervous my knees were shaking as we neared the beginning of the canoe trip. Papaw finally pulled off the road and stopped at the end of the lane near the river. A path took us to the river's edge. We unloaded the canoes and carried them the fifty feet to the river. We placed the canoes with the front end in the water and the back sitting on the ground. Purty threw his canoe in the water and the canoe began drifting away.

"There goes your canoe, Purty!" Junior yelled out. Tucky ran to the water's edge and dove into the river and caught the canoe before it drifted out of sight. He swam it back to shore.

"What are you thinking, Purty?" Randy yelled at him.

"I thought it would stay there," Purty explained.

"You don't quite understand what a river is, or does, do you?" James Ernest mocked.

Purty muttered to himself. We had decided on each day we would have a different canoe partner. On the first day I was going to canoe with Randy, Junior with James Ernest, and Purty with Tucky. Randy and James Ernest were going to steer the rear in their canoes. Purty and Tucky argued over who would steer the back of theirs. Purty played the seniority card and ended up winning the argument. Purty had told Tucky that he was the most experienced canoeist and was an expert at going down rapids. We all stared at Purty when he said it.

Clayton suggested that he lead us in prayer before we shoved off. We all agreed that it was a good idea, especially if Purty was our most experienced canoeist. Clayton prayed, "Father, I pray that you will be with these young men as they enjoy your wonderful creation. I pray that you will protect them and keep them from harm. Watch over them; keep them safe. And, Lord, keep your hands on them and bring them home safely. Amen." Papaw amended it again.

I began to believe that Clayton was a little worried about our safety on the trip. I hoped he was wrong, but I did appreciate the prayer.

Junior, Tucky, and I took our spots in the fronts of the canoes. Coty jumped into the middle of my canoe. We had debated on whether to let Coty come on the trip. We knew how much he hated water, but he almost always went on our adventures if it was possible and he was a member of the Wolf Pack, so he came along. Randy pushed the canoe into the water and hopped over the side and into his seat. James Ernest did the same with no problem. Our expert Purty pushed his canoe into the water and as he tried to jump in, he tipped the boat over and dumped Tucky into the river.

"My foot caught on the side," Purty explained as Tucky swiped the water from his Mohawk. Tucky turned the canoe around and made Purty get in first. Tucky then shoved the canoe away from the shore and quickly jumped into his seat and they floated to the middle of the river.

Purty shouted, "Hey, a big fish just went under our boat!" He leaned over to watch it swim and the canoe tipped over again and spilled the two boys into the river. Tucky swam over to Purty and grabbed Purty by the head and yelled, "Here, get a good look at it." He stuck Purty's head under the water.

I heard Papaw say to Clayton on the shore, "You better pray some more."

Purty and Tucky were finally in their canoe again and we waved at Papaw and Clayton and off we paddled down the great Red River. Who knew what would happen during the three days? That's what the adventure was all about.

The water was clear and green. At this point the river was only around twenty-five feet wide, but we knew this was near the start and later the river would get a lot wider and deeper. Randy and I were leading the way. James Ernest and Junior were close behind, and Purty and Tucky were doing circles somewhere in the distance behind us. Our expert didn't quite have the perfection down on steering the canoe. I heard a lot of yelling. Coty went from side-to-side looking at the shore and the water gliding by as we moved quietly in the water. Not long into our trip, large rocks began showing up in the river. It reminded me a lot of the large rocks that were in Licking Creek and Devil's Creek. Some of the rocks were ten to fifteen feet high and almost as wide. We had to maneuver around them.

We heard aluminum hit rock behind us and we knew that Purty had maneuvered his canoe right into one of the rocks. A little later they caught up with us and Purty was now sitting in the front with Tucky steering in the back.

"Six times! Purty has turned us over six times!" Tucky exclaimed. "How many times have you guys turned over?"

James Ernest raised his hand and had formed it into a zero. Randy said, "Not once yet."

Purty was still smiling as he looked at us. He finally said, "There's a lot of pressure trying to keep up with you guys."

"The only reason we're having trouble keeping up is that we're always out of the canoe," Tucky said. Junior was laughing his head off.

"Does anyone want to trade me for Purty? Anyone? Please!" Tucky begged. We began to paddle faster. "Coty, I'll take Coty for him!" he yelled.

Coty whined and hid his head under the gunwale.

"What will happen to us when we get to the rapids?" Tucky shouted.

I was wondering the same thing. If they couldn't stay afloat in calm waters, what would they do in rapids?

James Ernest told them that we should stop at the top of the rapids and take a look at them before going through. I agreed and Randy agreed. Purty didn't agree, and we didn't pay any attention to his objection.

"I need to pee," Purty said, all of a sudden.

"You've had six chances to pee," Tucky scolded him.

"I was busy saving your life," Purty said and grinned.

Tucky looked up at the sky and said, "Why me?"

"I think something is wrong with our canoe," Purty offered.

We all laughed at him.

It was the ideal day to start our trip. The weather was perfect, mideighties and sunny. We saw no one else on the water. The trees were green and towered over us as we passed by. We saw large mountains on all sides and the tall rock cliffs stood as if they were watching us float by. I leaned back in my seat and relaxed, letting the current take us while Randy leisurely steered the canoe on its path.

I looked over at Junior and he was doing the same thing, but with a huge smile across his face.

Suddenly, I heard white noise ahead of us. I could see eruptions of water and large rocks standing out of the water. "The rapids are coming up!" I shouted to everyone.

"Let's paddle over to the shore and walk up to see them," Randy directed. He angled the canoe toward the bank and the others followed his lead. We carefully got out and pulled the canoe onto dry land. James Ernest did the same. Soon Tucky and Purty were upside down in the water. We helped pull their canoe ashore while they managed to swim ashore. Tucky whacked Purty hard across his butt with the paddle. "You dumb wit."

We walked nearly a hundred yards to get to the top of the rapids. Coty marked spots along the way. The rapids were a lot bigger than what we thought they would be. My eyes almost popped out of my head as I saw the drops and waves and large rocks that blocked our path.

"This is going to be so much fun," Purty announced over the roar of the water.

I had never seen anything like it except in books or on adventure programs on TV.

"Could we carry the canoes around the rapids?" James Ernest asked.

"I don't think so. It's just large rocks and stonewalls. How would we do it? I think we have to go down the rapids. We need to pick a path and follow it," Randy said.

"They told us the first one was the worst," I said.

James Ernest studied the rapids and soon had a plan. He told us where we should enter the rapids, and which way to steer the canoe, and where to paddle faster, and where to let the current take us and not force anything. We went over it four times and everyone had to repeat the plan to make sure everyone had it down pat.

"I'll lead the way if that's okay," James Ernest said and we all agreed. "Tucky, you come down next and then Randy and Timmy can bring up the rear. Wait until each canoe is all the way down before the other canoe comes, in case someone turns over." Everyone looked at Purty.

We all took the opportunity to pee and then we walked back to our canoes. We held Tucky's canoe while they got in and we shoved them away from the shore. When we all were in, James Ernest and Junior began paddling toward the opening he had picked out. We moved the canoe closer to the spot so we could watch them go through the rapids.

We had to back-paddle to keep the current from taking our canoe down the rapids. Coty was pacing in the boat. I had to tell him to lie down. They hit the opening fast and James Ernest quickly turned the canoe to the left and around a large rock. They then steered the canoe to the right and through a tunnel of water, soaking both of them. They quickly dropped out of sight but then popped up as they tackled the next set of obstacles. It looked like James Ernest had been doing it his entire life. He then eased up and let the current push the canoe to the bottom and into quiet water. They raised their arms in triumph and yelled a war whoop.

I applauded and yelled for my friends. It was Purty and Tucky's turn. I heard Tucky tell Purty, "Let's do exactly what they did."

Purty shook his head in agreement and then they did it nothing like the first canoe. They missed the correct opening by going right of it, which made it harder to go around the big rock so they slammed into it. The canoe ended up backward and the current took it wherever it wanted. And it wasn't anywhere near where the boys wanted to go. A large body of water flipped the canoe over and we saw Purty flying through the air and over the drop. Tucky had managed to grab the canoe and was surfing behind it, trying to stay above water. The paddles went who knows where.

The canoe hit one giant rock broadside and we thought it was going to bend the canoe in half, but Tucky was able to swing the canoe to the left to get it off the rock and then he crashed against another boulder as the canoe snapped around the stone. We saw Purty floating in the river below the falls, watching Tucky direct the canoe through the rapids. When Tucky finally made it to the bottom, he began swimming after Purty and yelling his guts out. Purty turned and started swimming away from him. At least, for the time being, they were alive.

"You ready to try it?" Randy asked.

"We can't do any worse than that," I said and laughed.

"That's very true," Randy agreed. Coty's head popped up over the gunwale so he could see what was happening. I knew there was no use trying to get him to lie down.

We hit the opening just right and followed the lead of the first canoe. The canoe swung and spun and kicked and whacked against rocks. I wondered what Coty was thinking. I tried my best to paddle hard when I needed to and let Randy steer when I needed to. We dropped over the ledge of water and then floated to safety, next to James Ernest and Junior. What a thrill! My first time canoeing rapids, I loved every moment of the excitement. Our canoe chased down one of the missing paddles and James Ernest went after the other one. Purty's canoe looked like it had been through war. It had indents where it had slammed against the large rocks and black marks where it had skidded along them.

Tucky never did catch Purty, and he waited for us to catch up with his canoe. He jumped in and began explaining, "Just as we got to the correct opening, Purty says, 'I think we would be better off on this side of the rock' and he swung the front end to the right before I could correct it. We missed the opening and then everything went haywire. I thought I was going to die."

"You did a good job getting the canoe down the rapids without destroying it," Randy told him.

"I'm going to kill him," Tucky promised.

We got side-by-side and held onto each other's canoes and floated down the river like that. The river was widening as we went. We had Tucky's canoe in the middle.

"Where is Purty?" Tucky asked.

We all looked around for him, but he was nowhere in sight. A few minutes later we were floating toward a large flat rock that stuck out two feet above the water. I saw his head on the rock.

"Purty," I called out.

He stood up and there he was in all his glory. Just like the day he was born—nude from head to toe. Junior said, "That white boy is the ugliest thing I've ever seen. That just ugly as sin."

We all began laughing uncontrollably.

"That just ain't right a'tall," Tucky agreed.

12

The Bottom Brothers' Noose

The rock was large enough for all of us to get on and have lunch. We made Purty put on his pants. Purty was disappointed but didn't argue much. Once we all were up on the rock, Tucky caught Purty close to the edge and he pushed Purty back into the river.

"Hey, why did you do that?" Purty sputtered.

"I figure you like being in the river. That's where you had us spend the whole morning," Tucky said.

"You were steering the canoe," Purty argued.

Tucky shook his head after realizing there was no winning against Purty, no matter how wrong Purty was. Purty climbed back onto the rock and began eating his lunch. I gave Coty some boloney Mom had sent for him.

It was warm on the rock, but a nice breeze blew upriver making it tolerable. I was already having a great time and we had just begun the canoe trip. Suddenly, Randy said, "There's a boat coming this way."

We looked downriver to see a small, faded blue, wooden boat being pushed by a small outboard motor coming toward us. As it drew closer I could see two young men in the boat with fishing poles hanging over the edge and a rifle leaned against the side. I was hoping it would just go on past, but it headed straight for the rock we were on. Coty barked as they neared. I finally told him to stop.

We waved when we knew they were coming to talk to us. The man in the front made a halfhearted attempt at returning our greeting. They slowed when they got near and threw out an anchor and cut the engine.

"Are you guys Injuns?" the guy in the front asked and then laughed. I figured he thought our Mohawks were reason to poke fun of us.

"No. I guess I could figure why you would guess that," Randy answered.

"What are you doing on the river?" the man asked. He wore bibbed overalls but no shirt and had the bibs unhooked and down around his waist. He was muscular and had a hardened look to him.

James Ernest answered in his deep voice, "We're canoeing and doing a little fishing."

"Where you from?" the man asked.

"Lee County, near Beattyville," James Ernest lied.

"Where's your fishing poles?" he asked.

"At the campground. Didn't want to take them down the rapids."

The man looked at his buddy in the back of the boat and they laughed like they had a joke between them. Junior was sitting behind us so there would be less chance of them seeing him. Henry Junior made the mistake of poking his head around to look at the men. I could see the man in the front crane his neck and then stand up in the boat.

He then said, "What are doing with that colored boy?"

"He's with us," I chimed in.

"What is he doing with you?"

James Ernest jumped in, "He serves us. Whatever we tell him to do."

The man in the front of the boat rubbed his chin and asked, "Why does he have a haircut like the rest of you?"

I was nervous. I wasn't sure what James Ernest would say.

"He has a haircut like us because we told him to get a haircut like us. He does whatever we tell him to do."

"This is our section of the river. We don't want no colored boy polluting the water. Keep him out of the water."

The man in the back of the boat finally spoke and I didn't like what he had to say, "If we catch him in the water, there's a big tree downriver where we like to string Negros up. You can't miss it."

"I agree with you," Randy said.

"If he gets in the water, we'll help you tie the noose," James Ernest said. Coty ran to the edge of the rock and began growling at the two men.

"We'll be keeping an eye out," the muscular man said as he pulled the anchor up and the other man started the engine. They turned the boat around and headed back down current.

As the boat headed downriver, Randy said, "I'd like to string them up."

"Sorry about that, Henry," James Ernest said as we all turned to look at Henry Junior. I could swear I was looking at a white boy. He was as pale as Purty. The color had left his face, and he was shaking with fright. I couldn't blame him after what he had heard. "We had to say those things to keep you safe."

"I's want to go home," Henry Junior said, his words shaking out of his mouth. I couldn't blame him; I kind of wanted to go home myself.

"We just need to go on down the river and get out of their section. I don't think they'll follow us once we leave," James Ernest tried assuring Henry. I wasn't very assured and I knew by looking at Junior shaking that he wasn't assured either.

"I was ready to jump on them," Purty announced.

"You should have done it naked. That would have scared them away," I said. It made everyone laugh, though we were scared to death. The beautiful day and the fun of canoeing and going down the rapids were distant memories as we considered what could have happened and what might still happen. The sky was still as blue as before and the river was green and pretty as before, but the day had turned ugly as though dark clouds had rolled in and a storm was brewing.

We quickly gathered our stuff and got back into the canoes and headed downriver. We knew that was the same way the two men went back, but we had no choice but to go that way. We couldn't paddle upstream and our tents and supplies were waiting for us farther downriver. I kept my eyes open as we traveled the river looking for a sign of the blue boat, or the two men. We came to a series of smaller rapids that two of the canoes had no trouble getting through. Purty and Tucky turned over in all of them. I could see the frustration and growing aggravation on Tucky's face.

We all got hot in the warm afternoon sun, but we weren't about to stop and go swimming with the chance of Henry Junior being seen in the river. I couldn't believe that the two idiots thought a black boy would contaminate the river by swimming in it. I guessed a fool is just a fool. I became angrier as I paddled and thought about the threat. All we wanted to do was have fun.

Purty and Tucky were the only ones getting to cool off from the heat as they capsized every so often.

We went under the shade of a big tree whose limbs stretched halfway across the river. A rope was hanging from the biggest limb. The end of the rope was frayed. There was no noose there now. I wondered if someone had cut the noose off the end of the rope. We just stared at it as we passed under.

"I feel really stupid," Randy said as we floated, waiting for Purty and Tucky to catch up.

"How come?" I asked.

"Because those two men reminded me of myself a couple of years ago. I was so dumb," Randy explained.

"But you've changed," I said. I wasn't real sure what else to say.

"It's hard for me to believe I felt the same way that they do. I'm ashamed of myself," Randy said as a tear fell down his face.

Randy had felt the same way as his dad when the Washington family moved into the community. They wanted to run the black family out of the county. Randy had even quit the Wolf Pack because the rest of us disagreed with him, even Purty.

"Uncle Morton told me something once. He said that it took a real man to admit he's wrong and change his actions. You did that. I admire you and your dad for changing the way you did."

"But there are still times I have bad thoughts about blacks," Randy said.

"I think we all have thoughts we're ashamed of. The difference is that we're ashamed of them. It would be different if we weren't embarrassed by them. You're a good guy, Randy."

"Thanks, Timmy. You're a good friend."

Purty and Tucky finally caught up and paddled past us. Purty turned around to say, "I can't believe you guys are so slo…"

We never heard the end of the word because Purty's weight shift tipped the canoe over again. We laughed and splashed him with our paddles as we went by him. I heard Purty tell Tucky, "You are the worst steerer in the world." I knew Tucky probably wanted to string Purty up in the tree.

Randy and I were paddling next to James Ernest and Junior when we came upon an old fisherman in a lawn chair along the river. We stopped paddling and sat in the middle of the river as James Ernest asked the old man how far our campground was. James Ernest explained where we were headed and the old man said, "Y'all are probably two miles from there. Y'all will be there way before dark. There's a rope up ahead on the right that's fun to jump from the bank—a deep hole there. You could spend some time there."

"You catching anything?" Henry asked him.

The old man lifted a stringer out of the water filled with catfish.

"Wow," Henry said.

"I thought you guys were Injuns when I first caught glance of you," he said and laughed.

"Naw, we just like the style," Purty told him just after they arrived.

"You boys be careful on the river. There are a couple of men that aren't too thrilled with coloreds being on the river, or anywhere else for that matter. You be careful," the fisherman warned us.

"I think we've already met them," James Ernest told him. "They threatened us earlier. Where do they live?"

"You passed their house on the right just before the last rapids. We call them the Bottom Brothers."

"Is Bottom their last name?" Randy asked.

"No. It's actually Hatchet, Rupert, and Luther. We just call them the Bottom Brothers because God had to dig to the bottom of the human race barrel to find them two. They're meaner than two snakes. They won't bring their boat down here past those last rapids. They stay between the rapids. They think they own it."

"We didn't see the boat when we passed the house," I said.

"They pull it up to the house and hide it. They's afraid people will steal it," he told us and laughed. "The two biggest cheats and crooks on this earth, 'fraid someone will do sumthing to their crummy boat. But they will watch this part of the river from the banks and roads at times, especially if they know there is a colored boy on it, I reckon."

"Thanks, mister," I said as we left him.

"Have fun," he said and waved back.

As we moved the canoes away from the fisherman, I looked over my shoulder and asked him one last question, "That tree back there with the rope hanging from it, have they ever hung a person from that tree?"

"Yep, many years back though. It's mainly there to scare folks now," the old fisherman answered. "But that colored boy is the first black I've seen on this stretch of river since then."

I nodded my head up and down; my knees shook against the sides of the canoe.

We paddled without talking for the next few minutes. I knew that everybody was pondering the situation we were in. We wanted to have fun and fish and swim and float down the river on our backs, but we couldn't do that and leave Henry sitting in the canoe. That wouldn't be fun, or right. I realized then that we probably shouldn't have asked Henry Junior to come on the trip, but he had just as much right to enjoy the river as I did. I was so mad I took the paddle and smacked it on the water sending a loud echo down the river, much like a beaver slapping his tail on the water.

Randy quietly said from the back of the canoe, "I agree with you."

A little while later we came to the swinging rope on the bank of the river. We all gathered in the center of the river and debated whether to stop and use it.

"What does everyone think?" Randy asked.

"It looks like fun," Purty offered.

"But it can easily be seen from the road," James Ernest pointed out.

"We can't let those Bottom feeders bully us," Purty argued.

"I promised to look after Junior, and I don't want to take the chance," James Ernest stated.

"I'll stay on the shore. I don't have to use the rope. You guys can have fun," Junior said.

"That's a good idea. As long as Junior doesn't get in the water we'll be okay," Purty kept arguing.

"Haven't you been in the water enough for one day? You've got to be waterlogged," Tucky asked him and we all laughed. I looked at Purty's fingers and they were wrinkled from the water.

"It does look like fun. And that's the reason we came on this trip," Randy suddenly said, and then added, "We haven't hardly seen any vehicles on the road. We can take turns listening for cars, and if we hear one we'll make sure Junior is on the bank."

"That sounds okay. I don't want us not to have fun 'cause of me," Henry said.

I could tell that James Ernest was totally against it, but I was sure he didn't want Henry to feel guilty about keeping the Wolf Pack from having fun, so he decided to agree to the plan. Purty jumped out of the canoe and headed for the rope as soon as he knew the plan was agreed to.

"You could have helped me paddle the boat to the shore, you goofball," Tucky yelled.

"Just leave it there," Purty yelled back.

I guessed Purty really didn't understand the principle of a current in a river and that a canoe would float away by itself. Either that or he didn't care or didn't think. The rest of us paddled to the bank and tied the canoes off to trees so they wouldn't float away.

Purty was already on the bank and he grabbed the rope and backed up to get a running start. He ran and jumped from the bank and swung out and over the water. The strange thing was that he didn't let go of the rope. Instead, he slid down the rope a few feet and held on and swung back toward the bank until he slammed into the muddy bank. He then let go and slid down the bank and into the water. I laughed so hard I thought I might pass out.

James Ernest began walking toward the road. He called back, "I'll take the first watch."

I grabbed the rope next and backed up as far as I could. I then ran for the river, grabbing the rope as high as I could before I made the riverbank and I swung far out over the river and I let go. I flew through the air and then splashed down into the water. Boy, it was fun! The rope swung back to Henry Junior who grabbed it and did it exactly like I did. Soon, he was splashing into the water beside me.

"Who's next?" I yelled.

"I'll go!" Purty screamed out.

"You had your turn. Wait until everyone gets theirs," Randy directed.

"But I did it wrong. I didn't know I was supposed to let go of the rope," Purty told us. We all laughed.

Tucky took hold of the rope as he said to Purty, "You are the strangest boy I've ever known. You are the strangest of the strange."

When Tucky let go of the rope, he did a flip in the air before landing in the water. We all began clapping and yelling our approval of this flying acrobat. Randy was next and just jumped like Junior and I did. Purty was now attempting his second try. He went as far back as he could and began running. He did manage to let go, but he tried to do a flip like Tucky. He only managed to get a quarter of a turn before he slammed into the water on his belly, doing a giant belly flopper.

I now had tears flowing down my cheeks as I laughed at Purty's stupidity. James Ernest yelled out, "I hear a car coming!" Junior began swimming toward the bank as fast as he could. Before he could scramble up the riverbank, the car passed by. It didn't look like the Bottom Brothers. We continued taking turns jumping from the rope. Tucky amazed us with the tricks he did off the rope. Purty continued to amaze us with how many different ways you could jump from a rope the wrong way. He lost his grip once as he started his jump and just tumbled off the bank and into the water. Coty roamed the banks searching for anything that moved.

Randy went to the road to relieve James Ernest who came and began soaring through the air and out into the river. Henry finally said he was tired and told us that he was done and that Randy could come back. We ended up spending around two hours jumping off that bank having a blast. The sun was getting lower in the sky and we decided we had better head downriver to our campground. We had planned to eat fish every night for dinner and we needed enough time to catch the fish once we arrived at the tents.

Just as we were all finally in our canoes, after Purty tipped their canoe again, a rusty pickup stopped beside the road and we saw the Bottom Brothers jump out and run up to the riverbank.

"You boys come back here! Y'all hear!" one of them yelled.

We kept paddling. James Ernest and Henry were out in front and digging deep with their paddles. I looked back to see one of the brothers lift a rifle up and fire a shot toward Henry. I saw the bullet enter the water two feet from the canoe. Henry dove to the middle of the canoe and James Ernest kept paddling faster than anyone I had ever seen paddle. The man didn't fire another shot. He dropped the rifle to his waist and they began laughing and then headed back to their truck.

I thanked God right there and then that we had left before they got to the swinging rope. I wasn't sure if he was firing a warning shot or if he intended to shoot Henry Junior. It scared me so bad that I couldn't paddle without the paddle hitting the side of the canoe due to my hands and arms shaking so badly.

We finally caught up with James Ernest, and Randy asked Henry, "Are you okay?"

Henry had returned to his seat. He looked plumb scared to death. I felt real sorry for him.

"Do you think they'll follow us down the river?" I asked James Ernest.

"Maybe, but I doubt it. He only fired one shot, so I think he was just getting his point across. But I think we'd better move our tents farther down the river and find a place that's not so open to the road. I don't want them coming into our camp tonight."

"That's a good idea. What about calling home this evening? We promised to call home," I said.

"I'll try to sneak to a phone booth while you guys are taking the tents down. We better be quick about it."

Purty and Tucky had caught up with us and James Ernest explained the plan to them as we paddled. Purty complained about being hungry. Tucky told him to shut up.

13

PREACHING TO THE HOGTIED

We made it to the campground around seven. We knew we still had two or two and a half hours of daylight left. James Ernest entered the tent and then left for the nearby store where there was a phone booth.

Purty told him, "Get me some snack cakes and candy bars."

James Ernest ignored him and took off in a flash. We began loading two of the canoes with the tents and supplies. Randy and Tucky decided to not put any of our needed supplies in Purty's canoe. I thought it was a great idea. Why take a chance of his canoe tipping over again and losing our stuff?

We had most of our gear stored in the canoes when we heard the sound of a truck coming down the lane. We became frantic. We didn't have time to get in the canoes and paddle away and there was no good place to hide. We decided to stand our ground. We weren't even positive it was the Bottom Brothers, but we soon found out that it was them. The two men stopped the truck in front of us and they slowly got out of the truck. Both of them had rifles this time.

I took a step backward toward the river in case I would need to jump into the water. Randy stood tall between us and the two men.

The younger man, who we found out later was Rupert, said, "I thought we said to keep the colored boy out of the river." No one said anything.

"We got a report that he was seen in the water," Rupert continued.

"He stunk. I told him to get a bath. We couldn't stand the stink any longer," Randy lied, trying to appease the men.

"Where are you boys going in such a hurry?" Rupert asked.

"Didn't like this lousy campground, moving on downriver," Randy told them.

"I think you're lying to protect this Negro boy," Rupert said, as he walked up to Randy with the rifle pointed at his chest.

"We're going to take him now and teach him a lesson."

Purty began throwing up. Henry Junior was shaking so bad I thought he was going to kneel over. We all looked over at Purty who was on his hands and knees puking like a dog. Coty had gone off into the woods and I wasn't sure where he was. The next thing I heard was the voice of James Ernest.

"You're not taking anyone, anywhere," James Ernest said. I turned to see James Ernest standing behind Luther with a pistol against Luther's back. Where did James Ernest get a gun? Rupert's head whipped around and saw the gun at his brother's back.

"You had better lay that gun down before someone gets hurt," Rupert told him.

James Ernest replied, "You took the words right out of my mouth. Lay both of the rifles down slowly."

"I don't think so," Rupert said just before James Ernest fired a shot right between Rupert's feet. Rupert began dancing.

Rupert quickly laid his rifle at his feet. Luther slowly knelt to place his gun on the ground. Randy hurried over to collect the rifles.

"You boys are going to be sorry you ever saw our faces," Rupert said.

"I was sorry the first time I saw your ugly face," Tucky told him. "Did your mama not have any normal kids that lived?"

Randy found a long rope in the back of the Bottom Brother's truck. James Ernest directed the two men to climb into the bed of the truck. He first tied their hands behind their backs and then he cut the stinky t-shirt off Rupert. The shirt looked like he had wiped motor oil and fish guts on it. James Ernest cut it into two long strips and tied them around each of their heads and into their mouths, gagging the two men. He then cut the rope into smaller pieces and tied the brothers back-to-back and laid them down in the bed of the truck. He then tied their feet together so they couldn't get up. He tied a rope from their feet to each corner of the tailgate and from their necks to each corner behind the cab. They were then secure in the middle of the pickup bed. They looked like two sardines in a can. They weren't going anywhere until someone found them.

I was hoping it would be a mountain lion or a bear that found them. Giant buzzards were my next choice.

Before we left, James Ernest told them, "We now have two rifles and a pistol and we do know how to use them. I suggest when you get untied that you go back to your pitiful lives and forget about us. If you guys don't mention this, we won't either. Secondly, I pray that you guys ask forgiveness for your sins and turn to Jesus. It's not too late for you to become a child of God." Not only did James Ernest hogtie the two men, but he preached to them after doing it. I felt he should have sung *Amazing Grace* to them, but I was in a hurry to get away just in case they had any friends who were out looking for them, which I strongly doubted.

We jumped into the water and climbed into our canoes. I yelled for Coty and he came running.

Henry Junior yelled out, "Hey, I'm in the water and it ain't turning black."

We laughed as we headed down the river. It was nearing dark. We happened to pick three days for our trip that was in the dark moon. We would have no light except for the stars above us. Flashlights and a fire would have to give us light.

My adrenaline was sky high. I had questions, but James Ernest was moving fast in the water. Where did he get the gun? How did he sneak up on the two men? Although I knew if anyone could do it, it was James Ernest. He could sneak up on anything.

I knew that James Ernest was looking for a new place to camp for the night and that he would let us know when he found it. I found it hard to breathe normally; my heart was beating fast from the excitement and scary moments we had just had. We were now paddling hard in our getaway. I couldn't imagine how fast Henry Junior's heart was beating.

In the darkest part of my soul, I wanted James Ernest to kill the two men, to do the world a favor and get rid of the two scabs on humanity. But in my heart I knew he had done the right thing. He could have called the police, but then it would have been our word against theirs. So he embarrassed them, warned them, preached to them, and left them in a place where someone would find them. Hopefully we wouldn't see Rupert and Luther, the Bottom Brothers, ever again.

James Ernest slowed and let everyone catch up. We held onto each other's canoes as we floated in the middle of the river.

James Ernest spoke first. "According to the map, the river leaves the road soon. No one will be able to see us from the road then. I'll be looking for a spot on the opposite side of the river for us to camp. Maybe, that way, they can't walk from the road to find us. I'm not sure if we'll have time to catch fish for dinner. Any suggestions?" James Ernest asked.

"I could fish as we canoe, except I don't have any bait with me," I said. We knew we couldn't keep worms alive in the hot sun, so we had planned to find night crawlers, or dig worms, or catch crawdads.

"Purty and I will go get dinner. We'll meet you at the campsite," Tucky said. Before we could voice our objection, he let go of our canoe and began paddling toward the roadside riverbank.

I looked at James Ernest, whose face was already turning green with the thought of what delicious critter Tucky would return with.

"Let's hurry and find that campground. Maybe there'll still be time for me to catch some fish," I told the guys. The four of us began paddling faster than we had when we were trying to get away from the Bottom Brothers. This seemed like more of a life-or-death situation.

Within twenty minutes, James Ernest spotted an open area along the left bank with easy access from our canoes. We unloaded the canoes first and James Ernest put up the two tents end-to-end like we had done before. Randy began making a fire pit with stones he and Junior carried up from the river. They told me to find some bait and start fishing. I dug a few worms with a small folding shovel that James Ernest had brought. It was near dark before Coty followed me to the riverbank to start fishing. He laid there by my side watching me cast into the rolling water. He seemed to be tuckered out.

I didn't really like the looks of the spot I was at to catch fish. There was no cover for the fish and I figured about all I would be able to catch there was catfish, so I didn't use a floater and let the worm drift along the river bottom. I was right in that it wasn't a good spot. I didn't get a bite over the next half hour.

I was worried about Purty and Tucky. They still hadn't arrived at the campsite. I knew they couldn't have passed us by. James Ernest called out for me and I called back. He came over and plopped down by my side.

"Any luck?" he asked.

"It might be a good campsite, but it stinks as a fishing hole," I told him.

"Sorry."

"I got a feeling we're all going to be the ones who are sorry," I warned. "No telling what Tucky will return with for us to eat."

"I'm not very hungry anyway," James Ernest lied. I knew I was starving after all the hard work we had done and the long day without much to eat. It seemed as though the day was seventy-two hours long.

"I'm as hungry as I've ever been," I said.

"Me too, I'm just trying to convince my body it doesn't need any food tonight. We'll be able to fish as we canoe tomorrow. We'll have a mess of fish for lunch and supper tomorrow," James Ernest said.

Just as he finished his sentence, we heard laughter coming from upriver. I knew it sounded like Purty laughing about something. When they got close enough, I yelled out, "Over here."

It was almost completely dark by then. James Ernest turned on a flashlight so the guys could see where to head the canoe. Just before hitting ground, Purty decided to reach behind him for something and the canoe tipped over. The water exploded with arms and legs trying to get to the surface.

"Where did it go?" Tucky yelled out.

"What?" I yelled back.

"Our dinner," he shouted back.

James Ernest shined the light a few feet down river and saw something floating slowly in the current. It looked like some woman's drowned ugly wig. Tucky was off in a flash after it. Tucky finally grabbed hold of it and made his way back to the bank, where he climbed out holding the varmint by its tail.

"What in the world?" I almost screamed.

"It's a big ol' possum," Purty proudly said. "Isn't it purty?"

It was the furthest thing from purty that I had ever seen. In fact, it was ugly, gross, disgusting, foul, rank, and stinking. I wondered how long it had been dead. I wondered if it had tire tread marks across its back. Coty slinked over to it and smelled it and then ran to the tents.

"We can cut it up and cook strips of meat over the fire or cut it up into chunks and make a soup," Tucky said as he pulled his big knife from his pocket. I looked over at James Ernest. He was standing there with the flashlight pointed toward the dead animal. I knew that he wanted to throw up, but he probably didn't have anything in him to do it. "You guys can decide which way to cook it. We could do both. This one is a big'un. Don't want to waste nothing."

We were walking toward the camp when we heard Tucky say, "Have you guys ever tried Possum liver? It's gooood! Just wait."

Purty stayed with Tucky to hold the flashlight so Tucky could butcher the possum and cut it up for our meal. My legs felt like Jell-O as I walked to the fire pit. We didn't need the fire for heat, but we did need it for cooking food and some light. Randy had brought a lantern and had got it lit and placed it near the pit. We had brought a wire grate to place over the fire so we could cook our fish, which we didn't have. Instead, Tucky would be using it to cook a possum. Oh, boy!

"Where's the fish?" Henry asked.

"No luck," I told him and Randy. I could tell they were as disappointed as I was.

"Did Purty and Tucky bring anything back for dinner?" Henry asked.

"Yep, they're cleaning it now," James Ernest said.

"What did they find?" Randy ventured.

"A dead possum they found on the road," I answered. I knew the words wouldn't come out of James Ernest's mouth.

"Possum meat ain't the worst thing in the world," Henry Junior exclaimed.

"You've eaten possum before?" I said surprisingly.

"Yeah, when there wasn't much else to eat," Henry told us.

I decided not to complain any longer about the possum. I guessed people ate whatever they had to stay alive. Who was I to judge?

"We need to heat a pot of water," I finally said. I took the pot and a flashlight and headed for the river. I dipped the pot into the water upriver from where they were skinning the possum and carried it back to the fire.

While the water heated, James Ernest and Randy were able to drag the canoes out of the water and hide them. We didn't want to take the chance of having our canoes seen or stolen by someone during the night.

The four of us were sitting near the fire on logs Randy had found, when Purty and Tucky arrived with the meat.

"Well, how do you guys want the meat cooked?" Tucky asked.

We decided to go half and half. He laid strips of meat on the grate and let it brown over the open fire. The rest he cut up into bite-sized chunks and dropped them into the boiling water. We had small containers of salt and pepper. Tucky seasoned the water with some of each. We also had a container of flour we brought to fry the fish. Tucky told us that he would add some of the flour into the pot to thicken it once the water cooked down and the meat was tender. I wondered if possum meat ever got tender.

He said the meat laid across the grate would probably end up being like jerky. I thought, *Yum yum, possum jerky!*

"While we're waiting for the upcoming possum meal, what do you think the Bottom Brothers are doing right now?"

I asked. I figured *upcoming* was the right word to describe the meal that awaited us.

"I think they're still in the back of the pickup," Junior said. This was the first time that we had a chance to discuss what happened. He then added, "That was pretty great what you did."

"Where did you get the gun?" I asked.

"I bought it with some of the money we got from the coins we found," James Ernest answered. "I grabbed it out of the tent before I went to place the call. I was worried I might need it," he explained.

"Boy, did we," Henry said and smiled.

"I think they got loose and they're out here looking for us. They want revenge," Purty said in a ghostly voice.

"Maybe they did realize their wrongs and asked God to forgive them," I suggested.

"I doubt that. I think they're back at their shack thinking how they hope they never see the Wolf Pack again," Tucky said. And we all began whooping and hollering in agreement.

"Forever the Pack!" I yelled out over the roar of excitement. Everyone began yelling together, "Forever the Pack! Forever the Pack!"

Coty began howling at the moonless sky. We all joined in. This excited Coty even more, and he started jumping around in circles and barking. We all were laughing uncontrollably.

I loved the Wolf Pack. I would do anything for any of the members and even Junior, who wasn't a member yet. As we settled back onto our logs around the fire, I looked into each of their faces. We had seen the best and worst of each guy and still we loved each other. Yes, it was love. I would probably not say that word to them except for maybe James Ernest, but I knew I loved each of them.

That was what the Wolf Pack was all about. Looking out for each other, sharing adventures, correcting the wrongs we each had, easing the heartaches we each endured. We were brothers of life, sons of the outdoors, and kindred spirits of Mother Nature. We all wanted to matter to each other and share in something more than just our own life.

The boyish smile of Purty made me want to smile. The goodness and manhood of James Ernest made me want to be better and grow up to be like him. He showed me God. The strength of Randy and the willingness to change gave me strength I needed to face things.

Tucky's ability to go with the flow and make something good out of nothing made me realize I could be anything I wanted to be. Coty filled my life with unconditional love—a great lesson to be learned. The Wolf Pack made me complete, made me a whole person. I would be forever grateful to each one of them my entire life.

Tucky was turning the strips of possum over on the grate. The topside was now brown and hardened looking. He left the area for a few minutes and came back with some greens in his hand. He cut them up and placed them into the pot.

"What was that?" Junior asked.

"Wild onions. They'll make it a little better."

Tucky sat back down and turned toward me and said, "So my sister Rock is your new girlfriend now?"

"Wait! What! This is news to me," Purty shouted.

"They were holding hands at his birthday party. And I saw her kiss him," Henry Junior told him and smiled real big.

"You had a birthday party? We weren't invited. I thought we were best friends," Purty went on.

"You were at Rhonda's party, and I just had a small party. You couldn't be at both and I knew which one you would choose," I told him.

"Rhonda's," Purty quickly said.

"Yeah, I know, best friend," I teased.

"She has prettier stuff than you," Purty explained.

"What prettier stuff?" Henry Junior asked.

I waited to see how Purty would answer. Finally Purty was smart enough to ask, "Is the soup about ready?"

The fire was poppin' from the possum grease falling into it.

14

WHAT'S IN THE SOUP?

Once the soup cooked down, Tucky added some flour to thicken it. He checked the strips of meat and announced that they were done. They were less than half the size they were when he placed them on the grate.

"How do you know that the meat didn't go bad before you found it?" I asked.

Tucky didn't even flinch before answering. "There weren't many insects on it. If it had been there very long, the bugs and birds would have gotten to it. Also, it wasn't bloated."

"What does that mean?" Henry asked.

"If a dead possum is dead in the sun too long, the stomach will swell up like a pregnant lady. You never want to eat a possum with a belly 'bout to burst. Haven't you guys ever gone possum poppin'?"

"Possum poppin'?" Purty questioned.

"Dad takes us for rides in the truck looking for possums to pop. If you see a possum on the side of the road all bloated up, you drive over it fast with your tire and the possum will pop real loud, like a big balloon. It's fun. I can't believe you guys have never done it. 'Bout as much fun as a person can have," Tucky told us.

Made me hungry just thinking about it. I wondered what all I'd missed in my short life and how much more there was to learn. I looked at the strips of meat and doubted if I could actually put it in my mouth. I knew that people ate possums. I knew that folks ate skunks and raccoons and groundhogs, but that didn't mean that I did.

Randy took a fork and shoved it into a piece of the possum. He blew on it to cool it. He looked at it from all sides and edges. He lifted it toward his mouth. He lowered it and blew on it again. Purty grabbed a fork and pierced a strip and shoved it into his giant pie hole and chewed. Possum grease eased out of the corners of his mouth. He chewed, and chewed, and chewed, and chewed. I waited for him to either swallow it or spit it out. He chewed some more. All eyes were on him. Randy had found another reason to delay taking a bite.

I reached for a strip, blew on it, and gave it to Coty. He dropped to the ground and chewed on it.

Finally, Purty swallowed the possum strip and announced, "It tastes like chicken."

"Really?" Henry asked.

"No, of course not. It don't compare to anything else I've had except maybe Mom's potato waffles."

We all began laughing. Randy took a bite of his possum and began to chew on it. James Ernest decided to try it. Henry Junior stared at it.

"Why aren't you eating any of it, Tucky?" Purty asked as he grabbed another strip.

"I like the soup better. I'm gonna grab my cup and get some," Tucky answered as he looked for his cup.

Suddenly, we heard noise coming from the trees to the east of the fire pit. James Ernest pulled his pistol from his waistband and stood, staring in the direction we heard the noise. Coty barked at the sound. We all froze in our spots.

"Hello, hello," a voice came from the trees. "We come in peace, don't shoot."

I knew it wasn't the Bottom Brothers. The voice belonged to an older man. Randy stood and lifted the lantern above his head to shine light on the incoming strangers. There were two shapes coming toward us. I soon saw that it was an old man and a woman. They were holding hands and smiling as they neared the fire. The man held a shotgun pointed toward the ground in his other hand. They seemed harmless. I was relieved.

As he neared us, he announced, "I'm Clifford, Clifford Brown, and this lovely woman is my wife, Margaret Ann. We live up on the ridge, over yonder." He pointed straight away from the river.

James Ernest had lowered his gun and proceeded to introduce each of us to the Browns. Each of us stood and shook hands with Cliff and his wife.

"Please have a seat. What brings you out here in the middle of the night?" James Ernest asked them. James Ernest scooted over next to me and gave them his log.

"I saw the firelight and wondered who would be out here on this dark night. I told Margie I was going to investigate and she wouldn't let me come without her. So, here we are," Clifford Brown told us.

"We're from Morgan County and we're on a canoe trip down the Red River," Randy explained.

"No adults with you? Please don't take offense," the kind woman said.

Purty decided to tell them that we were the Wolf Pack and that this was our summer adventure and just about everything else he thought they might want to know. They nodded their heads politely. I was sure they were wishing they hadn't left their house.

"What are you boys eating this evening?" Cliff asked as Tucky was filling his cup with the possum soup.

I didn't want to answer. After a moment's silence Tucky said, "I made Possum soup and jerky this evening. I had a possum liver, but I ate it."

"I didn't see you cook the liver. When did you cook the liver?" I needed to know, but Tucky said the thing I didn't want to hear.

"I ate it raw. It's better like that. I should have saved you guys some." We all quickly said it was okay.

"It's Rock's favorite treat, raw possum liver." I knew then and there that I needed a new girlfriend, or my old one back.

"We have possum maybe once a week. Great in a stew with sweet potatoes," Margaret told us.

"Would you like some?" Tucky asked. Purty grabbed his cup and began filling it. I decided to pass on the soup also.

"No, thank you. We had supper a bit ago. You boys are mighty kind."

Clifford began, "From time to time we have trouble from a couple of brothers up the river. We wanted to make sure they weren't down here starting trouble again."

"You talking about the Hatchet Brothers?" I asked.

"Yes, do you guys know them?" Mr. Brown asked.

"We had a couple of run-ins with them today," Randy said.

"They are always stealing stuff from everyone in the area, but we haven't been able to prove it. They think they own this river and everything along it," Cliff said, his voice getting louder as he talked.

"I think they may be tied up for a while," Purty said as he placed a spoonful of possum meat in his mouth.

I shot him a look, but he was concentrating on his so-called food.

"They probably weren't real thrilled with Junior here being on their river," Mr. Brown stated.

"No, sir, they weren't," James Ernest answered.

"You boys need to stay clear of them, best you can," Margaret Ann told us in a grandmotherly way.

"We plan to. That is one reason we camped over here away from the road," Randy told her.

"Good thinkin'," she agreed.

They sat and talked to us for nearly an hour. He told us there would be good fishing on down the river, told us about a couple that would help us if we needed anything, told us about another good campground away from everyone.

As they were leaving, Mrs. Brown said, "If you boys need anything in the morning, just mosey on up to the house. Happy to have you."

I thought gravy and biscuits with sausage would be nice but kept my mouth closed. I figured feeding six hungry boys might be a bit of an imposition. We thanked them for all the info and for coming to visit. They quietly left into the darkness of the woods. I pondered who would arrive from the darkness next. I was tired. I saw Purty's head nodding as he tried to stay awake. We had traveled from Morgan County after getting up early; we canoed around twelve to fifteen miles, set up camp twice, and had the run-in with the Bottom Brothers. It had been a long day. I was bushed and hungry. I decided to go to the tent and get some needed sleep. Coty stayed near the possum strips.

I relieved myself on a tree at the edge of the woods and told everyone good night. Purty laughed at me and said something about me needing my beauty sleep. I didn't care what kind of sleep it was. Junior said he was ready for sleep also and followed me.

He placed his sleeping bag in my tent beside me and we scooted into our beds. I was almost asleep when Junior asked, "Are you asleep?"

"Not yet, almost. What's up?" I said.

"I thought I was going to die today," Junior said.

"It was scary," I said.

"I don't much understand why people hate me and my family," Henry Junior said. I could hear him sniffle. He was crying there in the dark.

"I don't either," I said.

"But we done nothin' to anyone," Junior continued.

"Uncle Morton told me once that people are scared of things they don't know anything about. Some white people have never been around coloreds."

"You never been either, but you weren't mean to us. You were nice," Junior reasoned.

"I was scared the first day I met you guys, but Mom had taught me that y'all were just people like we'uns," I told him. Then I added as Junior thought about what I had said, "Maybe no one ever taught them like my mom did me."

"Are people going to want to kill me my entire life? Are they going to hate me?"

I wasn't sure what to say. How did I know? I thought about it for a moment and then answered, "I don't think so. Things are better than they used to be, and I think things will get better all the time. Randy and his dad wanted to run your family out of the county, now they don't and they like you. I think we all have to make an effort to get to know each other."

A minute later Henry asked me, "If I died today, would I gone to heaven? It would make me feel better if I knew they let black boys in heaven."

"I think so. I heard Pastor White say one Sunday that we are all equal in God's eyes. I think heaven is for everyone who wants to go."

"I want to go. Is that all you need to do is want to go?"

"I'm not sure. I think there's more to it than that, but I think that's a big part. There's something about being 'washed in the blood.' I'm not even sure if I'm going to heaven."

"Don't you want to be sure?" Henry Junior asked me.

"I guess I do," I said as I thought about it.

We both laid in the darkness for a couple of minutes before Henry said, "I thought the Bottom Brothers were going to wash me in blood today."

I laid there and wondered what it would be like to have been born black. I was sure Junior had wondered how different his life would be had he been born white. A couple of minutes later we both were asleep.

TUESDAY, JULY 31

I woke up when the roosters crowed. I figured it was Mr. Brown's roosters. A few minutes later I heard a noise outside the tents. I could tell it was daylight without unzipping the tent.

"Boys. Boys." I heard someone whispering, trying not to startle us. I looked over to notice that James Ernest's sleeping bag was empty. Coty was gone also. I squirmed out of my bag and unzipped the end of the tent and looked out.

There was Mr. Brown holding a plate of what looked like sandwiches. I quickly rolled out of the tent and stood to greet him.

"Good morning, Mr. Brown."

"It is a good morning. I thought maybe you guys could use some BLT's this morning. Mrs. Brown thought you might be tired of possum."

Junior quickly rolled out of the tent with a big smile on his face. "Is one of them for me?"

"Sure is." Mr. Brown laughed as he answered Junior. Junior and I took one of the sandwiches from the tray that Mr. Brown held. I took a big bite. Nothing had ever tasted any better, except maybe Mamaw's cherry dumplings.

"Mrs. Brown insisted on getting up early and fixing you boys some grub before you took off this morning. Sorry I woke you. Wanted to make sure I caught you before you left."

"We sure appreciate it. That was mighty nice of her."

"I smell bacon," I heard Purty say inside his tent. The next thing I knew Purty came rolling out of his tent completely naked. He stood up and said, "Did someone make bacon?"

Junior began laughing and almost gagged on his first bite of the sandwich.

"Put some clothes on, Purty. We have a guest this morning," I told him.

"What's the big deal?"

"Put on some clothes. No one wants to see that."

Purty bent over and crawled back into the tent. I was certain that no one wanted to see that.

Mr. Brown began laughing. "He likes to go around naked," I explained.

"We don't like it so much," Henry Junior told Mr. Brown.

"I can see why," Mr. Brown said.

"You haven't seen James Ernest have you?" I asked Mr. Brown.

"No. Why? Is he gone?"

"He wasn't in the tent when I woke up," I said. "It's nothing he doesn't do all the time."

"You boys are a strange bunch, but we like you," Mr. Brown said, and smiled.

All three of the members of the Wolf Pack rolled out of the other tent and said good morning to Mr. Brown. Purty had his clothes on. Mr. Brown passed out sandwiches to each of them.

"I'll eat the one left over if no one wants it," Purty offered.

"We'll save that one for James Ernest, you glutton," Randy said.

I heard barking and then saw Coty come bouncing out of the woods, followed by James Ernest.

"Where have you been?" Purty asked with his mouth full. Mr. Brown presented the sandwich to James Ernest. I noticed the pistol in James Ernest's waistband. Mr. Brown then reached into his pocket and brought out a bag with bacon strips in it for Coty. Coty took the strips in his mouth, looked up at Purty, and went in the opposite direction. James Ernest ignored Purty's question.

"Thank you so much, Mr. Brown," Randy offered as Mr. Brown was saying his good-byes.

"You boys be careful and come back some time to see us," he said and then added, as an afterthought, "Here is our phone number in case you need anything. Don't hesitate to call. It doesn't hurt to have a friend nearby."

We agreed, and we all shook his hand and told him to thank Mrs. Brown for us. James Ernest took a seat near the died-out fire pit. I walked over and sat next to him.

"Where did you go?" I asked him.

He looked around to see if anyone else was near. When he saw that everyone was back in their tents he said, "I went back to check on Rupert and Luther. I wanted to make sure they weren't dying in the back of that truck."

"Were they?"

"No. They got loose somehow. The truck was gone."

"You think they'll come looking for us?" I asked.

"Don't know. They may want revenge, or they may decide to not mess with us any longer. Who knows what goes on in minds like theirs?"

"They may want to get their rifles back," I said.

"No. I took their rifles and left them on their front porch."

"Why did you do that?" I questioned. Why would James Ernest give them back their rifles?

"I didn't want them coming after us to get them back."

"But they could shoot us with them," I said in disbelief.

"Not with those rifles, unless they can shoot around corners."

"What?"

"I bent the barrels at ninety degrees."

I began laughing, slapping my legs. "I figured they wouldn't come after us to get the rifles back and they couldn't use them against us either," James Ernest said.

"Are you going to tell the others?" I asked.

"No need to right now."

"Did you get any sleep?"

"No. I'm canoeing with you today. You can steer the canoe and fish. I'll get some sleep."

We went back to the tents and began taking the tent down. The others were either back to sleep or packing their gear. Soon, we had everyone up and getting ready to shove off.

Purty was going to canoe with Randy. Randy said he would smack Purty upside of his head if he kept tipping the canoe over. That left Junior canoeing with Tucky; Tucky was happy to be canoeing with anyone other than Purty. He even asked Junior if he wanted to try taking the back of the canoe. The stretch of river we were canoeing was supposed to be gentle and flat with good fishing. I really looked forward to it. Despite the Bottom Brothers, I was still having the time of my life.

We divided the gear among the three canoes, securing the bags to the crossbars in case we did tip over. Before we shoved off everyone got their fishing poles ready and at arm's length. Junior and I had gone and dug some fishing worms for everyone. We had to use our drinking cups to put the worms in. We figured we could rinse the cups out later. A little worm dirt and scum wouldn't hurt any of us. I had a small container of artificial bait. I hardly ever used them but thought the river might be a good place for the small spinner baits as we drifted. We even found a bunch of crickets under some rotted logs in the woods. We also knew we could catch minnows in the shallows if we needed to.

Mist was rising from the river as we shoved off. The sun was still hidden behind the tall stone cliffs that rose around us. We might not see the sun for a few hours. I was full of excitement as I dug the paddle into the water and steered the canoe down river. I looked over to see a smile spread on Junior's face as he steered his canoe between the far-reaching banks of the Red River. We paddled in almost complete silence except for the gentle drops that flowed off the tips of the wooden paddles when we lifted them from the cool water.

The tall trees and cliffs on both sides of the river made me feel as though I was at the bottom of an envelope being sent downriver to a small Kentucky town. James Ernest pointed to the water's edge and I saw a Great Blue Heron standing in the water fishing for his breakfast. His tall legs moved lazily in the water as he waded along, paying no attention to us.

A dragonfly landed on the lip of the canoe, her wings spread out as though drying in the movement of the canoe. I watched her sit there flickering her wings and saw the rainbow of colors that sparkled in the morning light. I couldn't imagine a more peaceful, magical moment being possible. Before I wanted, the dragonfly flew away, and I drifted the canoe toward Junior's.

Without even saying a word, we grabbed each other's canoe and floated together down the middle of the river. A hawk swooped from its perch high on the stone wall and fell down toward the water. I pointed to it and we watched it soar and then flatten out and fly over our heads to somewhere behind us. My senses were full and open and every twitch or movement I caught and wondered at its magic.

Ahead we could see large rocks rising from the water as though God sprinkled them in the river with His huge hands. I told the other three, "I think it's time for fishing." I let go of the other canoe and we floated away. I cast a worm into the water and watched it fall into the slow current. James Ernest was leaning back in the canoe and I figured he was getting some needed sleep. I saw that Henry and Tucky were hooking worms and getting ready to fish. Coty was lying in the middle of the canoe with his head leaning against one of the packs, asleep. I knew he was tired also. He had been out all night with James Ernest.

I could see Purty and Randy floating around one of the large rocks ahead of us. I tilted the end of my rod up and reeled the worm in a little. I did it over and over until the bait was back to the canoe. I then flipped the worm at the large rock on my right and watched it fall. Two seconds later my line began zipping from my reel. I put my thumb on the brake and jerked the pole up to set the hook. The large smallmouth bass bent the rod into a large horseshoe and the battle was on. The fish rose from the depths of the river and flew into the air trying to shake the hook from his lip.

I heard Henry yell out, "Timmy's got one!"

I looked over to see Tucky and Henry watching me battle the large bass. Randy and Purty swung their canoe around to watch the encounter. The bass pulled our canoe sideways and then the fish came right toward the canoe and went under it. I had to swing the tip of my pole around the back of the canoe hoping the line wouldn't catch on the bottom of the canoe and break.

The bass came up and jumped again just as I got the pole on the left side. James Ernest and Coty were both awoken by this time and they both shouted encouragement. Coty would bark loudest when the bass came out of the water. I wasn't sure Coty wouldn't jump over the side to get it. "Stay, Coty, stay," I yelled. The bass made another leap for freedom and Coty made a leap for the fish, jumping out of the canoe straight for the fish, which had dove to the bottom by the time Coty was in the water. Coty swam and turned his head all around wondering where the fish had disappeared to.

James Ernest called for Coty to come and he helped Coty back into the canoe. I had to lean my body to the right while he leaned to the left to grab hold of Coty. While I was pulling on the pole and leaning, the fish was deciding what to do next. He decided to head for the front of the boat and go under again. I handed the pole to James Ernest and he moved the pole around the front end and handed it back to me. The fish was finally feeling as though it was getting tired. I knew my arms were.

I began reeling the bass in. We didn't have a net with us. I knew I would have to wear the fish out to get it into the canoe. The bass resisted for another few minutes and then gave in to his tiredness. I reached over the side of the canoe and put my thumb in its mouth and lifted the four-and-a-half-pound smallmouth bass into the canoe. We had lunch. *No leftover possum soup* was the first thing that crossed my mind. The guys began clapping and hollering at the same time.

I was hoping this was the first of many big bass we would catch during the day. It wasn't long before Tucky had a fish on his line. I could tell it wasn't nearly as big as the one I had caught, but he had a blast reeling it in. It was nearly a two-pound smallmouth—a nice bass. Junior was excited. I could see him almost bouncing in his seat as he waited for his first fish.

I could hear Randy and Purty fishing. Purty was making the loudest racket I'd ever heard anyone make while fishing. He kept banging his pole against the railing of the canoe. Every time he cast he let the rod go down against the canoe. The only good thing was that Randy had kept him from tipping the canoe over. I had seen Randy many times quickly sway to one side or the other to compensate for Purty's quick movements and weight shifts. Randy's concentration was on keeping the canoe upright.

As we drifted past the tall rocks, I would flip my bait alongside the rocks and wait for the next big bass to grab the worm. James Ernest finally jerked quickly and landed a nice bluegill.

"It's not quite as big as yours, but I'll take it," James Ernest said.

I soon noticed that Junior was also reeling in a fish and he had a big bluegill. Tucky then reeled in one. We had found a bluegill "honey hole." We had floated past the area, so we circled back up river and floated back through again. Each of us caught another big bluegill. Junior and Tucky did the same thing with the same results. Purty and Randy kept drifting downriver without any results.

The morning was beautiful; the surroundings were even more breathtaking. The day was sunny, but it was cooling on the water. The tall walls rose hundreds of feet above us on each side of the river; it was majestic. We were in a gorge. The large rocks stuck out of the water like tall buildings on a city street. Moss clung to the north side of the rocks and tiny plants and flowers grew out of crevices they had found to take root in. I had never seen anything so pretty, except maybe Susie.

And then it hit me. Susie was no longer my girlfriend. For the past two years, that had been the one constant in my life—Susie being my girlfriend. When my dad died, Susie was my girlfriend. When I wasn't sure what our family would do, Susie was still my girlfriend. When danger came my way, I knew always waiting for me was my girlfriend—Susie. Sadness hit me there on the river. Why had I thought of her? I was having one of the best times of my life and then Susie popped into my mind. How did I lose her as my girlfriend? I reeled my line in and just sat there looking up at the giant walls that surrounded us. It suddenly felt as though they were closing in around me.

I knew it would take a while to get over losing Susie as my girlfriend. I had hoped that the trip would take my mind off her. Rock had helped a little, but I couldn't help but think about her every day. I couldn't help but think of the plans we had made. I knew I wasn't the first guy to lose his childhood sweetheart, but that didn't make it feel any better.

We drifted on past the bluegill hole and I steered us around another big boulder in the middle of the river. James Ernest flipped his worm beside it and soon he was battling a large catfish. Before I realized what was happening our canoe was flipped around and the canoe was heading upriver. I knew it was a catfish because of the way the pole bent and it didn't come to the surface. I wondered if he had a giant one on his line like Sam Kendrick caught, whose head was as big as Leo's. All James Ernest could do was plant his feet against the front of the canoe and hold on. Tucky and Junior were whooping and hollering and paddling as fast as they could to follow us upstream.

"It's going to break my line!" James Ernest yelled back to me. I knew that James Ernest used a lot heavier line on his pole than I did. I used an eight-pound test line. I figured his to be at least a twenty-pound test line. I couldn't believe that this fish was any less than fifty pounds the way it was pulling our canoe upriver. Suddenly, the fish got tired of swimming upstream. James Ernest's line went slack and he thought he had lost the giant fish.

Just as abruptly, the line jerked the pole backward and hit James Ernest in the face and whipped the pole toward the back of the canoe and our canoe swung around with such quickness that I thought for sure we would tip over. But somehow we stayed afloat and were heading downstream straight at Tucky and Junior's canoe. Henry steered the boat sideways, trying to get out of the way, but I was unable to swing the boat around them, due to the pull of the fish, and our canoe hit them broadside.

I heard them scream as they capsized and we continued downriver at full speed ahead. We were heading toward Randy and Purty. A big rock was ahead of us. The catfish was going to the left side of the rock when he decided to go to the right. I figured it was the Purty of the Red River fish. Our canoe didn't have enough time to change direction and we slammed into the left side of the boulder and over we went. James Ernest held on for a moment, but then the line tightened against the rock and broke, sending the fish to freedom and sending our fishing gear through the water.

Randy was reaching with his paddle to try and grab my tackle box when Purty yelled out, "So, you guys can't keep your canoes upright. What do you have to say now?" He quickly whipped around in his seat to scold us and they tumbled over into the water. All seven of us were now in the water. Coty was dog paddling toward the shore. The only trouble was, there were no shores. The banks went straight up on both sides of the river and there was nowhere for Coty to get out of the water. I was scared he was going to drown. I took off after him, leaving the gear to collect at a later time.

I could see Coty near the bank searching for a spot to get out of the water. He looked frantic. I was swimming as fast as I could with the bulky life jacket on. I saw Coty's head go under the water.

"I'm coming, Coty! Come here, Coty!" I yelled. I tried to get Coty to swim toward me. He was panicking and I knew he didn't know what to do. We had always been able to get up on the bank when we were at the creek. I could hear him whining as I got closer. I saw his head go beneath the water again. "Keep your head up, Coty!" I screamed.

I could hear the guys behind me screaming instructions I couldn't understand. I wasn't sure they were yelling to me or to Coty. Coty's head appeared again when I was almost fifteen feet from him. I thought I was going to make it to him, and then his head disappeared for good. I swam harder than

I knew I could to the spot I last saw him. I dove underwater, but the life vest kept me from going very far under. I saw Coty struggling under the water, but I couldn't get to him. I popped to the surface and ripped the life vest off and dove under the water again. I grabbed Coty and swam back to the surface. As I treaded, I pushed on his stomach trying to get him to cough up the water he had swallowed, trying to keep my head above the surface. James Ernest arrived just in time and grabbed Coty from my arms. I then was able to keep myself from drowning, but tears were flowing down my face.

James Ernest took hold of Coty's back legs and held his lifeless body upside down and jerked him up and down a couple of times. Water came gushing from his mouth. Coty began whimpering and coughing. Coty was alive and breathing. I quickly wrapped my arms around him and hugged him.

I will never be able to explain how James Ernest treaded water high enough to hold Coty by his legs without his face being in the water. It took inhuman strength or divine intervention to do what he had done. How does someone tread water and at the same time hold a seventy-pound dog up out of the water by his legs? I saw it. I couldn't believe it. Coty was alive. That was all that mattered at that moment.

15

DONE AND CRISPY

Randy had turned our canoe upright and paddled it over to us. I placed Coty in the center. Randy jumped out of the canoe and I took his place. James Ernest then pulled himself over the side and into the front seat. It took us about an hour for all of us to find our poles, fishing gear, cups, and paddles. We had to catch up to a couple of them, which had floated down the river. We still had the fish we had caught. They were on stringers that had been tied to the crossbeams of the canoes and hung over the sides of the canoes.

We lost all of our bait. So we decided to paddle until we could find a spot to build a fire and have lunch and dig more worms. We had plenty of fish for a big lunch but would need to catch more for supper. I also wanted to get Coty off the water and let him dry out next to a fire. He looked worn out and haggard. He wasn't very fond of water to begin with and I felt this episode might make him totally scared of it.

The gorge continued for another hour. The scenery was magnificent, but I was anxious to find a spot. Every rock and overhang we came to I figured had another huge bass hunkered down beside it. Finally, the south side of the river opened up and we found a spot to tie up the canoes and build a fire for lunch. While the rest of the guys searched for wood and started a fire, James Ernest and I cleaned the fish. Papaw had taught me how to fillet bass and bluegill, therefore we didn't have to worry about getting fish bones caught in our throats.

I hated to fillet the big bass. I wanted to have it mounted and hang it in my bedroom. James Ernest assured me that I would catch many larger than it in my life, which made me feel good.

Coty was lying next to me. He didn't want to leave my side and he fell asleep as soon as his head hit the grass. When we were nearly done cleaning the fish we smelled wood burning, and I looked up to see smoke rising. We knew they had started the fire. James Ernest left me in charge of finishing while he went to get the coating ready for the fish fry.

We each hung some of our wet clothes on limbs to dry while James Ernest was cooking the fish. Purty just spread his out on the ground since he was too lazy to find a tree. We had put our sleeping bags in plastic bags so they made it here fairly dry.

"I've got some fish done—enough for a couple of guys." Purty ran toward the fire pit wanting the first batch of fish. He tripped on a rock in his path and went sprawling on his fat face—served him right for being so selfish. James Ernest yelled for Junior to come and get some also. I was willing to wait. My worry over Coty had diminished my appetite, but I knew I needed to eat. It would be a long afternoon and evening before we ate again.

I spotted some briars in a field near where we had stopped. I wanted to check them out. I thought berries would make for a nice dessert. Coty followed me as I walked to the place I saw. Sure enough, there were canes of blackberries shooting up from the ground and they were ripe. I picked a few and ate them, and then I gave a handful to Coty. He loved the sweet berries. I left knowing I would come back again before we left. I needed something to put the berries in.

It wasn't long before James Ernest had more fish ready. It was as tasty as any fish I had ever eaten. James Ernest had cooked the fish so the outside was crispy and the inside was flaky and tender. It was so good, and everyone went on and on about the fish. We ended up having enough where everyone got all they could eat, even Purty. Coty gobbled it down like he was starving. Almost drowning must have given him a big appetite.

I was wondering if I had made a mistake bringing Coty on the canoe trip. I had debated whether to take him or not. I knew he didn't like water much, but he always went on Wolf Pack adventures. Also, he was good protection for us. I was so happy he hadn't drowned, but I wondered how many lives he had left.

As we were sitting on the ground eating, Purty said, "This river is so purty."

"I've never seen anything like it," James Ernest agreed.

"It's purty purty," Tucky said.

"We should do a different river every summer," I suggested.

"We could canoe every mile of river in Kentucky before we die," Purty added.

"I'm not sure if Coty would agree with that. He almost died today," Randy said.

"How long do you think the Wolf Pack will exist?" I asked.

"As long as one of us is alive the Wolf Pack will be alive. Members for life, unless you quit or get kicked out," James Ernest told us. We all agreed.

"Thanks for bringing me on the trip," Junior meekly said.

"We love having you with us"—I thought I spoke for all of us.

"You add a little color to our group," Purty said. We all started throwing rocks at Purty.

I told the guys about the berries and where they were. Tucky, Junior, and Randy took a pan to fill up. Purty was put in charge of drowning the fire and cleaning up the area. James Ernest and I began looking for fishing bait. We dug worms and overturned rocks and logs looking for crickets. When we thought we had enough for the afternoon we went back to the fire pit.

The others had returned with a pan full of blackberries. The guys were pigging out on them. James Ernest and I were lucky to get any at all. After the berries were gone we loaded up the canoes and were off again, floating down the Red River. The sun was hot. None of us had on our life vests. Randy and James Ernest were working on their tans. I kept my shirt on, taking it off and soaking it in the river every so often to keep as cool as possible. The afternoon fishing was slow, so we found other fun things to do.

An hour after returning to the river we found a spot that was great for floating down the river on our backs. There was a swift current with a sandbar that we could walk back upstream. We tied off the canoes, put on our vests, and floated down the current time-and-time again. We splashed each other, dunked each other, and mainly tried to drown each other. Coty searched the sandbar while following us up and down the river. I was happy to see that Coty seemed to be recovering well from almost drowning. We spent almost two hours at the spot and had a tremendous time. We all were worn out and ready to get back into the canoes. The last half hour Purty had just laid in the water along the shore and let the water drift over him, too lazy to walk back up the river.

We all floated downriver holding onto each other's canoes. We laughed, made fun of each other, mainly Purty, and relaxed in the afternoon sun. We seemed to be leaving the gorge and heading into a deep forest area. The river was slower and shadier in this section, which I welcomed. I had loved the tall sandstone walls that lined the river with the large boulders scattered in the water, but this part of the river reminded me more of Devil's Creek or Licking Creek.

Parts of the river ran along country roads, while other sections bent away from the roads and sent us into what felt like the wilderness. I had no idea where we were. I was sure James Ernest could have told me, but I didn't want to know. I wanted to dream that we were exploring a new river that had only been paddled by earlier Indians. In fact, each time we rounded a bend I expected to see Indian warriors coming toward us, or at the least I thought I would see a village of teepees standing in a clearing beside the river.

I was lost in my dream world when a paddle full of water splashed into my face. Tucky had flung his paddle into the water trying to wake me from my fantasy world.

"I asked you a question," KenTucky said as I wiped the water from my face with my hand.

"What do you want?" I asked as the others laughed.

"Who would you want to be canoeing with right now—Susie or Rock?" he asked me again.

Why in the world did he ask me that? Why bring up girls when we were on a great adventure on a river? And there was no good answer to the question. I wasn't even sure what the answer was. Deep in my heart I knew I missed Susie more than I did Rock, but I had known Susie for so much longer. She had been my girlfriend for a long time. I missed her every day. But she had made it clear that she was done with me. I had blown it, big time!

"Rock," I lied, hoping it was the answer Tucky wanted to hear.

"The question that was asked was, who, at home, do you miss the most?" James Ernest cleared up the confusing interruption to my exploration.

"Well, that's not what you asked me," I said to Tucky.

"We figured it had to be one of those two, girl magnet," Tucky said, sending laughter from the canoes down the river.

"I would have answered, Janie," I said.

"Yeah, right," Purty yelled out, making everyone laugh again.

"Who did you guys say?" I asked.

"Purty said Rhonda," Randy answered. "I said Sadie." We all laughed at that.

"I said I missed my little brother, Luck," Tucky told me.

"Let me guess, I bet James Ernest said Raven, and Junior said Samantha," I said.

"You got that right," Randy said.

I decided to do a little fishing. I grabbed my favorite pole and placed a worm on it and cast it into the water near the bank. James Ernest was soon asleep in the front of the canoe.

The other two canoes were moseying on down the river. I noticed Junior started fishing after seeing me. It wasn't long before everyone in the other two canoes had bait in the water. I reeled the bait in and noticed that we were coming to a brush pile in the river. I flipped my line close to it and let the worm fall. I moved the worm a little and then I felt something pull the line. I set the hook and had a fish on the line. It didn't take me long before I reeled in a large crappie.

It was the first crappie we had caught on the trip. I knew from listening to other fishermen that if you found a crappie hole that there were usually a large group of them in the same hole. I paddled the boat back upriver and woke up James Ernest long enough to have him tie the front of the canoe off to a tree limb that hung out over the water. The rear of the canoe wound up perfect, around ten feet from the brush pile. I placed a bobber on my line and then cast another worm near the brush.

It wasn't thirty seconds before I was reeling in my second large crappie. The other two canoes came paddling back upriver to see what I was catching. Tucky and Junior tied their canoe downriver from the brush. Randy said he would go on downriver and see if he could find another brush pile. It wasn't long before all three of us were catching fish. Crappies have small mouths for their size and paper-thin lips. Another of the names they're called is papermouths. You had to be careful not to jerk too hard because you could rip the hook from their thin lips.

Junior was having the time of his life catching the large crappies. I was amazed at how many were around that brush pile. We ended up catching a dozen, enough for supper at the campfire. James Ernest never did get in on the fun. He slept the entire time, after being awake all night checking on the Bottom Brothers.

I had to wake him to untie us from the tree so we could continue down the river. He went back to sleep as I paddled us. We found Purty and Randy capsized in the river shortly after we left the crappie hole. Randy was yelling at Purty about sudden jerky movements. Apparently their fishing didn't go well. Randy was chasing Purty with a paddle in his hand. We helped them reload their stuff and turn the canoe back over.

We continued our trip.

The sun glistened in the waves made from the canoe wake. Birds chirped from the trees that grew on the banks of the river. Dragonflies followed the canoes as we drifted along. But late in the afternoon I noticed banks of clouds coming toward us in the distance. We were going west and heading directly into them. James Ernest woke up in time for me to show him what I thought looked like a storm approaching.

I wasn't wrong. As I was showing him the huge black clouds, we saw lightning inside the billowing white pillows cascading down into the black bottom. Coty's ears had perked up and he was standing in the boat.

"That storm is going to hit us," I said.

"Sure looks like it."

"What should we do?" I asked.

"I'm not sure, but I do know we need to get off the water." James Ernest began yelling at the guys ahead of us. I began paddling faster trying to catch them.

When we caught them we all headed for the shore. The storm was getting closer. The thunder was echoing in my head.

It sounded as though it was right on top of us. We jumped out of the canoes and tied them off to trees and climbed the banks.

"Doesn't lightning hit the tallest things—like these trees we're under?" Tucky complained.

I thought he was right.

"We should find cover in low bushes. Stay as close to the ground as possible. Let's split up and take cover," James Ernest yelled.

We ran away from the trees as we searched for cover. The rain began pelting us. Lightning and thunder was striking all around us. It was deafening. I dove under a yellowish bush with Coty by my side. Junior dove right next to me. We huddled together on the ground. Junior was holding onto Coty with a hug. Coty licked his face as if saying everything would be okay.

"Where is everyone else?" I asked him.

"Don't know. Don't care right now," Henry Junior replied. "Purty was trying to talk guys into climbing a tree with him. I knew I needed to follow someone smarter."

"Thanks," I said, even though I wasn't sure it was a compliment. The bush we were under was smarter than Purty.

Junior was shaking with fright. I knew I wasn't much better. I tried taking his mind off the storm by asking him, "Are you having fun on the trip?"

It was probably a silly question. He had almost been strung up by the Bottom Brothers, and here he was dodging lightning bolts.

"Best time of my life," he said as a *ka-boom!* went off above us.

He hid his head in my chest. We both were lying on the ground staying as low as we possibly could. We stayed that way for the next few minutes when suddenly the clouds seemed to veer to the north and before we knew it they were no longer directly over our heads. We could hear the thunder in the distance as it moved away. Junior and I stood and watched the storm clouds blow away. The sun had returned. We began to walk back toward the river. Tucky came out of hiding and joined us. Soon James Ernest was walking with us.

We yelled out for Purty and Randy.

"Over here, guys," Randy yelled out.

When we got there we saw one of the funniest and scariest sights I had ever seen. Purty was sitting on a rock with smoke coming out of his hair. His hair and eyebrows were singed and burnt. His face was blackened. He then smiled and we could see his white teeth beneath the char.

"That last lightning strike blew him out of that tree," Randy announced. "He tumbled down through the limbs and landed in the tall weeds. I heard him grunting like a pig when I walked by." There were two large trees side by side and lightning had struck the tree next to the one he had climbed. The tree had a large strip of bark blown from its trunk and there was a large hole where the lightning bolt exited the tree. The stripped bark lay at the base of the tree.

"Why in the world did you climb a tree?" I asked dumbfounded.

"He's always thought that since lightning looks for a ground he should be up in a tree away from the ground. I can't convince him otherwise."

"Maybe this will convince him," James Ernest said.

Purty wasn't saying a word. I was beginning to wonder if he could speak.

"Was he struck dumb?" I asked.

"I think the correct question is, was he struck dumber?" Tucky corrected.

I would have laughed if I hadn't been so worried about Purty.

"Are you hungry?" I asked.

"Yeah, I could eat something," Purty said. I knew he was okay.

I could tell Henry Junior was beginning to feel like one of the guys when he said, "Too bad you weren't carrying the fish with you. They would be done and crispy."

We all laughed at that. Junior had a big smile spread across his face.

16

THEY'RE YUCKY

It was late afternoon before we returned to our canoes. We did have to bail out the rainwater in the canoes before we continued our trip downriver. The river was a little darker than it had been, but not muddy from the rain. It hadn't really rained all that much. It had been a quick, sudden outburst and now the sun was back out, scorching everything as it moved west across the sky toward evening.

James Ernest told us that we needed to make up for lost time. We hadn't been canoeing as far as he had expected. He said it was going to be hard for us to make our final destination so we decided not to fish and just paddle. We still watched the beauty around us, but we focused on paddling the canoes. We had enough fish for the evening meal, but I still missed fishing the river. I thought of all the fish we were paddling over.

"I can't believe Purty climbed a tree," I said as I paddled.

"He was lucky. He should be dead," James Ernest stated.

"Nothin' can kill Purty. He's one of those guys that can do anything and not get hurt. Remember our fight with the boys of Blaze? All of us got hurt except him. He jumped up and peed on trees. He jumped from the cliff into the swimming hole without a scratch. Sugarspoon shattered his arm. He shoots at a squirrel and a raccoon falls out of the tree, almost landing on his head. Randy told us he escaped a rattlesnake strike. Pudgy Purty was fast enough to crawl backward so that a rattlesnake missed him. You can't tell me he's not watched over by someone."

Our paddle strokes were in perfect unison as we canoed along in the water. The other two canoes were trying their best to keep up.

"Do you believe in guardian angels?" James Ernest asked me.

"I think so," I said. "Do you?" I knew that James Ernest knew a lot more than I did about the Bible and God. James Ernest had gone forward and had been saved. He even prayed a lot.

"I'm not sure. I like the idea of having a guardian angel, but then why doesn't everyone have one? If that was true, no one would ever get hurt." James Ernest made a good point. Why would God only give certain people guardian angels? "Maybe God blesses some people and not others, like His chosen people."

"Concerning Purty, it could be just dumb luck," I said. We laughed, while agreeing.

"You said you think you believe in guardian angels. Why?" James Ernest asked me.

"Well, remember when the Tattoo Man was chasing me and I led him back to the cave?"

"Yeah."

"I never told you this, but I was standing behind a tree looking for the Tattoo Man when I suddenly heard a loud voice say, 'Duck, Tim.' I ducked just as the Tattoo Man was swinging a large stick at my head. It crashed against the tree and I got away and climbed into the cave."

"Wow."

"I first thought it was you telling me to duck. I had never heard the voice before and I had never heard your voice so that's why I thought it was you. But then later when I had time to think about it I knew that you would have come to help me. You wouldn't have yelled for me to duck and then just left me to battle the Tattoo Man by myself. My only explanation is that it was a guardian angel that told me to duck."

"That's amazing. I think you may have heard the voice of God, Himself," James Ernest said in a shaky voice. He stopped paddling and turned to look at me. I didn't know what to say, or how to act, him telling me I may have heard God's voice. That seemed bigger than a guardian angel looking after me— God watching over me. I was nobody that God should care about. At that moment I realized what Jesus and the Bible and God was all about. It was about the love that God has for each one of us. It was about God sending His one and only Son to die for me. No matter who I was—God loves me and cares about me.

James Ernest then said something that I would remember for the rest of my life—"God saved you from the Tattoo Man for a reason. He has a big plan for you."

I flashed back to what Uncle Morton had told me, "God is testing you for something bigger."

We canoed in silence for the next two hours, my mind racing and my heart pounding in my chest. I wasn't sure if I wanted God to have big plans for me. What if I couldn't do what God wanted me to do? What if it wasn't what I wanted to do?

I was in deep thought when a large splash of water smacked me in the face, waking me from my deep thoughts. I looked over to see Henry Junior with a big smile on his face.

"Gotcha," he said as he and Tucky laughed.

I quickly began trying to splash him back with my paddle, but I was too late as Tucky swung their canoe away from us. It had been a "sneak attack and retreat."

"Run like the cowards you are! I'll get even!" I screamed across the river.

Evening was approaching. The storm had left the air hot and sticky, but it seemed like a cooling front was moving in behind it. As the sun dipped in the sky the air cooled and the few clouds moved slowly across the sky in different white shapes like big marshmallows for our campfire. It was a great evening to be on the river.

"Let's go swimming," I suggested to James Ernest. He agreed.

We yelled our plans over to the other canoes and soon we all had our canoes tied off and we were diving into the river, swimming and floating. The river was fairly deep where we stopped and there were no large rocks that we could see under water, so diving and jumping off the banks was a blast.

I got even with Junior by jumping on him from the bank and dunking him. It felt good being in the water cooling off. Purty tried to wipe the char off his face. He probably was going to need soap to get it off. He was fortunate to be alive. He argued that his plan of climbing the tree was still a good one. He explained that he was just unlucky this time. We argued that he was lucky this time.

We played in the water for nearly an hour before James Ernest reminded us that we needed to continue downriver and find a phone and a campsite. We shoved off and we were back on the adventure. It took us another hour before we found a spot where we could get off the river and call home. We happened to find a grocery store right near the river. We all went inside looking for a snack.

I bought a Clark candy bar and a RC Cola. I also got Coty a few slices of boloney. Everyone was getting something except Junior.

"Why aren't you getting anything?" I asked him.

"I didn't bring any money with me," he said. "I didn't know we would need any."

"What do you want? I've got some extra," I told Junior.

"No, that's okay," he quietly said and walked out of the store.

I knew he liked grape pop and Milky Ways. I added them to my purchase but came up a dime short. Randy gave me a dime. When I went outside James Ernest was hanging up from the phone call and I found Junior down by the canoes. I gave him the pop and candy bar. He took them and thanked me.

"I'll pay you back when I can," he said.

"No need. A gift," I said.

"Thanks."

When James Ernest came back down to the canoes, I asked him, "Who did you talk to?"

"Your Papaw," he said.

"What did he say?" I asked. By then all of the guys were standing around listening.

"I told him we were having fun and everyone was okay. I also told him we were only about halfway. I said we might have to stay another day."

Everyone began talking at the same time. We were filled with excitement and concern at the same time. We all would spend as much time as we could on the trip but would our parents go for us staying an extra day?

"So what did he say to that?" I asked.

"He said everyone was okay, but everyone missed us."

"What did he say about us staying another day?" I said in disgust.

James Ernest smiled and said, "He didn't see a problem. He said he would talk to all the parents and if there was a problem he would pick us up tomorrow; if not, then he would see us on Thursday."

"I'll drink to that," I said as I put the RC Cola to my mouth and took a big gulp. The other guys did the same thing. The RC tasted so good after going two days without anything cold to drink. It made me almost miss home.

The news meant that we were only halfway done with our big adventure. It was great news. I was excited to know we had an extra day on the river. We got into our canoes and headed on down the river to find a campsite.

James Ernest told us the storeowner had told him of a good place not far down the river where we could stop for the night. When Purty got into the canoe he placed his pop bottle between his knees while he picked up his paddle. His knees came apart and his pop spilled onto the bottom of the canoe. He frantically tried to catch the bottle as it rolled under and behind him. His sudden weight transition flipped the canoe over.

Randy was hollering at Purty as we paddled past them. James Ernest told Randy we would see them at camp. I heard Purty tell Randy, "I'm not going anywhere until I buy another pop."

I knew that Randy was about to lose it.

We left them yelling at each other. We had only paddled a few minutes before James Ernest pointed to the campsite he had been told about. It was again on the opposite side of the river away from the road. The river had veered away from the road since we left the store, but we knew it couldn't be far away. Tucky and Junior were beside us as we turned into the bank. We quickly unloaded our gear and began setting up camp. We had at least an hour before the sun set below the western trees. After putting up my tent we began searching for firewood and a few large rocks to make a fire pit. James Ernest and Tucky carried a couple of big logs from the woods for us to sit on around the fire.

We heard Randy and Purty paddling up to the bank. Purty was still going on about how it wasn't his fault the canoe was wobbly and easy to turn over. I worried that I would have to canoe with Purty soon. Randy threw Purty's pack of clothes into the river and said, "It wasn't my fault the river was there."

"Oh, man," Purty said as he splashed down the river to get his pack before it floated away.

Randy came up the bank and entered the campsite with an exasperated smile on his face. He threw the tent down and turned to go back for another load. After helping him put up his tent, I began filleting the crappies. Randy and James Ernest built a fire. Tucky and Junior were doing other camp chores while Purty was laying out his clothes to dry in the evening warmth.

Tucky came down to the creek a little later and began helping me fillet the fish. He was almost as good at it as I was.

"Did you have fun canoeing with Henry today?" I asked him.

"Yeah, he's a good kid. I had never been around colored folks before meeting the Washingtons. In fact, I had never seen one, except on TV. After a while you just kind of forget what color he is."

"I know what you mean," I said.

It didn't take us long before we were done with the fish. We rinsed the fillets off in the river and stacked them on a plate and headed back to the fire pit. James Ernest had everything ready to begin coating and frying the fish. The sun had dipped below the trees and the evening shadows had crept upon our site.

"This is a purty campground," Purty said as he plopped down next to James Ernest with his plate and fork. I knew he was waiting for the first fish coming out of the pan. It wasn't long before all of us were settled around the fire waiting for our evening meal.

James Ernest announced, "I think the first is done. C'mon, Junior, let me fill that plate."

"I was here first," Purty hollered out.

"You can wait a little longer. Junior is the youngest and our guest on this trip," James Ernest told him. No one argued. Purty sighed liked he had lost out on a chicken dinner and was left with Spam. James Ernest filled Junior's plate and gave the rest to Tucky. He quickly began frying the next batch. I had a few slices of meat left for Coty and fed them to him. He then laid down by my feet.

"Two more days on the river," I said to anyone within earshot. "I love being on the river."

"Purty loves being in the river," Tucky said and we all laughed.

"Better than being up a tree in a lightning storm," Junior said between bites.

"You can say that again," Purty said with eyebrows burnt and frizzy. Junior repeated it. "I bring excitement to the Wolf Pack," Purty added.

"Can't argue that," James Ernest said as he flipped the fish over.

"This crappie is really gooood," Junior said, making Purty's mouth water.

As we ate our supper around the fire, Tucky asked Randy, "Do you have a girlfriend?"

"Brenda," Randy answered.

"You mean Susie's sister?" Tucky followed up. Randy nodded yes and Tucky said, "I didn't know that."

"You've liked her for a long time," James Ernest said.

"Almost two years," Randy told us.

"Has she ever let you kiss her?" I asked, remembering the day Brenda hit him for trying to kiss her.

"I don't kiss and tell," Randy said.

"That means no," Purty blurted out.

"It does not," Randy argued.

"So you have kissed her?" Tucky questioned.

"Of course," Randy shot back, and then he asked Tucky, "Who is your girlfriend?"

"Bernice," Purty answered. Tucky, who happened to be sitting next to Purty, shoved Purty and he went sliding off the log and his fish flew into the air. Purty quickly caught it with his plate without it falling to the ground, not that it would have mattered. Coty was disappointed none of it fell to the ground.

"Bernice, the skunk," Junior said. We all began laughing and pointing at Tucky.

"A guy can kiss a girl without her being your girlfriend," Tucky stated.

"Is that right?" I asked, wanting to know the answer.

"Yes. You can kiss as many girls as will let you. It doesn't mean you have to make them your girlfriend," Randy explained.

"Really," I said softly, almost under my breath. I had a lot to learn about girls.

"I've got my eyes on Susie now that she dumped Timmy," Tucky announced. I cringed, but tried not to show it. I couldn't picture Susie ever kissing Tucky after he kissed Bernice in the school outhouse. I didn't even want to picture him kissing Bernice in the wooden poop shack.

Probably the most stable boyfriend and girlfriend in our group were James Ernest and Raven and they wouldn't even say they were a couple. So was young love in our community. Purty loved Rhonda. Rhonda hardly acknowledged Purty. Randy liked Brenda and she acted like she couldn't care less. Tucky was looking for someone, mainly my ex-girlfriend, and I wasn't sure what I was doing. I liked Rock, but I still loved Susie, but she was through with me.

"Do you have a girlfriend?" Tucky asked Henry Junior.

"They're yucky and have girl cooties," Junior answered. We all shook our heads in agreement, despite each of us wanting one of them to love us.

17

Junior and the Crappie

I needed to get away from the talk of girls. I didn't like being reminded of Susie, and I sure didn't want to hear about Tucky wanting Susie as his girlfriend. The night was dark. I was tired. I decided to go to the tent and get some sleep. I watered a tree along with Coty and we unzipped the tent and I slipped into my sleeping bag after ripping off my clothes.

I lay there in the dark thinking about Susie. I knew I wanted her back as my girlfriend. Rock was nice and pretty and I liked her, but she wasn't Susie. I knew Susie. We had made dreams to be together forever. It wasn't supposed to be like this. But I wasn't smart enough to know what I could do to get her to be my girlfriend again. I wanted to look up into the sky and count the stars to help me go to sleep, but it wasn't going to happen inside the tent. I reached for Coty and rubbed his neck. I could tell he liked it.

I was soon asleep.

I walked out of the tent and saw a big bonfire and couples all around it. They had coolers of pop and kids were roasting marshmallows. A few were holding hotdogs over the fire. James Ernest was holding hands with Raven. They smiled as I walked by. Randy was sitting on a log with Brenda in his lap. They were kissing. Rhonda was giving her burnt marshmallow to Purty and they were laughing. I then saw Tucky, Kenny Tuck Key, standing in the shadows of a tree kissing Susie.

She looked happy. She had her arms wrapped around his neck. Her hand was playing with his Mohawk. She looked at me and then looked away. Rock was standing by herself. I started to walk toward her, but when I got within ten feet of her, Daniel Sugarman walked over to her and took her by the hand and they walked away from me. Sadie was even there with Monk Key. I realized I was alone. I wondered how I ended up without a girlfriend. Then out of the cornfield walked a girl with dark hair with a white streak. She walked straight over to me, took my hand, and said, "There's my guy. Let's go to the outhouse again and make out. I'll let you kiss me as many times as you want to."

"No, Bernice. No!" I screamed. "Not in the outhouse. Not anywhere!"

I was still screaming when the sound of the tent flaps being unzipped woke me from the nightmare. James Ernest shined his flashlight in my face and asked, "Is everything okay?"

"No," I answered.

The nightmare had really scared me. I was shaking as if I had the flu, and my teeth were chattering. After everyone was settled into their bags, Tucky, who was beside me, asked, "So, you were dreaming about Bernice."

Purty began moaning and saying, "No, Bernice. No. Don't stop kissing me, Bernice."

All of the guys began cracking up. I hid deep in my sleeping bag. They all then began calling out, "No, Bernice. No, Bernice."

I stuck my head out long enough to say, "I wasn't having a dream. It was a nightmare."

Tucky then said, "Wait 'til I tell Rock you were dreaming of Bernice."

"At least I haven't kissed her in the outhouse, Tucky," I pointed out.

"Hey, that was supposed to stay within the Wolf Pack," Tucky corrected me.

"I'm sorry. I forgot about Henry," I sincerely said.

"It doesn't matter," Henry said, and then he added, "That's old news. Everyone in the school knows about it."

We all laughed.

"Who told?" Tucky said angrily.

"Bernice!" everyone yelled out and then laughed.

I knew after the nightmare that I had to do something. I either had to get Susie back or I had to make Rock my girlfriend and forget Susie. I couldn't end up with Bernice.

After the laughter died down, Junior asked, "You guys think the Bottom Brothers are looking for us?"

I think all of us had wondered the same question. The problem was we had no way of knowing the answer. I then wondered if staying on the river another day was a good idea. It gave them another day to look for us.

"I don't think they'll bother us anymore," James Ernest said, trying to ease Junior's mind. I didn't think it really eased anyone's thoughts. We knew men like that weren't smart enough to give up, especially after being embarrassed like they were.

To take our minds off the Bottom Brothers, I asked, "Who's canoeing with who tomorrow?" "Pick a partner. Just so no one ends up with someone they've already canoed with," Randy said.

"You mean you don't want Purty again?" Tucky asked. We all laughed.

"Can I canoe with you, Timmy?" Junior asked.

"Sure, that will be fun," I said.

"I guess that leaves me with Purty, since you two have already had your day with him," James Ernest said to Randy and Tucky.

"One day in Purty purgatory was enough," Randy said.

Purty came back with, "This is what I think of you guys."

I quickly hid my head deep in the sleeping bag as Purty ripped off a long fart. I knew what was coming.

"Go ahead and get it all out. Maybe getting rid of all that gas will help you stay in your canoe seat better," James Ernest said.

"You would think with all that gas he could float above the water," Tucky reasoned.

Purty farted again, and then again. Even being deep in the sleeping bag couldn't help escape the rotten smell. Coty stood up and began howling. He then walked over to Purty and began growling at him.

"Okay, okay. That was the last one," Purty told him. We laughed as Coty came back and took his spot.

Wednesday, August 1

I woke up sweating in the sleeping bag. I quickly got up and put on my shorts and shirt and unzipped the tent. I then found a spot to use the restroom. When I returned to camp the others were beginning to arise. I grabbed my fishing pole and leftover bait and asked Junior if he wanted to help me catch some fish. He flew out of the tent ready and willing.

I knew I was hungry and figured others would be also. We had eaten all the crappie the night before.

"Anyone else hungry?" I asked.

James Ernest said they would dig more worms and get the fire going for another fish fry. I hoped we would be able to find a few fish this morning. Junior and I headed out. I had seen a good looking spot upriver that we had passed just before we got to camp. I thought we could paddle back upstream and try it. Coty stayed at the campground.

It didn't take long to find the spot. There were rocks on the bottom of the river and a tree that had fallen into the river at the location I had picked. We tied the canoe to the downed tree and I told Junior that we should try bobbers on our line and maybe we would get into another mess of crappies.

It didn't take long before I had a bite. I jerked and brought in a large bluegill. Junior soon caught a crappie—not as big as the ones we had caught the day before, but I figured we would find big ones there. Junior soon had another fish on his line, except this one was fighting for all he was worth. Junior's pole folded nearly in half. The fish tried going downriver, pulling our canoe as far as it would go until the rope tightened. Junior held on tight. The fish then headed for the middle of the river. Junior tugged on it as it pulled the drag.

"Don't let it head under the boat toward the tree. You'll lose it in the tree branches," I yelled.

Suddenly, the fish turned back downstream and jerked the pole right out of Junior's hands. Luckily, somehow the reel handle caught on the edge of the canoe long enough for

Junior to gain hold of it again. I thought for sure Junior had a large catfish on his line. It hadn't jumped like a smallmouth bass. Junior battled the fish for the next ten minutes, keeping it from going under the canoe. It would head to the middle of the creek and then downriver and then back again. The fish finally began to tire and Junior was able to reel it in a little at a time. I thought Junior was going to pass out from tiredness long before the fish was in the boat, but he didn't. We finally got the fish to the side of the canoe where I could grab it. I still wasn't sure what it was even though I was looking at it.

I put my fingers inside its gill and pulled it into the canoe. We both sat there in the canoe with open mouths, our eyes bugging out of our heads. Junior had just caught a crappie that was well over three pounds. I had never seen a crappie anywhere near the size of it.

"That a crappie?" Junior excitedly asked.

"It sure is."

Junior stood up and began jumping up and down in the canoe. I couldn't blame him. If I had caught the fish I might have been doing the same. I placed it on the stringer and Junior finally calmed down. I had no idea if we could catch another fish there or not. Junior's jumping may have scared all the fish away from the spot, or maybe it woke them up. We decided to keep trying.

I knew the three fish we had were enough to feed us breakfast, but I wanted a chance to catch a crappie like the one Junior had gotten. At first we got no other bites. Junior was still beside himself. I had never seen someone so excited. I may have been that way a couple of times, but I couldn't see myself.

I told Junior, "I wonder how close that crappie is to the state record."

"What do you mean?" Junior asked.

"The state keeps records of the largest fish ever caught for each kind of fish," I told him.

"Really? You think it could be a record?" he asked.

"I don't know, and we don't have any way to weigh it," I said.

"I think it weighs 'bout ten pounds," Junior guessed.

I laughed. "No, it's probably between three and four."

"It looks like ten to me," Junior said and smiled.

"I'm sure it will by the time we get home and tell the men about it," I said and grinned. "Too bad we don't have a camera or a scale with us."

I knew we could paddle upriver to the store where we had bought the pop, but it would take way too long and the guys were waiting on us for breakfast. I then got a bite and hauled in another large crappie, meaning almost a pound, not three to four pounds.

We each caught another smaller crappie and we decided to head back to camp. We had enough to feed everyone and Coty.

"I'm sorry we're going to have to eat your big fish," I told Junior.

"I can't have it stuffed anyway. Maybe we can measure it," he said.

"Sure, we can do that," I said.

We quickly untied the canoe from the tree and paddled downriver to camp. I was so excited for Junior to show the guys the giant crappie, just as excited as if I had caught it.

Junior then turned his head around in the boat and said, "Thanks for taking me fishin' with you, Timmy. You're the one who taught me how to fish. You've been the best friend I've ever had."

There I was wishing I had caught the fish. Yes, I was happy Junior caught it, but deep inside, of course, I wanted to be the one to catch it. But when Junior looked at me with his big brown eyes and giant smile, I knew the right person caught the fish. I was ashamed of myself for wishing I had the caught the crappie.

I couldn't believe Junior considered me his best friend. He had other boys in his class that he played with, although they probably never came to his house. I hardly ever went to his house either, not because I didn't want to, but because I was busy. I had chores, I had a girlfriend, and I had the Wolf Pack keeping me busy. I really liked Junior and knew then that I would have to make time to do things with Junior.

It wasn't long before we drifted the canoe against the bank and got out. I tied the canoe off and we went to find the other guys. They had already taken down the tents and James Ernest had a fire going for the fish fry.

"We're back!" I yelled out.

"Did you get any fish?" I heard Tucky say from behind a tree. He was peeing. I then saw the other guys coming out of the woods with the shovel and bait cans. They had been digging worms.

We walked up to them and Junior held up the stringer of fish. The large crappie made the other fish look like minnows.

"Wow! Look at that giant fish. What is it?" Purty asked.

"It's a crappie. The biggest one I've ever seen," I said.

"Where did you catch it, Timmy?" Randy asked.

"I didn't catch it. Junior did," I said. And I added, "Took him fifteen minutes to haul it into the canoe."

The other four guys went on and on about the crappie and how it might be a record. Randy went to his canoe and got out a wooden folding tape measure he had in his tackle box. It measured over seventeen inches long. We finally decided we didn't have any other choice but to eat it. Tucky and I went back down to the river and began cleaning the fish for breakfast. We threw the guts and bones into the river as we filleted the fish. Suddenly, out of nowhere we heard a splash and when we looked up we saw two river otters crunching on the heads of the fish we had thrown into the river. They floated on their backs and held the fish with their front two hands and ate the fish as they watched us.

I thought to myself that they had to be the cutest animals in the world. Tucky was thinking something totally different. He said, "I'll sneak up to the camp and get James's gun and we'll have otter to eat for lunch."

He started to slink away and I quickly said, "No."

"What do you mean, no?" he said.

"I don't think we should kill an otter. We have plenty of fish to eat. Look how cute they are, I don't want to see them killed."

"Close your eyes," Tucky said as he slunk away toward the campground.

Hopefully, James Ernest wouldn't give Tucky his gun. I liked Tucky as a person, but his thinking that everything in the world is made for him and his family to eat was a little weird. I could understand it if we were starving, but we weren't.

Within a couple of minutes all five of the guys were standing on the bank. James Ernest had his gun at his side.

"Go ahead and shoot one," Tucky said.

I stood up trying to block the view of the otters and said, "No! We don't need the meat. We have plenty of fish. Look how cute they are." I could hear Purty and Junior *oohing* and *aahing* over the otters as they played in the river.

"Let me have the gun, I'll do it," Tucky said.

Randy then yelled out, "Stop it."

Everyone stopped what they were doing and looked at Randy. He said, "We're not going to kill otters. We don't even know if they're in season or if there is a season. It seems as though they may be protected. This is the first time I've ever seen one. Timmy's right, we don't need the meat."

"What do they even taste like?" Purty asked, almost as if he would be okay with shooting them if they tasted good. He would eat sun-baked cow patties if someone guaranteed him they tasted good.

Tucky looked at Purty and said, "I don't know. Never ate otter before."

I bent down and went back to filleting the fish. I threw the next head to the otters.

"We've got some fillets ready if someone wants to rinse them off and take them to the fire," I said.

"I will," Junior said. As Junior was rinsing the fish off in the river the otters came up closer to get a good look. Maybe they thought Junior would throw them some of the fillets. Junior was all smiles. Tucky was disappointed, but he didn't let it bother him. He smiled and went back to helping me.

When we finished and as we were washing off our hands, he said, "Sure would have liked to try otter."

I said, "Probably tastes like chicken."

We both laughed and went back to camp.

18

The Great Escape

By the time we ate the fish and cleaned up the camp and got everything loaded into the canoes, it was nearly ten that morning. But we enjoyed relaxing around the camp and that was what the adventure was all about, having fun. We had been on the river for two days and it felt good to sit around the fire and talk, giving our backs a break from the canoes. The guys went on about how big the crappie was, and I went into great detail about how Junior had fought the fish and how his pole was jerked from his hand.

He told them, "I's was diving in after it if the reel hadn't hung up on the canoe." We all laughed. I figured he would have.

"This afternoon I want to stop somewhere private and take a bath in the river. I can smell myself stinking," James Ernest said.

"We can smell you too," I said and laughed.

We all stunk and we agreed that it was a good idea. We had brought two bars of Ivory soap, which would float, to use. Junior and I and Coty hopped into our canoe and we were off. I heard James Ernest giving Purty directions again so they wouldn't tip over. Randy and Tucky were right behind us.

The sun was bright and hot, but it felt good on the water. I decided to take off my shirt and vest and get some sun as we floated. I looked back and saw that most of the other guys were following my lead. The river was flat and calm and lazy. It looked like it would be a casual, fun float down the river.

About an hour into our trip, we came near the road and a car pulled over to the side of the road when they saw us. A man and woman got out of the car and motioned for us to come over to them.

James Ernest spoke first when we got near enough. "How can we help you?"

"We're letting folks know that a young girl is missing. She lives in Frenchburg and came up missing day before yesterday. She's seven years old and we're out spreading word and giving out flyers," the gentleman explained.

James Ernest paddled over and got a flyer from the man.

He continued, "There's a phone number on there if you happen to see her. I doubt she would be on the river, but we want everyone to know about her."

"We'll keep an eye out," Randy told him. "Thank you for letting us know."

"You boys enjoy your trip. Sorry to bring bad news. Are you guys Indians?" he said before he turned to leave. We laughed and we all said, "No."

James Ernest held up the flyer with a picture of the girl so we all could see her. Under the picture was her name—Lydia Boggs. I agreed with the man. There was no chance of us coming across her on the river. James Ernest told the couple how sorry we were; we thanked them and wished them luck.

As we paddled down the river we saw the two otters playing on the bank. They slid down the bank and into the water without leaving a wake. We watched them circle and twist in the water making a hissing bark sound as though they were trying to talk to us. I wondered if they were thanking us for giving them food and not shooting them. James Ernest had put his gun in our canoe. He didn't want to take a chance of it getting wet or lost when Purty flipped their canoe over.

Junior and I decided to fish as we floated down the river. We put bobbers on our poles and cast them out, letting them float beside our canoe. My eyes were tired and I closed them for a while as we floated. It sure was pleasant being on the river with the sun tanning my skin and a breeze blowing up the river. I was having the time of my life. I missed my family, Mom, Janie, and Mamaw and Papaw. I missed watching my favorite shows on TV—what were Barney Fife and Opie up to? But I knew this was the life for me, being outdoors, exploring the wilderness, and having an adventure around every bend. Nothing was better than this.

I went into a dream state of mind where we were called on to find a small girl who was taken from her home by Indians. We were sent out to find her and bring her home. We wouldn't quit until the young girl was safe and home again. I was almost dozing off when Junior yelled, "Timmy, you got a bite!"

I shook my head trying to think of what that meant. I then realized what he was talking about and I grabbed my pole and jerked. A small smallmouth bass jumped beside the boat trying to get away. I played with it for a while, letting it jump and wiggle in the air trying to throw the hook from its lips. I then reeled it in and took the hook from its mouth and released it back into the water so it could get bigger. It was around eleven inches long.

I noticed purple martins flying over the river catching flying insects, their purplish blue color on their wings glistening in the sunlight. A dragonfly lit on the lip of the canoe. His wings spread out soaking up the sun as I was. Turtles were lined up on dead tree trunks that had fallen into the river. They were basking in the sun. Tall sycamore trees provided shade when we floated under their outstretched limbs. The smell of the river and the outdoors filled my senses. Either that or I could smell the stink of James Ernest and our gang.

I casted my line back into the river and watched the bobber stand upright in the water waiting for a fish to drag it under the surface. I was hoping some six-pound bass would do it.

I looked behind me to see that each of the canoes was doing pretty much the same thing we were. They were floating and enjoying the sunshine and nature around us. Tucky was probably thinking of all the things he could shoot and eat. I wondered what it would be like to be a part of his family. Would I look at things differently if I had been brought up eating roadkill stew? What would it be like to have three brothers and four sisters all living in a small house?

We all lived in different types of houses with different kinds of families. Some of us grew up with an alcoholic father. Some of us grew up without any outward love shown to us, like James Ernest did. Some of us grew up in big families, small families, black families, no mom or no dad, with twin sister brats, on a farm, or in the city. We didn't get to pick how we grew up or who our parents were. We just do the best we can with the circumstances we're given and most of us turn out pretty good, some of us don't. But I had learned that all of us want someone to care about us and love us. We all needed that.

When the sun was straight overhead we came to a section of river away from the road where a large flat rock came out of the bank and down into the water. James Ernest yelled out that it would be a good place for us to take a bath. We banked the canoes and tied them off and started taking off our clothes on the large flat rock. I was naked in a flash and jumped into the river. The water was only around four feet deep. It was the perfect place for a bath. James Ernest threw me one of the bars of Ivory soap and I began lathering up. I washed my Mohawk hair with the soap.

Junior was in the water and Purty had stripped all his clothes off and was stretching to the sky as if we all wanted to see his ugly naked body. James Ernest had thrown the second bar of soap to Junior. Purty finally stopped posing and jumped into the river. He then started begging for a bar of soap.

"I'm almost done. Just a minute," I said.

"Well hurry up," he said.

I finished by washing my butt with the soap and then threw it to him. He began by washing his face with the same soap. I said, "I just washed my nasty butt with that soap."

"So what?" he said.

"You then took it and washed your face. You've now got my butt on your face," I explained. The other guys began laughing and pointing to his face.

"That's gross!" Purty yelled out.

"Quit crying about it, butt-face," Tucky said, bringing laughter again at Purty's expense.

"That sure is a purty butt-face you got," Junior told him as we laughed.

Purty put the soap to his nose and sniffed it and then said, "It don't smell that bad." We laughed even harder. I had tears rolling down my cheeks I was laughing so hard.

Once we were all done bathing we began just floating around and splashing each other. We did cannonballs off the rock. As James Ernest was jumping into the river we heard a voice say, "Well, what have we got here?"

We quickly turned our heads to the woods and saw three teenage girls standing there watching us. They looked to be around fifteen or sixteen years of age.

"I think we found six naked boys in our swimming hole," a red-haired girl said.

"This is quite a surprise," the oldest looking girl said with a smile. "I'm Mary Jane."

The other dark-haired girl said, "I'm Valentine. We don't get to skinny-dip with boys very often."

We were standing there with our hands over our privates even though they were under water. I was even turned backward to the girls. I heard Coty bark and I turned to watch him run up to Mary Jane. She bent down to pet him. He began licking her face.

"Whose dog?" Mary Jane asked.

"Mine," I said, without raising my hand.

"He's so friendly and cute," she said.

"If you'll give us a couple of minutes of privacy we'll be dressed and out of here," James Ernest told them.

"No need to leave. We'll join you. My name is Ophelia. Everyone calls me Red," the red-haired girl told us.

Then Purty yelled out, "You girls are awfully purty. Come on in! The water's fine."

"Okay," she said.

The next thing Purty did was swim over to the rock and he got out of the water and began moving our clothes to make room for the girls' clothing. He was parading around naked in front of the three girls as if there was nothing to it. I was surprised that his naked body didn't scare them off, but they stood there and watched him move the clothes and Red said to him, "You're not bashful at all. Are you?"

All Purty could say was, "I reckon not, never have been."

The next thing out of his mouth was one of the most unbelievable things I had ever heard. He told them, "We have soap you can use if you girls want to take a bath."

The three girls looked at each other and began laughing. Purty looked up at them and smiled.

James Ernest told Purty, "Throw my clothes to me."

"Me too," I followed.

Purty threw James Ernest his pants.

"Now, that ain't polite at all. We just got here and you guys want to run off. Ain't you ever seen naked girls before?" the red-haired girl said as she began to unbutton her top.

"I never have," Purty told them, standing right there in front of them, naked as a jaybird. He then continued, "I once seen my aunt naked from the rear. But that's all."

"Well then, you are in for a treat," the girl said.

James Ernest had his pants on and he jumped onto the rock and began throwing the rest of us our clothes. I slowly began slipping my clothes on in the river while watching the girl undress. I knew it was wrong for me to watch her, but I was also a curious thirteen-year-old boy.

"Let's go, Purty," James Ernest demanded.

"Aw, c'mon. It ain't going to hurt to skinny-dip with these nice girls," Purty argued.

"Please stop taking off your clothes until we leave, please," James Ernest begged the girl.

"You're an old stick in the mud," she told him and then said, "and you're so cute also."

Junior and I made our way to our canoe and jumped in.

Randy and Tucky made their way to the rock and gathered up the rest of their clothes and got into their canoe. Purty was still standing there waiting for the girl to continue disrobing. James Ernest finally had to physically push him to the canoe. When we were a hundred and fifty feet away I looked back to see that all three girls were standing on the rock—completely naked. I couldn't see anything except that they didn't have any clothes on. They were waving good-bye. Purty was waving back at them. He was still naked sitting in the canoe.

19

LIONS AND TURTLES

As we paddled down the river making our getaway, Junior asked me, "Why didn't James Ernest want to swim with those three girls?"

I had forgotten that Junior grew up skinny-dipping with his sisters all the time. He didn't think anything at all was wrong with it. I had even gone skinny-dipping with them once. I wasn't sure how to answer him.

Finally I said, "Well, we didn't know them for one thing. Their fathers or boyfriends might have shown up and not been very happy about us skinny-dipping with the girls. James Ernest probably thinks boys and girls shouldn't skinny-dip in front of each other. He thinks we should be modest."

"What does modest mean?"

"It means we shouldn't be naked in front of girls and they shouldn't be naked in front of boys. In other words—we shouldn't see each other naked," I tried to explain. It was hard to say the words because a part of me sure wanted to see those girls naked. Even though, deep down, I knew it was wrong.

"You'll understand it better when you get older," I added.

"People tell me that all the time," Junior said.

I laughed and said, "Me too."

This section of the river was nearly sixty feet wide and lined with large trees that flung their shadows across the water. It was nice to have the sun's rays blocked as we canoed down the river. We had left most of the large boulders that had littered the river behind when we came out of the gorge. The river meandered through forest, along country roads, and across farmlands.

When we planned the trip, I had no idea we would come across so many people and things. I figured we would just paddle and fish and swim. Of course, our adventures never had turned out the way I expected them to. I thought the next two days would be nothing but canoeing and fishing until we reached the end.

I reached for my rod and reel and removed the hook and bobber and tied on a small spinning bait. Junior saw that I was going to fish so he quickly put a worm on his hook and cast it into the river. I wanted to do something other than watch the bobber. I began casting toward the bank, slowly retrieving the spinner toward me. We were the middle canoe. James Ernest and Purty were behind us.

The trees around us were full of singing birds. They flitted back and forth across the water from tree to tree, almost as though they were happy to greet someone on their section of the river.

Junior glanced back toward James Ernest's canoe and said, "James Ernest is fishing also."

"What is Purty doing?" I asked.

"Don't know. He's a strange boy, isn't he?" Junior said.

I laughed. "Yep, a person could say that without being too wrong."

"Even I know that swimming naked with those girls would have been wrong," Junior said, surprising me.

"His brain isn't wired up exactly like ours. He's always thinking different. But I like him," I explained.

"I like him too. He's fun. I think he makes God laugh."

"You do?" I said, thinking what a strange thing for Junior to say.

"Yep. Why else isn't he dead by now? I think God keeps him around so he can laugh at what all he does," Junior said. I had to agree with him.

We both looked back at the canoe just in time to see Purty stand up to put his pants on. James Ernest was yelling at him to sit down. We watched Purty lift a leg and try to put it in his shorts when he toppled over the side, tipping the canoe over.

"I'm sure God laughed at that," Junior said as we both laughed.

I threw the spinner toward a stump in the water and began reeling it in when a smallmouth bass grabbed it. I jerked my pole upward and set the hook in his jaw. The bass exploded out of the river and twisted in the air, shaking his head from side-to-side trying to release the hook. He then splashed back into the water and dove into the river, hoping to swim away. I tightened the line and pulled him back toward the canoe. He came straight up in defiance and hurled his body toward the blue sky trying to fly like the songbirds that were watching him.

His body came completely out of the river and hung there like tinsel against the dark green of the trees along the river. He then crashed back into the water and, without any time to rest, the bass burst through the surface again looking for freedom that was not going to come. Junior *oohed* and *aahed* each time the bass jumped. I was finally able to reel him into the canoe and placed him on my stringer, but not before giving him a kiss for the fight he had in him.

"I ain't ever seen a fish fight like that," Junior said.

"Only the smallmouth bass will fight like that," I told him.

For the next two hours we fished, Junior with his bobber and me with my spinner bait. We ended up with a fairly nice stringer of fish for supper. Randy and Tucky had caught a few also. We noticed that the water began moving a little quicker and it looked as though the landscape was changing. Rocks began to reappear in the water. Sandstone cliffs appeared again along the banks of the Red River. I was afraid that we might be coming up on another set of rapids. James Ernest told us that he didn't think so.

Junior and I needed a break and I needed to pee. So we paddled over to the other guys and told them that we wanted to stop whenever we could and get out. They agreed that it was a good idea.

As we paddled to find a good spot to stop, Junior asked me, "Who do you think I'll be in a canoe with tomorrow?"

"I don't know. Who haven't you canoed with yet? I know the plans were for everyone to be paired with someone different each day."

"I like being with you," Junior said. "We have fun."

"I like it too," I said, feeling happy that Junior felt that way.

"I haven't canoed with Randy or Purty. Please don't let them put me in the canoe with Purty. I don't want to die," Junior said with a half smile on his face.

"I haven't canoed with Purty or Tucky yet," I told him.

"You take Purty," Junior said and grinned.

"You really love me, don't you?" I said.

"You'll have more fun with Purty and I'll be safer with Randy. I'm thinking about both of us."

"That would leave James Ernest with Tucky. Have they been together yet?" I asked.

"He was with me and you the first two days and Purty today. So that leaves Randy and Tucky. It would work out," Junior figured.

"Okay, but you owe me big time. We'll run it by the guys later."

We came to a shallow spot in the river where we could pull the canoes up on a sandbar. We all relieved ourselves and stretched our muscles. Three days in a canoe had made our backs sore. The surrounding area was heavily forested and had large boulders along the river. A crane was wading along the sandbar fishing for lunch. Coty had gone off exploring the site when we unexpectedly heard him barking like he was in trouble. He then began growling. We ran toward the sound.

As we neared we suddenly heard a louder growling, hissing sound. It made us stop in our tracks. James Ernest told us, "Wait here." He turned and ran back toward the canoes. The growling and hissing continued.

Within two minutes James Ernest returned with his gun in his hand. We then rushed to the sounds. We came to a dark spot that was covered by dense trees and had boulders tossed around the tree trunks. Coty was standing outside two boulders and barking at something inside the rocks. We went around the rocks and I stuck my head to where I could see inside and there stood two baby mountain lions. Their backs were arched and they were baring their teeth and growling with all they had. They were around thirty to forty pounds each and looked very healthy. We knew that we needed to get Coty away from them as quickly as possible.

I grabbed Coty by his collar and started pulling him away from the lions.

"No, Coty! No!" I yelled over the noise the three of them were making.

If the situation hadn't been so dangerous I would have loved to watch the baby mountain lions for a while. Randy helped me drag Coty away. When we got him to where he couldn't see the babies, we turned him back toward the river and there crouched Mama.

She was showing her large incisor teeth and she didn't look very happy with our being there. James Ernest raised his gun and aimed at the lion. I knew he didn't want to shoot the cat, but he also didn't want to have his friends or himself mutilated by the large cougar. It was the first time I had ever seen a mountain lion, except on TV. She was so large and beautiful, but she looked like she could tear us to pieces any time she wanted to. And I was quite sure she wanted to at that moment.

Our numbers may have stopped her from charging us, plus the fact that we were backing away from her babies. Randy motioned for us to go sideways away from the line that stood between the family joining back together. Coty was barking and growling again as soon as he saw the mother. I didn't try to quiet him, thinking it might help keep her from charging us. The large cat stood as we slithered sideways and she slinked around us and toward her babies. We ran.

When we arrived back at the canoes we quickly got in and shoved off. The safest place for us to be was in the canoes, on the river. I was so frightened I needed to pee again. I stood up in the canoe and peed over the side. James Ernest and Purty were ten feet away at our side. When Purty saw what I was doing I guess it made him need to go. He suddenly stood up and unzipped his pants and then lost his balance and the canoe flipped over. James Ernest was screaming as they splashed into the water. James Ernest still had his gun. He must have been able to grab it as they turned over and he held it above the water.

"You stupid knucklehead," James Ernest yelled when his head came out of the water. We paddled over to where James Ernest was and got the pistol from him. I wrapped it back up in plastic and tied it to our canoe. Purty began screaming and slapping the water.

"What's wrong?" I yelled, knowing it could be anything.

"Something has my toe! It's biting me!" he shouted back.

If it wasn't one thing it was another with Purty. Randy and Tucky came up beside us and Tucky said, "That boy is as dramatic as a chicken coop with a fox inside."

Right then Purty pulled his foot out of the water and connected to his big toe was a turtle. He started yelling, "Get it off! Get it off of me!" Tucky stood up and dove into the water and swam over to Purty. He grabbed the turtle by its neck and stuck his finger in the turtle's butt. The turtle let go of Purty's toe and Tucky swam back to the canoe and threw the turtle over the side and into the bottom of their canoe.

Purty was still whining about how bad his toe was injured. We didn't pay a lot of attention to him. I was more interested in what Tucky was going to do with the large turtle. Junior beat me to the question when he asked, "What are you going to do with that, Tucky?"

"Have you ever had turtle soup?" Tucky answered by asking Junior.

"I don't reckon so," Junior answered.

"You guys will love it," he promised.

James Ernest got the canoe over to where we could hold the one side down and he had Purty get in first and then he jumped into the back. He then took his paddle and whacked Purty upside of his head with it.

"Hey! Why did you do that?" Purty said in a sad voice.

"Because now I have to eat turtle soup," James Ernest told him.

20

ZERELDA

It had been quite a morning on the river. We came across three girls wanting to skinny-dip with us, a mountain lion and her cubs, and saw Purty with a turtle stuck to his toe. The day was hot, the sky was blue, and the water was refreshing, so Junior and I decided to jump in and float for a while. We put on our life vests and let the current take us down the river. It didn't take long before the others began doing the same thing.

I held onto the rope that was tied to the front of the canoe and let the canoe pull me along. I was lying on my back relaxing, almost asleep, when I heard voices ahead on the river. It wasn't long before I saw a black woman and man sitting in old lawn chairs fishing off the banks of the river. We were floating in the middle of the river. When our eyes first met I waved a greeting and they waved back. The couple looked as old as the dirt they placed their feet on.

"Catchin' anything?" Junior yelled out.

"Bugs and heat," the old man yelled back.

I knew that Junior was probably surprised and relieved to see other colored folks at the river. We swam over to the bank below the couple and tied off the canoe and then swam back upriver and floated past them again. Coty jumped out of the canoe and ran up to the couple to be petted. The other guys hadn't caught up with us yet.

"Nice friendly dog," the lady said.

"His name is Coty," Junior told them.

"You folks live here?" I asked.

"We'uns lives in a little town near here. We'uns come over two times a wik and fish for our dennurs. They's sum good fishin' in this old river," the old man said. When he spoke his mouth opened up real big like he was trying to get the words more room to tumble out of his mouth. I couldn't see any teeth.

"We been catchin' fish for our dinners too," Junior said.

"Are you boys Injuns?" the woman asked us.

Junior and I decided to swim over to the bank and talk to the couple. It was too hard staying in one place and difficult swimming back upriver. We climbed up onto the bank and settled in the grass next to them.

"No. We have a club and we all got Mohawk haircuts for fun," I explained.

Junior then said, "I'm not in the club. I got one because I was coming on the canoe trip with 'em."

"They won't let you in their club because you black?" the old man asked. Close up I could tell the old man didn't have any teeth. His mouth moved one way and the words weren't what I expected to come out when he spoke. It was the weirdest thing I'd ever seen. It was like he was gnawing on something tough, but words came out instead.

"No. I think because I'm too young," Junior told him.

The old man rolled his eyes to Junior's answer. It made me wonder if Junior thought we hadn't asked him to be a member because he was black. He was right; we hadn't considered asking him because he had been so young. He had just turned ten. I would bring it up at our next club meeting. He had proven on the trip that he would make a great new member to the Wolf Pack.

"Don't see white boys and colored boys together much," the old woman stated.

"We live close to each other, and we go to the same church and school," I said.

"I never heard of such thing," the old woman said, showing that she doubted my story.

"It's true," Junior confirmed.

"The world is changin'," she said.

"It 'bout time," the old man said as he lifted his cane pole a little to move his bait.

"My name is Timmy and his name is Henry Junior," I said.

"I'm Claude and she's Hattie."

"Have you ever come across the Bottom Brothers?" Junior asked the couple.

She shook her head no. He gnawed, but nothing came out.

I added, "Their real names are Rupert and Luther Hatchet. They live along the river up that way a few miles." I pointed upriver.

"Yes'um, we came across them boys one day. They ran us off. Say they own that part of riv'r," Hattie told us.

"Not even nice 'bout it. Called us bad names and said they'd hang us from a tree if we came back ever agin'," Claude bumbled.

"Told me the same thing," Junior told them.

"How long you boys been on the river?" Hattie asked as she petted Coty again.

"This is our third day. Going home tomorrow evening, I guess," I answered.

"Ya'll regular Huck Finn," Hattie said and laughed. Hattie's bobber disappeared and she lifted her pole as quick as she could, which wasn't very quick at all, and she had a fish hooked. She dragged the fish up the bank through the mud and weeds. I went over and lifted it for her and saw that it was a sucker.

"You got a stupid sucker," I said and took it off the hook for her. "I'll throw it back for you."

I started to fling it back into the water when they both yelled, "No!"

"Put it in this bucket," Hattie told me, pointing to a bucket that sat between their plastic lawn chairs. I looked into the bucket as I dropped the sucker in and found that it had four or five other suckers and a couple of catfish in it.

I had always been told that suckers were awful eating, full of bones. I had never seen anyone keep a sucker to eat. A lot of fishermen would just kill them after they caught one to get them out of the water.

"You like suckers?" I asked. I knew I wasn't very good at hiding my surprise.

"Can't be picky. A person has to learn how to cook 'em," Hattie told me.

"We're havin' turtle soup tonight," Junior told them and grinned.

"I loves my turtle soup," Claude told us while smacking his lips and licking them. His lips didn't seem to have muscles.

They flopped back and forth like he didn't have any control in the direction they went. I figured out that was what made him look funny when he spoke.

The other guys had finally floated down to where we were talking with Hattie and Claude. I introduced the other four guys. They waved.

We said our good-byes and wished them good luck in their fishing. Hattie told us to be careful. Claude smacked his lips and said, "Sure looks like 'em Injuns."

Hattie nodded her head in agreement as we untied the canoe. Coty jumped in and we floated back into the river.

As we were floating away, Hattie stood up and warned us, "Keep your eyes open for the witch. Stay away from her."

I smiled, waved back, and said, "Okay."

"Did she say to watch for a witch?" Junior asked me.

"I think that's what she said. Or she could have said something about a ditch." We both laughed.

By mid-afternoon everyone was ready for a break. We had been floating and paddling the river all afternoon and decided to stop. We made our way up a bank on the far side of the river and I found a nice shade tree to lie under. Coty went exploring. Junior decided to fish off the bank. I had never seen a kid who loved to fish as much as Junior, unless I was looking in a mirror.

I fell asleep and quickly went into a dream world. I was sailing on a large raft with Huck Finn down the Mississippi River. Except in my dream his name was Huck Funn. The three girls—Ophelia, Valentine, and Mary Jane—were on the raft with us. Huck had a piece of hay in his mouth, chewing on it. Hattie and Claude were fishing off the back of the raft. They kept raising their poles out of the water and a sucker would fly over their backs and land on the raft and flop all over before sliding back into the river.

Over and over and over again suckers were flying through the air, flopping and reentering the river only to be hooked again and repeat the scene. The three girls were cheering each time a sucker was pulled in. Every once in a while a mountain lion would snatch one out of the air and feed it to one of her cubs who were playing with Coty. Huck Funn poked me in the ribs and asked, "Who are those crazy guys chasing us with guns a blazing?"

I looked upriver to see the Bottom Brothers shooting at us and yelling, "We told you to stay off our river."

I woke up when James Ernest poked me in the ribs and said, "It's time to go."

We had been there nearly three hours. Most of the guys had taken naps. Junior had managed to catch three bluegills and a bass. Coty was sitting beside him dozing and watching him fish.

We decided to paddle for a couple of hours and then look for a good campground. We didn't need more fish for dinner and we still had a ways to travel before our meeting place the next evening. It was decided we needed to make up for lost time. It was still warm, but a nice breeze blew upriver from the west keeping us cooled off. We decided to have races. We would pick a tree in the distance and line up in a row and then race our canoes to the tree. Randy and Tucky had a big advantage and they won every time.

Junior and I didn't have a lot of paddle power, and Purty kept James Ernest from ever winning. They turned over twice as Purty would lean too far out of the canoe to dig his paddle into the river. It was fun and we gained a lot of distance doing it.

About eight-thirty we found a flat spot on the far side of the river that looked like it would make a nice campground. We paddled over to it and James Ernest jumped out onto the bank to check it out.

"It's good," he called back. We went ahead and tied our canoes off and joined him at the campground. We unloaded our gear and Junior and Randy and I went to work putting up the tents. The others gathered wood and built a fire pit. It didn't take long to get the tents up and our gear stored inside.

James Ernest and I went into the woods to get a big log to sit on. I asked him, "What do you think about making Henry Junior a member of the Wolf Pack?"

"I think it's a great idea," James Ernest answered. I then told him about the conversation we had with Hattie and Claude. I told him how they had more or less told Henry he wasn't a member because he was colored.

"But that's not true," James Ernest said. He looked upset about it.

"I know, and Junior knows that also. Or at least I think he does," I said. I then added, "You think we should bring it to a vote tonight or wait till our next meeting?"

"If we could get all the members together without Junior and discuss it first, we could do it tonight. If not, then I think we should wait. I don't want to bring it up and then have someone vote no with him there. We'd want to be sure it's unanimous before voting in front of him."

"That's smart," I agreed. "I don't think anyone would vote no, unless maybe Randy. But I don't think he would."

"I don't think so either, but better off not taking a chance."

"Okay," I said as we lifted a large downed log.

Tucky and I then filleted the fish. Junior wanted to watch us and learn how we did it. Purty went off into the woods to poop. James Ernest and Randy built a fire. We had fish frying before it got dark. Tucky had cleaned the turtle and we had a pot of turtle soup over the fire cooking. James Ernest had hidden a cabbage in his pack. He cut it into slices and made coleslaw to have with the fish. He said he had saved it for our last night.

As it got dark we ate the fish and coleslaw. The slaw was a great extra treat. The fish was so good. Later when Tucky said the soup was done we tried it. I couldn't get the first spoonful past by lips before spitting it out. Randy, Junior, and James Ernest had the same reaction. Something was either missing or turtle soup just wasn't that good. Purty and Tucky had two cups of it, but you could place anything in front of Purty and he would think it was tasty.

I asked Tucky how he knew to stick his finger up the turtle's butt to get it to let go. He answered, "There's an old saying, 'If a turtle bites you, it won't let go till it thunders.' So you have to do something and that always works."

"You amaze me, Tucky," I said.

The talk then turned to girls. First the guys discussed the three girls we met when we were taking our baths. Then they began discussing girlfriends and who they would like to kiss. They rated their top three girls in the school they would most like to kiss. Susie, Rhonda, and Sadie were on the top of most lists.

I soon grew tired of listening to the girl talk and when it came my turn to tell my list I said, "I'm going to go for a walk."

I found a pathway in the woods and followed it. I had my flashlight in my hand, shining it on the trail. Coty was searching the edges of the path ahead of me. It looked like it had been used often by people. It didn't look like an animal trail.

By then it was pitch dark. The only light was from the stars above and the weak light coming from my flashlight. I heard tree frogs and whip-poor-wills calling out around me. Crickets were chirping from the forest floor. I walked until I came to a clearing. A two-story farmhouse stood in the middle of the field. A large barn was to the side of it. I saw lights on in the house.

I didn't want anyone to see me and worry that I was a prowler up to no good. I quickly turned around and headed back to the camp. My heart raced as I made my way back. Something scared me about the house, probably not knowing who lived there, but it also had a dark, spooky feel to it.

Within a few minutes I was safely back to the campground. I said good night to the guys, who were still sitting around the campfire talking about girls, and went to my tent and slipped off my clothes and into my sleeping bag. Coty circled and settled next to me. I was tired from the day, I was a little scared after the walk in the woods, and I was still upset with the talk of kissing and girlfriends.

I must have drifted off to sleep quickly, because it wasn't long after that when I was awakened by James Ernest telling me to get up and come on.

"Why? What's up?" I said, but he was already gone.

I quickly put back on my clothes and slipped my feet into my old tennis shoes and unzipped the tent. Coty ran to catch up with the gang. I saw them talking to someone I didn't know. I ran over to them and Randy introduced me to a woman by the name of Zerelda Samuel.

"Hello. Pleased to meet you," I said politely. She looked to be in her sixties or seventies and seemed as though a smile might crack her face. She had, what I called, a pouty face. Her lips drooped down almost meeting her chin at the bottom of her face. I could only see a few teeth in her mouth. Her neck was wrinkled and hung loose like a gobbler. Her gray hair was parted in the middle and rolled up into a large bun at the back of her head. As we walked on the same path I had traveled earlier I noticed that she waddled like a duck heading toward water. Her large rear end swayed back and forth from one side of the trail to the other. No one could have walked beside her without getting knocked off into the bushes and trees that lined the trail. Her hair came undone as she walked and dropped down to the middle of her back.

I still wasn't sure what the seven of us were doing following this woman into the woods. I was walking next to James Ernest.

I whispered to him, "Why are we following her?"

"She needs help moving her husband to their truck. He's ill and she needs to get him to the hospital, but she says he's too heavy for her to move by herself. She saw a flashlight on the path earlier and figured there would be help at the campsite," James Ernest explained.

I was leery of the story for some reason. I wondered why she hadn't called a neighbor or a relative to come help, or even an ambulance. Why would she tramp through the woods to, by chance, find someone to help? It didn't make sense to me, but I had been asleep and didn't hear the lady's plea. I thought I might be dreaming, so I let it go.

We finally came to the same field that I had been to earlier. I knew it was my flashlight she had seen. We hurried across the clearing to the house. She asked that Coty stay outside. We walked through the back door and into the dark country kitchen. I noticed a big pot of water boiling on the stove. There were dead chickens hanging from the cabinets by their necks. There were jars of different herbs or something else filling the counter. One jar jumped out at me that looked like it was filled with eyeballs. It looked like they were staring at me. It freaked me out. I wanted to turn around and run. I knew this wasn't right.

"He's down there in the basement." She interrupted my thought and led us to an opened door that had claw marks running down the half-missing paint. She motioned for us to go through the door and descend into the basement. I wondered what was wrong with her husband. Did he have some disease that I didn't want to catch?

"There's a light string hanging at the bottom of the stairs," she told us. Once all of us were on the stairs, past the doorway, she laughed and said, "Now you're all in my basement. Enjoy the darkness."

She slammed the door behind us and I heard the sound of a lock sliding into place. I then heard a deadbolt lock click. The closing of the door left us in total blackness. It reminded me of when I had been inside the cave above Devil's Creek. I couldn't see my hand when I held it inches from my eyes. I could hear Coty outside barking as though something was wrong. He was right!

Purty screamed, of course.

"Where's the pull switch?" Henry asked with a shaky voice. I could tell that everyone began reaching above their heads trying to find the string. I joined them in the search to no avail.

Purty finally quit screaming and then unbelievably asked, "Where's her husband? How can we find him and carry him out in the dark?"

I heard everyone sigh. "There is no husband. She's trapped us down here," Randy explained to Purty.

"She wh-what? Why would she do that? What does she want us for?" Purty was asking questions all of us wondered but had no answers for.

We then heard her through the floorboards. "There's candy to the right of the stairs. Help yourselves."

I had an answer. She was trying to fatten us up.

"Oh, boy," Purty cried out through his sobs, "at least we won't starve." The only one she didn't need to fatten up was the most excited about the candy.

"Here it is," Purty yelled out.

"Don't eat any of that," I warned. "It could be poisoned."

"She's just being nice," Purty said, trying to argue his way into eating the candy.

Junior then said something I had forgotten about, "Hattie told us to stay away from the witch."

"What? Now's a good time to tell us," Randy said.

"Didn't you guys notice the big pot of boiling water in the kitchen? She's planning on eating us. This is like Hansel and Gretel. She got us into her house and now she's trying to fatten us up for her pot. She'll eat the fattest one first," I said.

"You're right," James Ernest said. Everyone began scrambling around the basement looking for a way out. Guys were bumping into walls and all kinds of things.

"There are no basement windows down here," Randy yelled out from the other side of the basement.

"We can dig our way out! The floor is dirt," Purty yelled out.

A few minutes later as it quieted down I heard sobbing in a corner of the basement. I made my way over to where it was coming from. I moved closer to the sound and whispered, "Who's there?"

No one answered. I then heard James Ernest talking to Randy and Tucky so I knew this had to be either Purty or Junior.

"Purty?" I whispered, figuring he would be the most likely to be whimpering in the corner. I got no answer.

"Junior?" I whispered, but still got no response. I then heard Junior's voice when he asked James Ernest, "You think the witch likes dark meat?"

James Ernest assured Junior that no one was going to eat any of us. This had to be Purty I was whispering to. Then I heard from the middle of the room. "She'll eat me first. I'm the fattest." He began weeping in a mournful way. It was hard to listen to.

So who was this person crying in the corner of the basement?

"We can help you. What's your name?" I asked the person in the corner.

A faint whisper came back, "Lydia."

It was a young girl. I was stunned. I was shocked. I was scared beyond scared. Then I remembered that the missing girl we had been told about was named Lydia. After getting over the initial surprise I said, "It's going to be okay, Lydia Boggs. We'll help you. We'll all be fine. Are you down here by yourself?"

"Yes," she said.

"How old are you?"

"Seven."

"How long have you been down here?"

"Don't know, a couple of days, a week."

I placed my arms around her and held her there in the dark. Her shoulders would rise and fall as she cried on my chest. I stroked her long greasy hair. I could tell she hadn't had a bath or hair washing since she had been there.

"Timmy!" James Ernest yelled out.

"Over here," I said loud enough for them to hear.

I heard footsteps coming my way. When they got close I stopped them and told them, "I have Lydia here. I found her in this corner. She's the girl that we were told about."

I couldn't see the expressions on their faces, but I knew they had to feel for the young girl. I could sense their sorrow and sadness for her.

James Ernest softly said, "We're going to get you out of here. Have there been others down here with you?"

We all wanted to know and waited to hear the answer to this very important question that I was scared to ask. I also wondered how this witch had gotten Lydia. It didn't seem very likely that she was nimble enough to catch a girl by herself. But then I remembered that she had just trapped six able-bodied boys in her basement cellar.

Lydia then answered, "No. I been all alone."

That was the first time I almost cried. The sorrow I felt for this little girl was almost too much to bear.

"You're going to be okay," James Ernest assured her with his deep husky voice. I'm sure she felt as though God was talking to her in the dark. Everyone settled onto the floor around her, like we were protecting her from harm.

"What's our plan?" I asked.

Randy began, "We could surprise her by sneaking up the stairs and trying to break down the door."

"She might have a gun," Tucky suggested.

"He's right. That could be risky," James Ernest said. "We could do that as a last resort. She must be planning to do something soon since the pot is boiling. We wait till she comes down to get one of us and then we overtake her. She can't make one of us go up and jump into the pot."

"Who is this Zerelda Samuel?" I asked.

"I don't think that's her real name." James Ernest surprised us.

"How come?" I asked.

James Ernest explained, "You know the outlaws, Frank and Jesse James?"

"Yeah," we all answered. Tucky asked, "So what?"

"That's the name of their mother, Zerelda Samuel. I think she's gone crazy and thinks she's an outlaw herself and took her name because it's associated with crime. But maybe she thinks she is a witch," James Ernest told us.

I was amazed that James Ernest would know Jesse James's mother's name.

"Maybe it is really their mother," Purty said in the darkness.

"No way. She would be 130 years old or more." James Ernest laughed.

"She looked pretty old," Junior said.

"It could be her ghost," Tucky suggested. That was all we needed now, to have a ghost thrown into this mess. I wasn't sure we were making Lydia feel any better. She had stopped crying in my arms. She just stayed there in my arms and listened to our plans and stories. I started to let go of her, but she quickly grabbed my arms and placed them back around her. I was sure she was relieved to have others trapped with her.

The door at the top of the stairs squeaked open and the old woman, or ghost, said, "I need someone to help me. Send up the plump boy."

"Don't say anything," James Ernest whispered to everyone.

"I said, **SEND UP THE PLUMP BOY!**" she screamed. We all jumped a little there on the basement dirt floor.

"Okay, if you don't send him up then send the girl up," Zerelda ordered.

Lydia tightened her grip around me. "You're not going anywhere," I whispered into her ear, which was right below my mouth, because her head was tucked tightly against my chest.

"I will then be forced to go outside and get the dog," she said and closed the door and locked it behind her.

We could hear her footsteps going toward the back door and then we heard the door open and I heard barking.

"*Run Coty, run!*" I yelled toward the stairs. All of us began yelling for Coty to run away. I heard Coty continue to bark. His barks got fiercer. I knew she was getting closer to him. We began yelling for him to run again. Suddenly, we heard his barks fade as we knew he was running toward the woods.

"Let's go break down the door," James Ernest told us. The five other guys jumped up and began feeling their way to the stairs. I heard one of them bump into something and scream. Lydia was holding me so tightly I couldn't go anywhere, plus I knew I would be no help knocking down the door. In fact, all five of them couldn't hit the door at the same time. I heard the footsteps going up the stairs and then I heard the door crash against the wall when they knocked it open. I listened for gunshots. I heard footsteps running across the kitchen floor and the door slam and lock.

I figured they had locked Zerelda out of her house, but I knew it would do no good if she was a witch.

21

I'm a Toad!

I could hear the guys scrambling around the house from room to room. I heard Zerelda banging on the front door telling the guys to open the door or they'd be sorry. It suddenly got real quiet. It scared me more than when there was lots of noise.

"Let me in!" Zerelda yelled from outside. Lydia and I jumped at the scream.

I then heard James Ernest tell Zerelda. "Drop your rifle on the ground and come to the door and we'll let you back in the house."

Everything then came to a stop. I stood up and Lydia and I climbed the stairs to see what was happening. We bumped into a large box. The guys had closed the door at the top of the stairs. It was pitch dark and we had a hard time finding the bottom of the steps. Lydia held onto the bottom of my shirt as I felt my way.

"Here they are," I said as I stumbled on the bottom step. I reached for her hand and we climbed the stairs together. I opened the door. There were no lights on. Apparently the guys had turned off all the lights so Zerelda couldn't see them in the dark. I wished I had my flashlight but I had forgotten it in the tent when I was awoken. I still was hoping I was in a bad dream. I tried pinching myself, but all it did was hurt me.

"Hey, guys," I whispered.

"Over here," Randy whispered back. "Stay low."

Lydia and I dropped to our hands and knees and crawled to where Randy's voice came from. He was huddled against the stove in the kitchen. Purty and Junior were beside him.

"What's happening?" I whispered. We talked in hush tones, not wanting Zerelda to know where we were.

"James Ernest and Tucky are looking for a back door. If they find it then James Ernest is going to head back to the camp and get his gun. Tucky is going to stay and guard the door."

"Why don't we all go through the back door?" I asked.

"We don't know where she is. It would be risky taking off and maybe running into her. It's better to have only one guy go and you know how good James Ernest is in the dark and sneaking around without being heard."

I thought it was a good plan, but I worried for my best friend. I also wondered what Coty was doing. I thought he would probably try to come back and the witch was out there with a gun. As we talked we heard the guys crawling back into the room.

"What's up?" Randy asked.

"There's not another door in this house and there's no windows except the ones here in the kitchen," Tucky told us.

"That's strange," I said.

"Tell me about it," James Ernest said.

"I know there're windows upstairs. I saw lights from them earlier when I went for a walk," I said.

"It must have been you she saw earlier. This is your fault," Purty blurted out.

"I wonder where the stairs are that goes to the second floor," James Ernest said before adding, "I'll be back."

We waited there in the dark. Lydia was still holding onto me. We listened to the quiet that surrounded us. It seemed eerie. The only sound I heard was the heavy breathing coming from Lydia and Purty. I noticed that the pot of boiling water was no longer boiling. I couldn't see if the pot was still on the stove or not. It was too dark. Within a few minutes James Ernest was back.

"There are no stairs leading to the second floor," he said.

"What?" at least three of us said.

"I've searched everywhere."

Why would a house have an upstairs with no way to get up to it? Everything about this place was creepy.

"Helllooo," a hollow voice rang out.

Lydia almost broke my ribs hugging me so tight. The voice seemed to come from above our heads. I looked skyward to see nothing but the darkness of the room.

"Who said that? Stop goofing around. This is no time for jokes. You scared Lydia to death," I said. I failed to mention to them how badly it had scared me also.

Everyone denied doing it. Not only was this a witch's house, but now we find out it was a haunted house to boot, with no back door or windows and no way up to the second floor. I felt sick. I wanted to throw up. I wanted to scream.

"I could go out the front door and run. She'd have a hard time shooting me in the dark," James Ernest offered.

"I think it's too risky. Maybe we should just wait her out. It's only a few hours before daylight. Then we can see where she is," Randy said.

"Yeah, and she'll be able to see where we are," Purty said. It was the first thing he had said this trip that made sense.

Randy then said, "She could be sitting on the front porch waiting for us. She knows there's no other way out." He was right.

"All we can do is wait," Randy said, and we all kind of agreed.

I then heard James Ernest begin to pray. I could hear his words. He didn't really pray for our safety or for us, he prayed for Zerelda. He prayed for forgiveness and courage and he prayed for God to use him as a witness to the glory of God. It certainly wasn't what I would have prayed for. I would have prayed for a gun. I would have prayed for something bad to happen to the witch. I would have prayed for Jesus to come down out of the sky on his white horse and rescue us. I had heard Preacher White preach about it. At least someone was praying.

The time clicked by a second at a time, and then a minute at a time, and then an hour at a time. I couldn't go to sleep. I was sitting against a bottom cabinet. Lydia had snuggled her head on my leg and was sound asleep. I heard other sounds of sleep scattered around the room. I knew most of the guys had drifted off. I wished I could, but I was too uncomfortable. I didn't want to move and wake Lydia.

THURSDAY, AUGUST 2

Hours later I saw dim light coming through the eastern window. A rooster crowed signaling the beginning of the day. I wondered if this would be my last day in this world. What did the witch have waiting for us? The light grew until I was able to see everyone around the room. James Ernest raised his head to the window and looked outside.

I whispered after he lowered himself back to the floor, "Did you see her?"

James Ernest scooted over beside me and said, "She's in the yard sitting in a lawn chair just off the porch."

"Is she awake?" I asked.

"Yeah. She has the rifle across her lap just staring at the house."

"What do we do now?"

I heard stirring and looked to see Randy and Tucky waking up and stretching. It wasn't long before all of us were huddled in the center of the kitchen floor trying to come up with a plan. Each of us took turns looking out the window. Lydia didn't want to look at the witch.

"Has she done anything to you since you've been here?" James Ernest asked her.

"The first day I got here she placed me in a chair and said something I didn't understand, like a foreign language, and then sprinkled some stuff on me. Then she got mad and put me in the basement."

"How did she get you?" I asked her.

"I was playing in my yard when she drove up. She opened up the passenger door and asked me how to get to town. It was only a block away. She offered me candy for helping her. When I reached in to take it from her, she snatched me with her other hand and dragged me into her car."

I always thought when Mom had told me not to take candy from strangers that it was just something moms said. I guess it was real.

Purty asked, "When she sprinkled the stuff on you did it do anything to you?"

"No. But it made me sneeze."

"Pepper. I bet she was seasoning you with pepper before she was going to cook you," Purty reasoned. Lydia began to shake.

"Stop it, stupid. You're scaring her. If she was going to cook her, she wouldn't have put her in the basement after putting pepper on her," I said.

"It was just a guess. Sorry," Purty said.

At that moment we heard a truck drive up on the gravel lane to the front of the house. We knew that we were about to be rescued or at the least be able to make our getaway. We all poked our heads over the counter and looked out the window.

Much to our disappointment the doors opened and the Bottom Brothers, Rupert and Luther Hatchet, slid out of the cab. They walked over to the witch. She rose from the chair and hugged the two men and patted them on their backs. I could tell that they asked her, 'Why are you sitting out here in the yard?'"

She answered them and pointed toward the house. All three heads turned to look our way. We all ducked. I wasn't sure what good it did. They already knew we were in the house.

"What are the Bottom Brothers doing here?" Purty cried out.

No one answered. No one had an answer. I slowly rose to look out the window again. The two brothers had walked back to their truck and gotten their rifles and the three of them started walking toward the house. I noticed that the barrels of the rifles had been straightened from when James Ernest had bent them. Each had a wave in the barrel.

I ducked and said, "They're coming."

Lydia began crying. Purty began crying. James Ernest stood and walked to the door and unlocked it. What was he doing? We all stood to watch what was happening. James Ernest walked through the door and met the three people with rifles on the porch. The brothers lifted their crooked rifles and aimed them at James Ernest.

They stood there and stared at each other, everyone seemed unsure what to do next. Randy and Tucky walked toward the door and joined James Ernest on the porch.

"What do you want with us?" James Ernest asked.

Rupert spoke first, "You come to our mom's house and lock her out of it. I should shoot you right now."

"I guess you could. But we only came to the house to help your mom. She lured us here to help carry her husband to her car. She told us he was sick and she needed help. Then she locked us in the basement with the young girl."

The two brothers slowly turned their heads and looked at their mother. "What young girl?"

"I needed a girl for my potions," Zerelda told them. They shook their heads.

Luther walked over to his mother and placed a hand on her shoulder and said, "Mom, you are not a witch."

"I am so. I can prove it," she barked.

"Okay, Mom, prove it," Luther said.

Rupert and Luther directed everyone into the kitchen. They jumped at the sight of Lydia and Junior in the kitchen.

Zerelda suddenly was full of vigor and zest. She told her sons to line the kitchen chairs up in a row. They had us sit in the chairs. What in the world was going to happen? When I got a look at the barrels of the rifles I saw that not only were they crooked but they each had an indent. I was almost sure that a bullet would never come out of the barrels.

"Where should I start? I could change one of them into a toad. I could change the colored boy. I could make his skin white. Would you like to see that?"

"Mom, this is crazy. You can't do that. You're not a witch," Rupert tried convincing her.

"Frank and Jesse, just watch, I'll show you," Zerelda said. The two brothers looked at each other with a puzzled look.

"You just called us Frank and Jesse," Rupert said.

She laughed and said, "I did? That's strange."

I thought maybe we should tell the brothers who she told us she was, but I decided to stay out of it. I figured James Ernest would know what to say better than I would. I knew that the brothers now realized how batty their mother was.

"I'll do that one. I'll change the little black boy into a white boy. That way, you won't need to hang him," Zerelda told them. I was sure at that moment Junior was hoping she was a witch. He would much rather be changed into a white kid than be hung from a tree.

She opened a book and read from it to herself and then she went to her counter and picked up two of the jars that were sitting there. She took a little of each ingredient from the jars and mixed them in a bowl. She then opened up a cabinet door and got out a bag of flour and opened it. She walked over to Junior. He was squirming in his seat. His eyes were wide with fright.

She stood over him and read, "Hocus, pocus, hullabaloo. Mucus, focus, I put a spell on you. Don't you fight, I'll make you white." She then sprinkled the contents from the bowl she had mixed onto his head and said, "Poof."

Junior was still a black boy with some weird stuff sprinkled in his Mohawk. Zerelda then carried the flour bag over to Junior and began throwing flour into his face.

"Look, look, he's turning white. I told you I was a witch." She then cackled with laughter. She sure sounded like a witch. I wasn't sure how I held back my laughter, but for my own good I thought it was best to hold it in.

"Now, let's change one of these boys into a toad. Which one will it be?"

She walked in front of us and looked at each one of us from head to toe and then she pointed and said, "This one. He would make a good toad." She was pointing to Purty.

"No! No! Not me! Please don't turn me into a toad. How about him? He would make a better toad," Purty begged while pointing at me. Purty was a true friend, save himself by sacrificing me. What would ever lead Purty to believe he would become a toad? What he was turning into was a big butthead.

"Okay, I volunteer. I want to be a toad," I said.

Purty let out a sigh of relief. He then looked down at his shoes. I was hoping in shame.

"No. I'm the witch Zerelda. I'll pick who I want—and I want you," she said as she turned and stuck her dark fingernail in Purty's face. He started weeping. I had never seen a sadder display from a boy. I was thinking that Purty should be placed in the loony bin with Zerelda.

The witch began mixing different things into a bowl. She opened up the large jar with the eyeballs and took one out with a spoon and placed it in the mixture. She pulled a hair from her head and added it. I saw James Ernest motion for Rupert to come close. James Ernest was whispering something to him. Whatever James Ernest said, Rupert agreed with and nodded his head up and down.

Zerelda carried the bowl over to Purty and began to chant:

> Toil, Toil, all the day in soil.
> Let me burn this boy in oil,
> If not the trust I put in you,
> To cast a spell upon this boil.
> Sun comes up, sun goes down,
> I praise you with this frozen frown.
> By all the might of heaven and hell,
> Grant me this one pleasure of spell.
> North, south, east and west,
> Make me the witch that is the best.
> Give me the strength to be so bold,
> To turn this boy into a toad.

Urine was soaking the front of Purty's pants. Sweat was dripping from his chin. He shook like Santa's belly. The self-proclaimed witch took out the eyeball and made Purty open his mouth. She placed the eyeball inside. I thought it looked bigger than a human eyeball, not that I had seen one outside of a skull. She then threw the contents of the bowl into Purty's face and yelled, "Poof!" She lifted her eyes and hands to the ceiling.

Purty began gagging and spitting and snorting and throwing his arms around in the air. The eyeball popped out of his mouth and rolled across the floor. He screamed out,

"Am I a toad? I'm a toad. Oh God, I'm a toad!" He dropped out of the chair and began hopping on the floor on his hands and knees. We couldn't control it any longer. We all burst out laughing. Even the Bottom Brothers were laughing at the sight in front of us.

Tucky said, "I've seen chickens with their heads cut off that were smarter than that boy."

Rupert made his way over to the phone book that was on top of a small table under the phone on the wall. He picked up the phone and placed a call. Zerelda had looked back down to see Purty hopping on the floor acting like a toad. She began wailing and picked up the jar of eyeballs and threw it against the wall. The eyeballs rolled across the floor. Purty began screaming as he looked into the eyes on the floor. A jar of preserved lizards and newts were thrown onto the floor, scattering glass and lizards and newts where Purty was hopping. I grabbed Lydia's arm and we ran through the front door and into the yard. Junior and Tucky were right behind us. I heard Coty barking and saw him running toward me from the woods.

James Ernest and Randy led Purty out of the house. We all stood on the lawn and listened to screams and jars smashing against the walls. Within minutes we heard police sirens and the cruisers soon were speeding down the lane. Two of the officers went inside, while the other two ran over to us. I introduced Lydia to the policemen. They told her that they had been looking everywhere for her. She clung tightly to me, not wanting to let go.

"The witch had me," she whispered to them.

22

A Law

We had to stay and tell the police the entire story. Rupert and Luther verified our story. The brothers were extreme bigots, but they did care about their mother and they knew she needed to be in a hospital, nursing home, or mental ward where she could get help. Somehow she had gotten obsessed with witchcraft and thought she had become a witch. She had gone nuttier than a walnut tree is what she had become. Her sons said she hadn't been right since their dad died four years earlier.

We asked about the ghostly voice we had heard upstairs and whether the house was haunted. The brothers told us and the police that their aunt, their mother's sister, was in bad shape and was bedridden upstairs and that she every so often would cry out. Rupert said there was a hidden stairway that went upstairs. An ambulance came to take her away.

We all were starving. One of the officers went to a nearby store and got us drinks and breakfast sandwiches and snack cakes to eat.

As we were eating we discovered that the pot of boiling water was for washing her undergarments. She had no intentions of eating us; she had left the candy in the basement as treats for Lydia. She wanted to try out her potions and curses, and needed live bodies. That was the reason she had kidnapped Lydia and had lured us to her basement. Zerelda had decided that Lydia was too small for the curses to work on her.

We also discovered that her real name was actually Zelda, but she had convinced herself that she was the mother of Frank and Jesse James. The police asked if we wanted to file charges against Rupert and Luther. The six of us got together to discuss it and decided since they had called the police there was no reason to charge them with anything. We couldn't file charges on them threatening Junior. They hadn't actually done anything to him. They were ignorant men who were big bigots.

The police had called Lydia's parents as soon as they found out who she was. Within an hour they drove down the lane and we got to see their reunion. Lydia's parents began crying as soon as they got out of the car and spotted her running toward them. They covered her face with kisses. The police introduced her parents to us. They hugged each of us and kissed us and thanked us over and over again. Lydia came over and held my hand.

"Timmy is the one who found me, Mommy," she said. "He protected me all night."

A tear rolled down my cheek when she looked up into my face like I was a hero to her. I just happened to be the first one to hear her crying in the dark. I had done nothing special, but to her I had. It made me feel great.

After being there almost three hours after the police arrived, they said we were free to go and asked if we needed a ride somewhere. We told them we needed to continue our canoe trip. We explained that we needed to call my papaw to arrange a place and time to pick us up. The officer got out a map and showed us a good meeting spot on down the river. They said we could easily be there by three or four that afternoon.

They then called the store for us and handed the phone to me. Papaw answered the phone and I quickly told him where to meet us and what time. I told him we were sorry we hadn't called the night before but we were kind of locked up.

"What?" Papaw asked.

"We'll explain this afternoon," I said.

The officer asked if he could talk to Papaw. I heard the officer ask Papaw if he had heard about the missing girl. He then told Papaw that we had found her and that we were heroes.

I knew the whole community would know about it within minutes. They would probably turn on the radio to hear the reports.

Before we left, Randy walked over to Rupert and Luther and asked if he could speak to them. They walked to the side of the house and talked. When he returned from the talk, we said 'our good-byes' and headed back to the river. Lydia gave me a long hug good-bye. The parents told me they would keep in touch.

The six of us began our walk across the field to the path we had followed to the house. We walked side-by-side with our arms stretched across each other's shoulders.

Tucky looked over at Purty and asked, "Why aren't you hopping, toad?" We all laughed.

"Yeah, Toad, you should be hopping. I'm a white boy now," Junior told him.

"How do you like being white?" Randy asked him.

"I feel a lot stupider," he said and grinned. He then said, "It gives me the urge to hop." He fell to the ground and began hopping and then yelled, "I'm a toad! I'm a toad!" We laughed so hard we had to stop walking.

"Hey, I did feel like a toad," Purty said seriously. We couldn't control our laughter.

We laughed all the way to the campground. All of our stuff was just like we had left it. We began taking down the tents and packing our gear. Tucky asked if anyone wanted him to heat up the turtle soup. Everyone except Purty yelled, "No!"

James Ernest told Purty, "That turtle could have been one of your relatives—since you're both amphibians." Purty smiled at me. I wanted to laugh, but I was about laughed out.

Tucky then asked, "Who's canoeing with who?"

I quickly spoke up, "Junior is with Randy. James Ernest is with Tucky, and I'm with Purty."

No one even questioned me. I guessed as long as none of them had to canoe with Purty they were okay with anything. We began loading the canoes. Most of my stuff I put in the canoe with James Ernest and Tucky. I didn't want to have to search for my stuff every time we flipped over. I even put my fishing stuff in their canoe. I didn't figure we would be doing any fishing.

It was almost eleven that morning before we shoved off onto the river again. Papaw said he would be at the meeting spot between three and four that afternoon. I had a lot of mixed emotions as we paddled down the river. I was anxious to see Papaw and to go home, but I also loved being on the river the past four days and would like for it to continue a few more days. The fishing had been great and the memories would last a lifetime.

Purty was in a sullen mood. As we broke down camp, guys teased him about being a toad. James Ernest asked him to hurry at one point and Tucky said, "He means hop to it."

Purty told us that he thought we were all going to die at the house. James Ernest teased him, saying, "You mean you thought you were going to croak, don't you?"

It was a beautiful sunny day. Coty sat in the middle of the canoe. His head swung from side to side watching the trees and birds go by. This had been my favorite adventure by the Wolf Pack. I began thinking about what we could do next summer. I would vote to canoe a different river, maybe the Cumberland or the Kentucky River. Randy was ready to get back home. He was trying out for the high school football team and practice was starting on Monday. He was trying to talk James Ernest into trying out. Purty said he might go and try out. He would begin high school this year in the ninth grade. Randy raised his eyebrows but didn't say anything.

I was beginning to get stronger and bigger. I would be going to Morgan County High School in another year. I wondered if I should try out for football then. I definitely wanted to try out for the baseball team and maybe basketball in high school. A bad thing about going to a one-room school is that we didn't have the chance to play junior high sports like they did in Ohio. But I gladly traded that chance in order to live in the country. I didn't mind being called a hillbilly, or a clodhopper. To me, they were names of honor.

We hadn't been on the river long before we floated under a swinging bridge. It was the longest one I had ever seen. It was probably a hundred feet long at least. I wondered where it led to. I looked for a spot to get out so I could walk across it but there wasn't a good spot anywhere near. We saw a doe and fawn drinking from the river at one point. They quickly turned and bolted when we got too close.

Around one o'clock James Ernest said we had around an hour of paddling left and we could stop and play in the creek for a while if we found a good spot. Fifteen minutes later we came to a deep hole with a large rock on the bank that looked like it had been used a lot for jumping into the river. This was where we decided to stop and have some fun.

We spent the next hour diving, jumping, and doing cannonballs off the rock. Purty went skinny-dipping. We didn't care. I just didn't look at him when he was out of the water. I grew tired of jumping off the rock after thirty minutes and got my pole out of the other canoe and walked down the river a little ways and began throwing a spinner bait. Randy decided to join me. He told me he wanted to watch what I did to catch all the fish.

"I like to fish, but I've never been very good at it. I thought maybe you could give me some pointers," Randy said.

It really made me feel good. I had really looked up to Randy since he changed his view on blacks. Since then he and James Ernest had been great role models. I was always learning from them. It felt good to be able to teach Randy something. I told him what areas of the creek probably gave us the best chance to catch fish. I told him how I would fish different if I were fishing with live bait versus the artificial bait I was using. I taught him how to hold his mouth. He laughed when I told him that it was a joke.

I then asked Randy, "What did you tell the Bottom Brothers when you pulled them to the side before we left?" I wasn't sure he would tell me. I caught a small smallmouth bass and released it as he began telling me what they had talked about.

"I thanked them for helping us. I then quickly told them how my dad and I were bigots and how we wanted Junior and his family out of the county. I told them what had happened and how Mr. Washington saved Billy's life. I told them how I had completely changed after that. I told them what a great kid Junior was and how I had seen the stupidity of my ways. I told them they should change also and that it wasn't too late."

"Wow. What did they say?"

"Nothing really. Rupert laughed at me and said I was crazy, but I could tell Luther was thinking about what I had said. At least he didn't laugh at me. I then turned and walked away. I had said all that I wanted to say to them."

"That was big. I'm really proud of you. You're a great guy, Randy," I said.

Randy turned away and began fishing in the other direction. I knew he didn't want me to see the tears that ran down his cheeks.

James Ernest yelled downriver, "We'd better be going."

When we got close to the canoe, Purty was taking one last jump from the rock. Randy looked at me and said, "He looks like a big old bullfrog jumping from the bank." We both laughed.

I then added, "He is. He is."

Purty had to climb back up on the rock and put his clothes on before we could shove off. He got into the canoe and we pushed off and Purty turned around to say something to me and he flipped the canoe over. We had to swim the canoe back to shore and get back in and shove off again. I told him, "You don't have to turn around to talk to me. I can hear you."

"I like looking at a person when I talk to them," he said as he half turned that time.

I watched the moss-covered rocks and tall trees on the banks pass by as we paddled down the river and I thought of how beautiful the trip had been. I stopped paddling and watched the beauty before me. I let Purty paddle while I steered the canoe and kept it in the middle of the river. I didn't want the trip to end. I wanted to take the Red River all the way to the Kentucky River and then follow the Kentucky River to wherever it went.

The time passed by and soon we were pulling into a sandbar that looked like it was used a lot for entering and exiting the river. We unloaded our gear and carried it up the bank to where the turnaround for cars and trucks was located. We then helped each other carry the canoes. As we were going back for the last canoe we saw Papaw and Clayton drive in and park their trucks. As we were walking back with the canoe, Clayton yelled out, "Here come the heroes again."

We dropped the canoe at the truck and I ran up to hug Papaw and I shook hands with Clayton and he rubbed my head like he always did. I was hoping a little that Susie had come with them to pick us up, but she wasn't there.

"We're heroes?" James Ernest questioned.

Papaw answered, "The radio is telling about the rescue on every station. They've been naming all six of you as finding Lydia and taking her from a woman who claimed to be a witch."

"Wow," was all I could say.

"One report I heard even said that the little girl wouldn't stop clinging to you, Timmy," Clayton continued the report. I just shrugged my shoulders.

We loaded everything into the trucks and headed home. Before we left I asked if we could stop somewhere for lunch.

"Hungry?" Papaw asked.

"Starving," I answered. We stopped at the first restaurant we came to in a small town. There was a small diner on the corner across from the town square. We tied Coty to a pole outside the restaurant. When I opened the door I noticed that each table was covered by vinyl-checkered tablecloths. A jukebox was playing against the back wall. The song *Breaking Up Is Hard To Do* was playing. I now could relate to the lyrics. We walked in and sat down. A waitress came running from behind the counter and told us, "Boys, we don't serve coloreds in here. You can order some food for him and take it outside to him."

Junior started to get up and leave.

"Sit down, Junior," I said. I looked up at the woman with mousey brown hair and black glasses. "We want to be served. We're not going anywhere."

Tucky and Purty were also sitting with Junior and me at our table. Papaw and Clayton were at a table with James Ernest and Randy. Tucky and Purty looked up at the waitress. Junior was visibly upset and looking at his lap.

"He leaves, or you all leave," the woman said. She looked nervous. Maybe even a bit worried.

"I think we'll stay. We're hungry. Isn't this a restaurant?" I said.

"I'm hungry," Purty said, looking back up at the waitress.

"It's okay. I'm not very hungry," Junior said, as he again started to stand.

I grabbed his arm and pulled him back down. "Yes, you are."

The waitress turned her head and yelled, "Frank, we have a problem."

There were only three other people in the small restaurant—an older couple at the table next to us, who kept giving us dirty looks, and a man at the counter who wasn't paying us any mind.

Papaw heard the commotion and rose from his table and walked over to our table just as Frank walked out of the kitchen. Frank was a short, fat, greasy-looking man in an apron. I guessed he was the cook, maybe the owner of the restaurant.

"What's going on?" Papaw asked.

"Sir, we don't serve coloreds in here. We'd be glad to fix food for him and you can feed him outside," the waitress explained. "This boy is refusing to obey the laws."

Papaw looked down at me. I knew he could see the hurt in my eyes.

Papaw then said, "First off, it is not a law. It may be your backward ways, but it isn't a law. This boy is as free and equal as you are. Secondly, you think we should feed him outside like he's a horse or a dog?"

"No. We allow dogs in the restaurant," Frank finally butted in. I could see the smoke coming from Papaw's head. I expected Papaw to slug the man. Right then Clayton took a glass of water from his table and quickly walked over and dumped it on top of the man's head.

I knew it was time to get up and go. I let go of Junior's arm and we stood. Frank was fuming and cussing. I kicked him in the chin as I walked by him. He began hopping on one foot. As we walked out of the front of the building, I yelled, "He's a lot better person than you are. He's even a hero." I was so mad I wanted to scream. I could hear the song, *Sherry,* by the Four Seasons playing in the background as we left.

Papaw didn't say anything to me. I could tell he was just as mad as I was. He just smiled at me as we returned to the trucks. We decided to wait until we got home to eat, where it was civilized. It wasn't that long of a drive anyway. Papaw did stop at a country store and treated us all to cold drinks and snacks.

We all stood in the parking lot and drank our pops. Junior was drinking his Orange Crush when Papaw said to him, "I'm sorry that happened in the diner."

"You didn't do nothing. I'm sorry I caused a problem and no one got to eat," Junior said.

"You didn't cause a problem, son. The problem is people who learnt that behavior from their folks. It's been passed down for so long they think it's right."

"I think I like it better at home in our community where almost everyone is nice to me. No one there ever wants to hang me from a tree limb," Junior told Papaw.

"Who wanted to do that?" Papaw asked.

Oh no. I knew I was going to have to tell Papaw all about the Bottom Brothers and everything that happened on the trip. I thought the Wolf Pack might never get to go on another adventure. We got into the trucks and on the way home I told Papaw all about Luther and Rupert. Papaw was really upset, but he laughed when I told him what James Ernest had done to the two men. When I was finished with the story, I said, "Please don't tell Mom about the Bottom Brothers. She'll never let me out of Morgan County again." I actually wasn't sure if I wanted to ever leave Morgan County again anyway, except I really enjoyed canoeing the river and wanted to canoe others. I knew I might have to wait until I was an adult to do it.

"I think it's best that we keep that part of the trip a secret from your mom and mamaw. Although, I think your parents need to know, Junior. Maybe I should tell them," Papaw said.

"Okay," Junior agreed.

"For now, let's remember that you guys are heroes," Papaw said and smiled.

23

MAKING OUT

The two pickups rolled through the communities of Mize, Grassy Creek, and Index before coming into West Liberty. We were nearing home. It was good to be coming home. We drove on through Wrigley and turned left on State Route 711 and we saw the waterfalls. We honked as we passed Tucky's house. He wanted to go on to the store with us. We drove through the tunnel and then we came to the store. It had never looked so beautiful.

I jumped out of the truck and ran into the store yelling, "Mom, Mom, I'm home."

Mom met me in the living room and she smothered me in hugs and kisses. I wasn't too old to still need and want the love that Mom showed me. "I've been worried sick for four days," she said.

She then went outside and hugged each of the boys as we unloaded the trucks. Mom even hugged Coty. After everyone got picked up and we got settled, Mom fixed us sandwiches and then had James Ernest and me sit with her at the kitchen table and tell her about our trip and about rescuing Lydia. Janie was spending the day with Mamaw. We spent the next hour telling Mom about everything that happened, except for the Bottom Brothers. Mom would often laugh and then get that worried look that mothers get. She began crying when we told her about finding Lydia and how she attached herself to me. She cringed when I told her about the witch and her potions and eyeballs.

Later, James Ernest headed for the Washington's to check on his garden and I knew he wanted to see Raven. I went up to the lake and picked up garbage. There were only two fishermen there on that late Thursday afternoon. I didn't know one of them and the other was Fred Wilson. Fred stopped me and began asking me about the trip and about Lydia. He told me it was the talk of the whole area. He said all of the radio and TV's stations were talking about it.

I gave him a quick version of how we had found her. Before I left him and continued around the lake, he said, "You're a hero again, Timmy."

"We were just in the wrong place at the right time. That's all," I said.

I knew I wasn't a hero. I thought if anyone was a hero it was James Ernest or Randy for taking up for Junior and standing up against the Bottom Brothers. I was just a scared boy who happened to hear a little girl in the dark. I knew that Junior was even more of a hero than I was. He's able to withstand the hatred thrown his way and stay happy.

I had read stories about some of the first great black athletes like Jackie Robinson and Hank Aaron in baseball, Jimmy Brown in football, and Bill Russell in basketball who had taken the abuse without losing their temper, for the good of other blacks who came after them. I admired that. I felt that way about Junior and his entire family. To take the hatred and abuse toward them and still smile, when I knew they wanted to scream or hurt someone. I knew they were heroes to me.

Coty spent the afternoon in the shade by his doghouse. He was worn out. I didn't blame him. When I got back to the store I found the sofa in the living room and was soon sound asleep. I didn't wake up until nearly seven-thirty when I heard a familiar voice in the store. It was Rock. I quickly got up and went into the store. Mom was behind the counter waiting on a customer. Rock threw her arms around me and hugged me when she saw me. I was embarrassed to be hugged in front of Mom by someone other than Susie.

"I'm glad you're back," Rock said.

Mom gave me a look that I wasn't sure I knew what it meant. She looked like she was trying to figure out what had happened.

"Hi, it's good to be back," I said.

"Let's go for a walk," Rock said.

"Sure." I looked at Mom and told her, "We're going for a walk, Mom."

"Why don't you walk to the spring and get us some water?" Mom suggested.

"Okay," I said, figuring I could kill two birds with one stone, taking Rock for a walk and doing a chore at the same time. Plus, I could get her to help carry the pail.

We walked through the back door and I grabbed the bucket and we took off for the spring. As soon as we started walking down Morgan Road, she took my hand in hers and said, "I missed you. Did you miss me?"

"Yep, I missed everyone," I said, being the romantic that I was.

"Kenny said he really enjoyed the trip," Rock said. For a second I had to think about who she was talking about—Kenny. We had been calling him Tucky for so long that I hadn't heard his real name for quite a while.

"It was really fun. I love canoeing," I said.

"You could take me canoeing on the lake. I think I would enjoy that," Rock suggested.

It actually wasn't a bad idea. We had the small rowboat, but it was a hassle to use on the lake. I hadn't even thought that I could now use the canoe on the lake. It would be fun.

"Okay," I said.

We had arrived at the trail that led to the spring. We followed the path to the spring. I placed the bucket on the ground and started to bend over to fill the bucket when Rock grabbed me and threw her arms around me and kissed me with a long, long kiss. It felt good to have a girlfriend who wanted to kiss me. She then kissed me again. Rock was really pretty too. She was tanned and a little mysterious looking. I then filled the bucket and we both held onto it and carried it back to the store.

On the way, I said, "We could take the canoe out now if you have time." It was a good time to take it out on the lake with not many men fishing.

"Sure, that sounds great to me," Rock said. As we walked toward the store we began talking about Purty thinking he was a toad. We laughed. She said Kenny had told them about it, and she said her whole family was rolling on the floor laughing about it.

When we arrived home I went into the store and told Mom our plans and asked if she cared. She told us to go ahead and have fun. But then she said, "Don't plan on doing anything tomorrow except watching the store and lake. I need to go to Morehead with Rebecca."

Rock and I carried the canoe to the lake and placed it in the water near the same place the rowboat was anchored. Rock and I both were good swimmers so I didn't see the need for life vests. Rock got in the front seat and I hopped into the back and pushed us off with my paddle. Rock said, "This is my first time in a canoe."

"Don't do any sudden shifts of weight. All you have to do is paddle on either side you want. I'll steer the canoe and paddle according to which side you're paddling on." We paddled out to the middle of the lake. The two fishermen had left for the day. Another had come and was fishing off the dam. We paddled away from him so not to bother his fishing.

The evening was nice for the first week of August. It wasn't too hot at all. A breeze blew slightly from the back of the lake, sending small ripples into the front of the canoe. The sun was already below the western hillside. It was dusk. We heard bullfrogs beginning to serenade us on the banks. It was almost perfect. I actually wanted a fishing pole in my hands.

"Have you seen Susie since you've gotten back?" Rock asked.

"No. I...I..." I started to say I had hoped she would be with Clayton when he and Papaw had picked us up but caught myself before I made the mistake.

"What?" Rock asked.

"Nothing, I haven't seen her or talked to her. No reason to," I told her.

She turned her head toward me and stared at me. "Are you disappointed?"

"No. Why would I be?" I said, as if it was the dumbest question in the world.

"I'm not sure, but your voice sounded like you were a little disappointed."

"No. No reason for me to be disappointed. I wanted to see you when I got back," I said.

"Then why didn't you walk down to the house to see me, instead of me having to come to your house?" Rock questioned.

There it was, girl logic, which I didn't understand. I guessed because I hadn't come straight to her house to see her it meant I didn't like her any longer and wanted Susie back as my girlfriend. It made me a little mad. I was unsure if I was getting mad because she figured me out and she was right, or because she was being a jealous ninny.

"I was worn out when I got home. We didn't get hardly any sleep last night and I fell asleep on the couch until I heard your voice in the store. I couldn't call because you guys don't have a phone," I explained, trying to get out of the conversation. She turned around quickly to look me in the eyes, almost turning the canoe over. I caught it just in time. She stared into my face. I was glad it was getting darker out. I wasn't sure what she would have seen.

What a day it had been. I went from watching a self-proclaimed witch make Purty think he was a toad, to Junior being turned into a flour-covered white boy, to being a hero, to being questioned by my new girlfriend about my loyalty. I was tired and decided not to answer any more questions. I was going to say the wrong thing. I pointed to an owl flying across the pond almost over Rock's head. The owl lived near the pond and I saw him fly across the lake most evenings I was there.

We paddled to the back of the lake near the slanted rock and then I turned the canoe around and started to head back. Rock then said, "Prove it to me."

"What?" I said.

"Prove to me that I'm your girlfriend. Let's park the canoe and get on the slanted rock and make out," she said.

Make out what? I didn't know what "make out" was. I was naïve as it came. I wasn't sure if she meant make it out of the canoe; I knew I could do that.

"Don't you want to?" she asked.

I still wasn't sure what she meant, but I said, "Sure."

So we paddled to the shallow rocks where the stream came into the lake and we got out. She took my hand in hers and led me to the slanted rock. She climbed onto the rock and then watched me as I climbed up. She then sat down on the rock and pulled me down to the side of her. I picked up a few pebbles at my side and began throwing them into the water.

"Well?" she said.

"What?"

"Are we going to make out?"

As far as I knew that was what we were doing. "I guess I'm not sure what 'make out' means," I admitted to her.

She smiled at me and said, "They told me you were backward."

What did that mean? And who told her that?

"It means we should have fun kissing and holding each other. Do stuff that other boys and girls do," she explained. I had no idea what other boys and girls were doing. I didn't object to kissing. I liked kissing, so I leaned over and kissed her on the lips. She pounced on me.

An hour later we walked to the front of the store. Rock was heading home. "I'll walk you part-way home," I told her. It was almost pitch black and I didn't want her walking home in the dark on the road.

I ran into the store to tell Mom what I was doing and Mom said, "No. I'll take her home. I don't want you kids walking down that busy road after dark. You stay here with Janie."

I walked back out and told Rock what Mom had said and then said, "I'll probably see you this weekend."

She kissed me just as Mom came through the front door. I pulled away. They pulled out of the lot and I walked inside to see Janie.

Janie was sitting in front of the TV watching *The Groucho Show*. I sat beside her and rubbed her head.

"Hi, Timmy. Were you and Rock at the lake kissing? Yuck," Janie said and wiped her mouth like she was wiping away kisses.

"You're funny," I said as Groucho said, "That's the secret word. You have just won a hundred dollars." Janie began clapping for the contestant that won the money.

It wasn't long before Mom returned from dropping Rock off. I told them I was tired and was going to bed. James Ernest walked in right behind Mom and followed me to bed. I heard Mom tell Janie that it was past her bedtime. Janie begged to stay up until the show was over. Mom gave in and watched it with her.

I climbed into the top bunk. The bed felt so good after being in the tent and the witch's basement for the past four nights. James Ernest said, "Boy, the bed feels good."

I answered, "Do you know what it means to 'make out'?"

James Ernest laughed and said, "Why?"

"Rock and I went canoeing and she said she wanted us to make out. I didn't even know what it meant," I explained.

"Did you make out?" James Ernest asked me.

"I guess so," I answered.

"I hope you didn't make out in the canoe," he said.

"No. How did you learn this stuff?" I asked him.

"Sadie taught me what making out meant," he said.

"How come girls know more about it than boys?" I asked.

"I don't know. Maybe it's more important to them than it is to us."

"Well, she showed me what it was tonight. She's not a bad teacher," I said and giggled.

I knew that we both laid there in the dark and thought about girls. I wondered if he and Raven had made out. I wanted to ask him but decided it wasn't a very nice thing to ask him. I wondered if Susie had made out with another boy, then I slowly fell to sleep.

24

Let's Drink to It

Friday, August 3

I slept late the next morning. I heard rain bouncing off the roof over my head. It hadn't looked like rain last night on the lake. The stars were out. I didn't expect James Ernest to be in his bed when I awoke, but I still leaned over the side of my bed and looked down to see him staring back at me.

"Boo," he said.

"What are you doing here, Casper?" I asked.

"My garden is getting watered this morning by God. So I decided to sleep in. I was tired."

"Me too. Mom is going to town with Miss Rebecca today. You want to help me in the store?" I asked.

"Sure," he answered. "I should go up and make baskets with Raven, but after canoeing with Purty I'm tired of getting wet."

"I'm just plain tired of being with Purty," I said and laughed.

I jumped from the top bunk and put my clothes on. I said a quick hello to Mom, who was sitting at the kitchen table. I hurried outside with an old umbrella that stood beside the back door. I saw Coty's nose inside his doghouse. I made my way to the outhouse. He was smart enough to not come out to greet me.

When I came back into the kitchen James Ernest was sitting with Mom at the table. I took a seat with them.

"Miss Rebecca is picking Janie and me up around ten. What are you doing, James?" Mom asked.

"I'm going to stick around here and help Timmy," he told her.

"I want to tell you two that I'm very proud of both of you. I was really worried about the trip, and I probably always will worry when you're gone on one of your adventures, but I know you will always do what's right. Lydia's mother called me and thanked me for both of you. She said she was so impressed by both of you and couldn't get over how Lydia had bonded with you."

"That was all Timmy. He was the one who found her and protected her all night and morning. He has a way with girls," James Ernest said and grinned.

"I just want to tell both of you that I trust you. You boys are becoming men. I love you," Mom told us.

"Thanks," I said.

"Thanks, we love you too," James Ernest told her. Why didn't I say that?

"Make sure both of you are here this evening. We're going up to Mom and Dad's this evening around seven for supper. They want to make sure both of you come."

"Okay," we both said.

"I'm going to get Janie and myself ready," Mom said.

"Want any breakfast?" James Ernest asked me.

"Yeah, how about sausage, eggs, pancakes, bacon, fresh-made biscuits, and sorghum molasses," I answered.

"Coming right up," James Ernest said as he placed Cheerios on the table and went back to the kitchen for the milk.

All day long we answered questions about rescuing Lydia. A newspaper reporter for the *Licking Valley Courier* even stopped by the store to do what he called an exclusive interview. We didn't have many customers, but we sure had a lot of folks just stopping by to talk. They did buy snacks and drinks as they listened to us tell about our adventure.

Our mailman, Roger Smuckatilly, came in with the mail and placed it on the counter. He paid for a Coca-Cola and I handed him back half of the mail that wasn't for us and he walked back out after exchanging pleasantries. He never even questioned why I gave half the stack back to him.

Around three o'clock that afternoon Sheriff Hagar Cane walked into the store. We talked about the same thing everyone else wanted to talk about for a while and then he said, "I actually came to talk to you guys about something else." He nervously began walking around the store. He fumbled for the words that he wanted to say. I wondered what I had done wrong this time.

His nervous behavior was making me awfully nervous.

I finally burst loose with, "What did I do, Sheriff Cane?"

He jumped at the suddenness of the question and then laughed uneasily. "I wanted to ask for your permission to ask Betty, your mother, your guardian, to marry me."

He then looked from me to James Ernest and back to me. He was sweating bullets. His armpits were wet. If we didn't answer soon he would soon look like Large Larry on a hot, humid day.

James Ernest assessed the situation and knew we had the sheriff right where we wanted him. He asked Sheriff Cane, "And what are your intentions for Betty and the family?"

"Wh-what? O-Oh I want to mar-marry her and make us al-all one-one big hap-hap-happy family," he stammered around his answer.

"And where would we all live—this big happy family?" James Ernest questioned him. I was loving how James Ernest was putting the sheriff on the spot. He had certainly turned the tables on the sheriff. Usually Sheriff Cane was the one who got to interrogate people. Now it was our turn.

The sheriff took a couple of minutes to think about the question before trying to answer. "I'm unsure. I guess Betty, your mother, and I would need to discuss that if she agreed to marry me, I guess."

I decided to join the fun. I asked him, "What if James Ernest and I or just one of us says *no*? Will you still ask her to marry you without our permission?"

I thought the poor man was going to collapse right there. His shirt was now wringing wet. His tongue was tied in knots and his hands were shaking so bad I hoped there was no reason for him to use his gun in the next hour. It would take him that long to settle down. He answered, "I guess I wouldn't ask her then."

James Ernest jumped back into the fray. "You can't let kids decide if you're going to ask a woman to marry you. Kids don't know anything about marriage. Get some nads. Do you love her?" he asked the sheriff.

I couldn't believe James Ernest told the sheriff to "get some nads." I nearly started laughing.

"Yes, yes, yes. I love her very much."

"Do you want to marry her and make her happy?" I jumped back in.

"Yes, yes, very much."

"Then I think you should ask her," James Ernest said. And then he added, "You have my blessing."

"You have my blessing also," I said.

Sheriff Cane hugged James Ernest. I stayed behind the counter hoping he wouldn't hug me. I didn't want his sweat soaking me like it had James Ernest. He walked over to the counter and shook my hand and said, "Thank you, thank you, boys."

I went to the pop cooler and said, "I think we should drink to it." I took out a Pepsi Cola for Sheriff Cane, knowing it was his favorite. I handed James Ernest a grape pop and I took an RC Cola from the cooler. We opened them on the pop bottle opener that hung on the counter and held the bottles up and clinked them together and I said, "To a new family."

"That wasn't so bad, was it, Dad?" I said after taking a long drink from the bottle.

Sheriff Cane looked at me and smiled.

I heard him quietly whisper, "Dad."

I couldn't imagine how he was going to ask Mom to marry him if he got that nervous asking us. I wondered if he would rather James Ernest and I asked her for him. I had never seen a man melt down before my eyes. It was sad and sweet at the same time. I really did appreciate him asking me and James

Ernest. I liked Sheriff Cane a lot, and I knew he would treat Mom and us really well.

James Ernest asked him, "When are you going to pop the question?"

"Maybe tonight. I'm supposed to come to the party, but I've got to get home and take a shower and 'find some nads,'" Sheriff Cane said, as all three of us laughed.

I then asked, "There's a party tonight?"

"Oh, no. I shouldn't have said anything. I'm not thinking right. Forget I said that," the sheriff begged. He was a mess.

"Said what?" I said. James Ernest and I then acted as though we hadn't heard him say it.

"Thanks, boys," the sheriff said as he slid out the front door.

As the sheriff drove away James Ernest and I cracked up.

"I guess there's a party tonight," James Ernest said.

"I love parties," I said. My next thought was, *I'll get to see Susie.* I couldn't help it. That was my thought. How could I ever get over Susie?

Mom returned from Morehead around three that afternoon. The rain had stopped around noon and the gravel road outside the store was already dry from the sun that came out afterward. It was a nice afternoon. The rain had dropped the temperature outside. It would be a nice evening for a party. I didn't mention to Mom that we knew about the party.

"Busy day?" Mom asked us as she walked through the store.

"No. We just got our first couple of fishermen a little while ago. It might get busy this evening," I said. Fishermen always liked fishing after a rain at the lake. They figured fish would be out looking for food due to the increased water in the lake. I didn't think it was particularly true, but I didn't tell them that.

Janie was all smiles as she walked in with a bag of stuff she had gotten in town.

"What did you buy us?" I asked her.

"Nothing. I guess we forgot about you two. I'm sorry about that," she said as she continued through. She didn't seem all that sorry. Fishermen began swarming into the store. We took turns running to the back porch and getting bait out of the fridge.

Louis Lewis came in and announced, "There's my heroes."

Fred Wilson came back. Sam Kendrick arrived to fish. Phillip Satch, Roy Collins, Billy Easterling, and Mud McCobb all arrived. I was shocked to see Harry the Mouse come into the store and say he wanted to fish. James and I hadn't seen him since we helped him and Large Larry tear down the barn last year.

Around six o'clock I went up to the lake and asked all the fishermen if they needed anything. I announced that the store would be closing at seven and they had better get what they wanted now or do without. I got all kinds of orders for pop and snacks and more bait. It was almost seven before I gathered everything and got it delivered to the fishermen.

I asked Mom, "Are you sure you want to close the store? There are a lot of fishermen up at the lake."

"It's okay. This one time we can do it," Mom said. I knew we would hardly ever close the store early just to go to supper. The sheriff was right. Something was up.

Mom wasn't ready to leave before seven-fifteen. We piled into the car and left for Papaw's farm. Mom drove past Papaw's lane.

"Mom, you missed your turn," I said. She didn't say anything as she continued and turned left into Homer and Ruby's lane. When we got to the house we saw cars and trucks parked everywhere.

Mom handed me and James Ernest bags to carry and said, "Take these to the barn, please."

When we walked into the barn everyone began clapping and yelling. There was a big banner strung across the barn that read, "Great Job—Wolf Pack." I was in shock.

I looked around to see all of our relatives and friends that lived in the community. The rest of the Wolf Pack, even Junior, was standing on a small stage waving for us to join them on the stage. Everyone was cheering and clapping as we took the stage. I looked out to see the faces of the Key family. Rock was cheering and blowing me kisses. I saw Uncle Morton standing and bowing to us. I then saw Susie standing with Raven. They both were waving their arms and shouting. I looked to the left and saw Lydia's family standing there. Lydia's father lifted her up to the stage and she ran over and wrapped her arms around me. I felt water on my cheeks and knew I was crying. I looked over to see that the rest of the guys all had tears rolling down their faces.

After a few minutes Papaw took the stage and raised his hands and everyone quickly fell silent. He then spoke, "We have all gathered this evening to celebrate the rescue of Lydia and the bravery of six boys. I am so proud of these six young men. There're two things I know. Number one is—if they go on an adventure, it's going to be a real adventure." Everyone began nodding their heads to each other and cheering again. "Number two—they will always do what is right." The inside of the barn exploded in cheering again. "We're here to celebrate with Lydia's family her safe return and to eat some good food. But first, hold up everyone; let's thank our God who protected our children. Pastor White."

Pastor White jumped up on the stage and prayed, "We are thankful to you, Father, for your watchful eyes and your caring arms that looked after and held our children in your love and protection. I'm thankful that you saw the boys' courage as useful in your service. We thank you for bringing everyone home safe and sound. We pray that you will bless this food before us and bless those who prepared it. Amen."

"Amen," everyone shouted back.

"Let's be polite and let our guests go first and then the boys," Papaw said after the prayer.

Robert Easterling yelled out from the back, "Don't let Purty up there first. There won't be any food left for anyone else." Everyone laughed.

The party was tremendous fun. I really appreciated all the pats on the back and the head rubs, but I didn't feel like a hero. I was a boy who went on a canoe trip and was trapped in a basement, nothing heroic about that. If there were heroes among us it was James Ernest and Randy. They stood up to the Bottom Brothers. They protected Junior.

I ate as much as I could get in my stomach without throwing up. I then let it settle and went back for cherry dumplings and a slice of coconut pie. Rock was sitting with me outside the barn on a big rock. She was eating a piece of chocolate cake.

"Everyone is really nice," Rock said.

I nodded that I agreed. I had a mouthful of dumplings in my mouth.

"Has Susie talked to you this evening?" she asked.

"No," I mumbled.

Around dusk I watched Mom and the sheriff walk away from the barn and down a path. I wondered if this was the moment. I stood up and ran to find Susie. Rock watched me run away. I searched frantically for Susie. Rock stood at the barn opening and watched me. I found Susie sitting with Brenda, Raven, James Ernest, and Randy.

"Can I talk to you?" I asked her. I knew I had to share what was happening with someone. I wanted *that someone* to be Susie.

She looked up and stared into my face. She could tell it was important to me. She said, "Okay."

Rock hurried over and started to say something, but I quickly said, "We'll be back in a minute." Susie and I left her standing there alone. The others at the table looked up at her and she turned and walked away.

Susie and I walked out of the barn and up the lane toward the main road. I stopped and Susie turned toward me.

"I had to tell someone," I said.

"What is it?" Susie asked.

"I think Sheriff Cane is asking Mom to marry him," I blurted out.

Susie became excited and asked, "When? Tonight?"

"Right now," I said. "I had to tell you."

"Why did you have to tell me?" Susie asked.

"Because," I said.

"Because why?" She wasn't letting me off the hook.

"Because I still like you. I still love you. I miss you," I said.

"You do?" she said.

"I think about you all the time," I told her.

"I thought Rock was now your girlfriend."

"She is. I mean—I guess she is, but when I'm with her I think of you all the time. I keep thinking how I wish it were you," I told her.

She lowered her head as if she was in deep thought. I continued, "I am very sorry. Please forgive me and be my girlfriend again."

Susie lifted her head and smiled. She threw her arms around me and kissed me.

"Timmy, Timmy." I heard Rock calling my name as Susie was kissing me. I heard her footsteps running up the lane toward us. Susie stopped kissing me and I turned my head to see Rock freeze in her tracks and stare at me. I really liked Rock. She had done nothing wrong. She didn't deserve for me to treat her like I did.

"Your mom is looking for you," she said and turned back toward the barn.

Susie and I turned and began running toward the barn.

25

POPPED THE QUESTION

As we neared Rock, I asked Susie, "I need to tell Rock. Okay?"

Susie nodded okay and ran on past Rock. I stopped and walked with her. She kept her gaze on the barn we were nearing. I had no idea what to say. I really liked Rock, but like a friend. She didn't make my heart flip like Susie did.

She finally turned her head toward me and said, "Go ahead and say it."

I hesitated trying to come up with the right words. Rock then told me, "You're trying to tell me that you want Susie as your girlfriend again. She's finally forgiven you and now you don't need me."

"I really like you, Rock. You're a cool person. I know I've always loved Susie. I'm sorry," I said.

"I like Susie also. She's been a good friend. I hope she doesn't dump you again. I still like you," Rock said. She left my side as we entered the barn. I looked for Susie. I found her standing with Raven and James Ernest in front of the stage. A few of the men were playing an old bluegrass song on stage. A few folks were dancing to the music. Mom saw me and hurried toward me.

She grabbed my arm and James Ernest and asked us to follow her. We walked toward Sheriff Cane, who was standing with Janie in the corner.

When we walked up, Sheriff Cane left.

"Are we leaving, Mommy? I'm having fun," Janie said.

"No. I need to ask all of you something," Mom said.

We both nodded. Mom continued then, "Hagar asked me tonight to marry him."

Janie said, "Wow." James Ernest and I just smiled. We knew what was happening.

"I want to make sure you kids are okay with him becoming your stepfather," Mom said. Her eyes were mixed with happiness and worry.

"We're great with it, Mom," I said and hugged Mom. The worry left her eyes. James Ernest hugged her and told her the same thing.

Janie asked, "Can I be the flower girl?" Mom picked her up and hugged her and began crying.

Mom asked me to tell Papaw that the sheriff had an announcement he would like to make. I ran. I ran to find Papaw. I relayed the message to Papaw and after the song was finished Papaw stepped up on the stage and raised his hands and said, "The good sheriff has asked to make an announcement. The stage is yours, Sheriff Cane."

I made my way back to Susie's side. We stood with Raven and James Ernest. I saw Mom and Janie at the side of the stage with Miss Rebecca. As Sheriff Cane walked up the steps, Robert yelled out, "What did the Wolf Pack do now?" The crowd began laughing.

The sheriff stood on the stage looking like he was completely naked. He looked very awkward and out of character. He took a handkerchief from his pocket and wiped at his eyes. The crowd grew silent and stood in anticipation as to what the sheriff might be announcing that would upset him so.

"It is my great honor to announce that Betty has accepted my proposal of marriage." The pack of people erupted in cheers, shouts, and whistles. I saw Miss Rebecca throw her arms around Mom. Sheriff Cane was trying to get Mom to come up on the stage. Finally, Miss Rebecca and Monie pushed Mom up the steps. Mom looked up and saw Hagar waiting for her at the top of the steps. She had tears flowing down her face. Hagar wrapped his big arms around Mom and the crowd cheered even louder.

"Way to go, Sheriff," Uncle Morton shouted out above the cheers.

"Kiss her, Sheriff," Homer yelled.

Susie threw her arms around me in excitement. I noticed that most couples in the barn were embracing or had their arms in the air cheering. The men on the stage began playing a happy song and the sheriff began clogging in his happiness. Mom stood there watching him and laughing in great embarrassment. We all were laughing. I even noticed that Buck and Winona Key were clogging behind us. A lot of their kids joined in. We had a real dance going. Rock was really kicking her heels up and was probably the best dancer of them all.

Susie ran over and asked Rock to teach her the steps. Rock took her hand and led her in the steps. It didn't take long for Susie to learn. James Ernest and Raven soon followed to the dance floor. Before it was over there were probably forty people clogging throughout the barn. Even Pastor White and Miss Rebecca took a turn at trying it. Delma and Thelma and Janie were doing something on the dance floor that was nothing like clogging, but they were having a great time doing whatever it was. Randy drug Brenda onto the dance floor and they gave it a try. Randy was a lot better than Brenda was.

The party lasted forever. It seemed as though no one wanted to go home. The weather was perfect. Everyone was having a terrific time. The musicians kept playing. I even slow-danced with Susie, and then Rock asked Susie if she could slow dance with me. Susie said yes. As we danced, Rock told me she wasn't upset with me. She said she always knew I would end up going back to Susie. She said Susie and I were meant to be together, and she wanted to remain friends with both of us. I told Susie what she had said. Susie smiled. Lydia then wanted a dance with me before she and her family left. I couldn't imagine there being a better night ever in my life. But then the night got even better.

Lydia's father announced before they left that there was a five hundred dollar reward for Lydia's safe return. He said since there were six of us, he was increasing the reward to six hundred so we each could have a hundred dollars. James Ernest, Randy, and I tried to give our portion back to him. We didn't even know about the reward and didn't feel we should have it. He insisted that we keep it. I decided that maybe I could buy Mom and Hagar a nice wedding gift with mine.

Near the end of the evening I got the five members of the Wolf Pack together and asked them about making Junior a member of the Pack. They all agreed that we should. We found Junior and asked him to come with us. We found a picnic table outside the barn and sat around it. Randy asked, "Would you like to become a full-fledged member of the Wolf Pack, Junior?"

Junior's smile lit up the dark night and he said, "Really? Are you serious?"

We all nodded and Junior said, "Yes." He began bouncing on the wooden plank.

"It will cost you a hundred dollars," Purty said.

Junior gave him a funny look and James Ernest said, "He's just messing with you."

"All those who vote for Henry Washington Junior becoming a member of the Wolf Pack raise your hand," Randy said. All five of us quickly raised our hands and we stood and put our hands together and chanted, "Wolf Pack, Wolf Pack, Wolf Pack, Wolf Pack, Wolf Pack, Wolf Pack, Wolf Pack, Forever the Pack!" We then looked toward the sliver of moon that was above us and howled.

"We assume that Coty would vote for you. When you come to our next Wolf Pack meeting there will be a couple of things you will have to do for your initiation and then you'll be an official member of the Wolf Pack," Randy told him. Junior was all smiles as we returned to the barn. I loved having Junior as a member of the Wolf Pack. He was such a fun, happy kid. He made us all better.

The party began breaking up around midnight. It seemed as though most people searched me out to congratulate me on finding Lydia and on the engagement of Mom, which I had nothing to do with, except giving my blessing, which they didn't know about. I finished off the cherry dumplings as a few of the ladies were cleaning up the final dishes and saying their good-byes. Mom was so happy and glowing.

When Susie left, she gave me a kiss and said, "I missed you, and I'm glad I'm your girlfriend again."

"Me, too. I've never wanted a different girlfriend than you."

SATURDAY, AUGUST 4

On the way home I told Mom that Susie and I were together again.

Janie was in the back seat beginning to fall asleep, but she managed to say, "It's about time."

Mom asked, "What about Rock? I thought you two liked each other."

"We're going to remain friends," I said.

"Does she know that?" Mom asked.

"Yes," I answered. James Ernest laughed. Mom laughed.

I didn't understand what they were laughing about. As soon as we got home I congratulated Mom again and headed straight out to Coty before going to bed. I told Coty about Junior becoming a member. I had brought some meat from the party to give him. He gobbled it down. I petted him and filled his water bowl.

I slipped into the top bunk and said goodnight to James Ernest. I then said, "It was a big night."

"It was a great night," James Ernest said in response.

It wasn't long before we both were in a deep sleep. I dreamed of Susie that night.

Morning came early. I heard Papaw's knock on our bedroom door before I heard the Tuttle's rooster. "It's going to be a busy morning," Papaw said through the door.

"Okay. Coming," I said sleepily. James Ernest groaned.

Suddenly there came a tapping, as if someone was gently rapping, rapping at my bedroom window. I looked over at the twilight that barely interrupted the dark and there was Bo standing on my windowsill. "Bo," I said as I slid out of bed and dropped to the floor. I hurried over to the window which was left open a couple of inches and flung it up to let Bo enter. Bo called out his familiar *Caw* and then flew up to the top rail at the end of the bunk bed and perched himself on it. James Ernest turned around in his bed and slid his body down and stuck his head out from under my bunk and looked up at Bo.

"Hello, Bo," James Ernest said.

Caw, caw, Bo returned the greeting.

James Ernest and I quickly got dressed and I opened the door as Bo flew over and landed on my left shoulder just like he always had. We walked into the store and saw the surprise on Papaw's face. "I thought I heard Bo in there," Papaw said. "How about giving me back my pocket knife, you thieving crow?"

"Bo took your knife?" James Ernest said surprised.

"I was whittling on the porch this spring and I laid it down on the arm of the rocker to get a Coke and, when I returned, he was picking it up and he flew away with it. He's bound to have a stash somewhere," Papaw said.

"Crows do that. They like shiny things," James Ernest agreed.

I looked up at Bo and asked him, "Where did you take all the stuff you stole, Bo?"

Bo blinked and cried out, *Caw*.

It didn't help one bit. I heard Coty barking on the front porch. I opened the door and Coty came inside. He looked up at Bo and barked. Bo flew off my shoulder and carefully landed on Coty's back. Coty's friend was back. I opened the door again and Coty went out with Bo on his back. Just then Mud McCobb and Louis Lewis pulled into the parking lot.

"That's a sight you don't see every day," Mud said when they opened the screen door.

"We offer our fishermen more than just fishing here at the lake. We have sideshows," Papaw teased.

"Speaking of sideshows, there's Timmy," Louis said and smiled.

"At least I'm not a freak show," I said.

"Martin, is that any way to treat a paying customer?" Louis asked.

"Well, I haven't seen any money yet and that's between you two. I think you could probably take him—if you could catch him," Papaw told him.

Louis laughed and said, "I don't think I could do either one. I'm just a lazy, woman-lovin' hillbilly."

"He got that lazy part right," Mud jumped in.

"I like it a lot better when the lovely Betty waits on us," Louis Lewis then said.

"She's off the market, boys," Papaw told them.

"What do you mean?" Louis huffed.

"She got engaged to Sheriff Cane last night," Papaw said.

"Engaged, and to a lawman to boot. I'll be," Louis said.

"He's a lucky man. No better available woman around than Betty," Mud said.

It was shocking to me to hear the men talk about my mom in that way. I knew Mom was pretty, but I never knew that men who came into the store were interested in Mom in that way—available. I wondered if the number of fishermen would slack off when word got out that Mom was engaged. This could be bad for our income and for my tips that I made when I waited on them.

Mom came into the store at that moment.

The two men tipped their caps when she walked in. "Good morning, gentlemen," Mom said. I watched the men's eyes follow Mom as she walked over to the door and looked out. Their eyes followed her as she walked behind the counter and hugged Papaw. It was like they wanted her to come hug them.

"I guess congratulations are due," Louis was finally able to say.

"Yes, me too," Mud agreed.

"Thank you, Louis, Mud. Word sure gets around quick," Mom said.

"He sure is a lucky man," Louis said.

I could see Mom blushing. I was getting embarrassed myself so I changed the subject. "Bo is back," I said.

"I thought that was what woke me up this morning. At first I thought I was dreaming. You boys want some breakfast?" Mom asked.

"Not me," James Ernest answered.

"Me neither. I'm still full from last night," I said.

Mom left the room and so the two men got their money out and paid for fishing and bought some bait. "You need any fishing lessons this morning? I give them for two dollars an hour," I told the men.

"You need to do something with your grandson," Louis said as he and Mud left the store and headed for the lake. I could hear them laughing.

Papaw just shook his head. He knew the men loved teasing me. After taking turns going to the outhouse, James Ernest and I spent the next three hours waiting on customers, running after bait, and checking around the lake for garbage. Bo sat on my shoulder as I walked around the lake. When it finally slowed down James Ernest left for Raven's. He said he needed to hoe his garden and make baskets. I told him I was planning to spend the evening with Susie and asked him if he and Raven might want to make it a double date. He said he would let me know. He also said he was glad I was back with Susie. I smiled.

26

You Can't Embarrass Love

⌒

The morning went by fast. We were extremely busy. Mom had folks stopping in all day congratulating her on the engagement. I saw disappointed looks on many men's faces when they heard word of it, especially the bachelors. So far, I had run all day from the store to the back porch, to the lake and back, and then back with refreshments. I made a lot of money in tips and discarded pop bottles.

When we got a break around two I asked Mom about spending the evening with Susie. She said I could leave around seven. She said that Papaw could drive me up to Susie's. Mom was going out with Sheriff Cane. They were going to dinner with Pastor White and Miss Rebecca to celebrate their engagement. Janie was spending the night with Mamaw and Papaw. Mom said Mamaw and Papaw were going to watch the store until closing time, which in the summertime usually wasn't until dark, nearly nine-thirty or ten.

I called Susie. Delma answered the phone. "Hello, this is the Perry residence, Delma speaking."

I tried to remember all the directions she had given me the last time I had called and messed up according to her. I began, "Hello, this is Timmy. May I please talk to Susie?"

"Why do you have to come back into her life? She was safe and happy without you. You had the right girlfriend, Rock. You know, like the thing you crawled out from under. I can't believe... Hey!"

I heard Delma yell just before I heard Susie say, "Hi, Timmy, sorry about that. What's up?"

"I was wondering if you would like to spend the evening together. I could come up there. James Ernest and Raven might make it a double date."

"That sounds like fun. Okay," Susie said.

"Be there around seven. I can't wait to see you," I told her.

We hung up. I was excited that I was spending the evening with Susie. Papaw was standing behind the counter eating a sandwich.

"So you and Susie are an item again, huh?" Papaw said.

"Yeah, I guess so. I'm going to spend the evening with her. Mom said you might take me up there around seven."

"I can do that. I need to go pick up Corie around then anyway," Papaw said. "I'm glad you two are together again."

I went behind the counter and made myself a boloney sandwich. I took an RC Cola from the counter and stood with Papaw and ate lunch.

The screen door opened and Uncle Morton walked in. "It's good to see you guys," blind Uncle Morton said. We greeted him.

He walked over to the cooler and opened it and pulled out a cold grape pop. He opened it and took a long swig. "Did you find what you wanted?" I asked.

"Yes, I did. I could tell it was a grape pop by the feel of the label. They're all different. When you're blind you have to find different ways to recognize things," he explained. I always marveled at Uncle Morton. The one person I looked up to the most was Papaw, but Uncle Morton was a close second.

"You want to fish, Uncle Morton?" I asked.

"No. I came to spend some time. I knew this would be a happy place, a place where love is in the air. It's a good place to be," Uncle Morton explained. "Betty's engaged and you're back with Susie. Happy, happy, happy."

Mom came into the store and hugged Uncle Morton. "See what I mean. This is a lady who is happy," he continued.

Mom told him, "Stop it, you're going to embarrass me."

"No. You can't embarrass love. When you're in love you want everyone to know and you couldn't care less what people think. Isn't that right, Timmy?" Uncle Morton asked me.

"I think you're right," I said, and then I added, "I think I hear fishermen calling my name." I took my sandwich and pop and flew through the door.

Around seven, Papaw took me up to Susie's farm. Clayton came out and asked if Papaw was going back to the store.

"Yes, after I pick up Corie."

"You mind giving Brenda a ride to the pastor's house. She's babysitting Bobby Lee this evening. Save me a trip," Clayton told Papaw.

"No problem," Papaw answered.

Susie came out of the front door and started walking toward me. She was so pretty. She had long bangs falling to her eyes. Her freckles glowed in the sunshine. Her strawberry blonde hair was pulled back into a ponytail. She had on blue shorts that covered a fraction of her tanned slim legs. Her blouse was a sleeveless white buttoned up top. I was again the luckiest boy in the world. Papaw drove away with Brenda. Delma and Thelma stood on the porch and shook their heads at us. I could imagine what they were saying to each other about us.

We decided to go for a walk. As I reached for Susie's hand and we began our walk, Susie and I looked up to see James Ernest and Raven walking down the lane holding hands. James Ernest leaned over and kissed Raven on the cheek.

I thought that maybe Uncle Morton was right when he said, "You can't embarrass love. When you're in love, you want everyone to know, and you couldn't care less what people think."

I turned to my right and we smiled at each other. The End under the last line. All of the books in the series have it.

THE END

Dear Readers,

I hope you enjoyed reading my new book.

Please visit my website: www.timcallahan.net for pictures and information on how to order other books.
    You can e-mail me at: timcal21@ yahoo.com with questions and comments.

> I love hearing from readers.
> Blessings and happy reading,
> Tim Callahan

listen|imagine|view|experience

AUDIO BOOK DOWNLOAD INCLUDED WITH THIS BOOK!

In your hands you hold a complete digital entertainment package. In addition to the paper version, you receive a free download of the audio version of this book. Simply use the code listed below when visiting our website. Once downloaded to your computer, you can listen to the book through your computer's speakers, burn it to an audio CD or save the file to your portable music device (such as Apple's popular iPod) and listen on the go!

How to get your free audio book digital download:

1. Visit www.tatepublishing.com and click on the e|LIVE logo on the home page.
2. Enter the following coupon code:
   96bc-c55d-6667-edbc-9b95-9a47-c0a3-f834
3. Download the audio book from your e|LIVE digital locker and begin enjoying your new digital entertainment package today!